PRACTICAL DREAMERS

Communitarianism and Co-operatives
on Malcolm Island

PRACTICAL DREAMERS

Communitarianism and Co-operatives
on Malcolm Island

Kevin Wilson

10 9 8 7 6 5 4 3 2 1

Printed in Winnipeg, Canada

Library and Archives Canada Cataloguing in Publication Data

Wilson, Kevin, 1969-
    Practical dreamers : communitarianism and co-operatives on Malcolm Island / Kevin Wilson.

    Includes index.
    ISBN 1-55058-306-9

    1. Communitarianism--British Columbia--Malcolm Island--History.
2. Cooperative societies--British Columbia--Malcolm Island--History.
I. British Columbia Institute for Co-operative Studies. II. Title.

HD3450.A3B75 2005   307.77   C2005-902842-4

Editing, Layout, Photography, Cover Design, Indexing: Ron Dueck

British Columbia Institute for Co-operative Studies
University of Victoria
University House 2 - room 109
PO Box 3060 STN CSC
Victoria BC V8W 3R4
tel. (250) 472-4539
email: rochdale@uvic.ca
website: http://web.uvic.ca/bcics

For the people of Malcolm Island.

Contents

Acknowledgements

This book is a preliminary examination of Malcolm Island's co-operative and communitarian heritage, an effort to appreciate the value of the social economy in creating wealth and stability. We at the British Columbia Institute for Co-operative Studies are very pleased to be associated with its development and publication.

Kevin Wilson has written this story but it has grown out of the efforts of many people. Within BCICS, Kathleen Gabelmann, the Institute's Research Director, has worked with several researchers, notably Laura Sjolie and Ryan George, for parts of two years on the co-operative experience of the people of Malcolm Island. We gratefully acknowledge the support we have received from the Social Science and Humanities Council to undertake this project within its New Economy Programme.

BCICS researchers have created a rich resource on the co-operatives of Malcolm Island, especially in the social economy experience. Kevin has used these sources extensively and well to write a popular history of the island's social economy, a good beginning to the work we are and will be doing.

We are indebted to Ron Dueck, a BCICS researcher and law student at the University of Victoria, for his careful and creative editing of the book, for his photographic skills, and for his efforts in guiding it through the publication process.

We are pleased to acknowledge the co-operation we have had with colleagues in the Faculty of Fine Arts at the University of Victoria, particularly through its Community University Research Alliance project, also funded by the Social Sciences and Humanities Research Council and under the direction of Professor Martin Segger. Grants from this project helped to make possible Kevin's work and that of other students as they worked with local communities in creating new resources on the cultural heritage of British Columbia. We wish particularly to thank Barabara Winters, the administrator of the CURA project, for her assistance and encouragement.

Finally, and most importantly, we wish to thank our community partners on Malcolm Island. This book is a joint project with the Sointula Museum and all profits from it will be shared equally between the museum and BCICS. In particular, we wish to thank Tom Roper, community volunteer, for his support and assistance throughout the project, for his help in locating resources, and for helping us to meet people to assist with the research on which this book is based. We wish to thank Marnie Crowe and Gloria Williams for their work in helping with the research and to express our appreciation to them and Pat Roper for reading drafts of the book. We are also indebted to all those whom we have interviewed formally with a tape recorder and informally over coffee in the Wild Island Foods Co-op.

Ian MacPherson
Director, BCICS

BCICS

Foreword

The history of Sointula has long been regarded as an exotic and fascinating story within British Columbia history. The story of the community's founding, its brave but ultimately doomed desire to create a "utopia," has captured the imagination of many who have followed. It is a quintessentially "BC story," at the forefront of what has been a long experience with intentional communities: a long list of religiously-inspired communities, early efforts to develop co-operative housing, and the communes of recent decades.

That is, however, only one aspect of the Sointula/Malcolm Island experience. When viewed in the longer context, beyond the failure of the original dream, the people of the island are not as different as they might appear to be. Like many in other BC communities – whether isolated by water or forest – they were adept at developing community strategies for survival and improvement. The people of British Columbia can be characterized as being inherently individualist and independent, carving often difficult livings from the land, seas, mines and forests, struggles that go back to the dawn of human experience in the province. They have also learned well how to work and live together through community action and sharing, patterns that stretch back to the potlach and forward to recent communal efforts to provide health care and social services.

Co-operatives have been an important part of the communal traditions and of particular kinds of associative individualism that form an important strand in the provincial history, a much more common trend within the province's development than the usual analyses of the provincial experience might suggest. When looked at that way, the people of the island were unusual only in their publicized understandings of the possibilities of communitarianism and in the particular ways in which they sought to realize its potential.

Ian MacPherson

Introduction

When looking at the history of Sointula on Malcolm Island, it is sometimes difficult to see past the dream. Formed as a socialist utopia in 1901, its very name – "place of harmony" – has embodied the idyllic vision of the Finnish immigrants who settled here. Committed to socialist and co-operative principles, the group developed a 'communitarianism' that has valued group security over individual profit, and local values over provincial norms. For the first half of the community's life, and the first half of the twentieth century, the absence of pubs, police, and churches revealed that these islanders took a different path from other British Columbians. They followed a dream.

This communitarian dream, far from being a whim, was born out of circumstances of necessity. For the first Finnish immigrants to the island from Vancouver Island, it was a chance to protect themselves against exploitation in the Nanaimo coalmines. For the fishermen who joined the community later, it was an opportunity to combat the power of large canning companies. Time and again, those who came found that, in the face of outside threats, their interests were best protected by forming alliances among the island's distinct groups. Excessive individualism and economic accomplishment became seen as a threat to the prosperity of the community as a whole, with each member's well-being wrapped up in the community's success.

However, as the members and needs of the community changed over time, so did the values that informed Sointula's communitarianism. Its communitarianism, spanning the twentieth century, can not be reduced to Finnish nationalism, union support, or co-operative principles. But what then does being a member of the Sointula community mean? What communal values does the community in fact share?

There is no one defining feature on Malcolm Island that has drawn its residents – no vast plains for farming, no gold deposits, no industrial base to provide stable and secure wealth. While it adequately supports mainstay fishing and logging industries, it does not do so any better than other British Columbia communities. In short, Malcolm Island has never lent itself to people of a purely material bent, and those who have been attracted to the island have shared this in common – including early twentieth century Finnish-socialists searching for a better life; 1960s 'hippies' seeking to get back to the land; and, most recently, American arrivals looking for a simpler, less competitive environment.

This common thread among these diverse migrations has made the island a natural place for co-operation and community promotion. In return, the island has given them a beautiful, rural, and relatively isolated home in which to do so. And so today, even in troubled economic times, the island itself serves as the connection for the community – a physical and symbolic reminder of over one hundred years of practical dreaming.

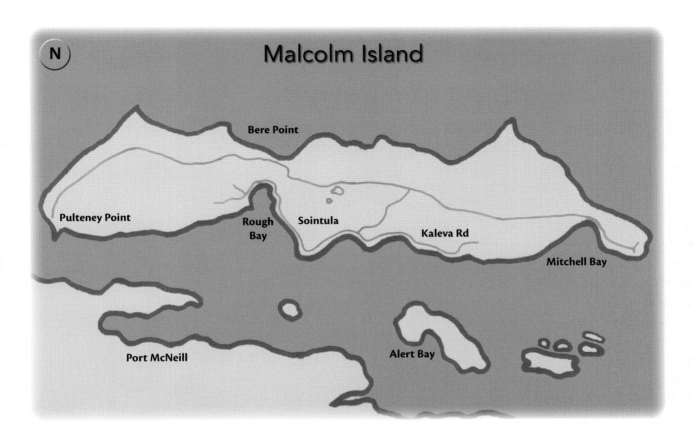

Malcolm Island

N

Bere Point

Pulteney Point

Rough Bay

Sointula

Kaleva Rd

Mitchell Bay

Port McNeill

Alert Bay

1. A Vision of Utopia

An agreement for the settlement of Malcolm Island was signed on November 29, 1901, between the co-operative Kalevan Kansa Company, representing a group of British Columbian Finns, and the Chief Commissioner of Lands and Works, representing His Majesty King Edward VII of England. From these formal beginnings arose a community that has stirred the public's imagination, giving rise to folklore that has, at times, taken on truly melodramatic dimensions. These tales have referred to the island as 'a free love utopia,' 'a hippie commune' and even 'the Communist state in BC.' However, though forgotten within this popular history, the real beginnings of Sointula lie almost a century earlier, in nineteenth century Finland.

In 1809, having been dominated by Sweden for hundreds of years, Finland finally gained a measure of autonomy under a new empire – and with it, a nationalism fueled by a new belief in the possibility of positive change. Backed by his powerful army, Tsar Alexander I of Russia tacitly made the Finns a proposition: in return for accepting him as Grand Duke of Finland (the title held by the Swedish monarch at the time) they would receive relative political and social control. Though many Finns felt a lingering loyalty to Sweden, particularly as Swedes remained a sizable minority within Finland itself, the majority of Finns had lost faith in the ability of Sweden to defend them, and saw possibilities for greater local autonomy under the Russian monarchy. Alexander's proposal was accepted.

As they had hoped, the Finns gained extensive autonomy under the Russians, permitting them to shape a national identity, which, while borrowing from those who had ruled over them, was distinctive. Pekka Hamalainen, a Finnish-American historian, has written that Finland:

> ...retained and developed further the political, social, and cultural institutions and traditions that it had inherited from its long association with Sweden. It had its own culture, laws, diet, government, civil service, military, monetary unit, official languages, educational system, church, and a number of other attributes which distinguished and separated it from the Russian empire.[1]

Inspired by the new horizons that this identity afforded, in 1835 classical scholar Elias Lonnrot published one of the most important cultural compositions in Finnish history, the national epic poem *The Kalevala* – drawn from Lonnrot's extensive collection of traditional Finnish runes, or folk song-poems. Roughly translated, the poem's title means 'The Land of Heroes,' whom it depicts working in a beautiful pastoral setting, striving for justice and a better life in the face of outside adversity. Its verses capture the spirit of an archetypal and ideal Finland,

By the turn of the twentieth century, *The Kalevala* had become a central text of inspiration for a Finnish nationalism that had made its way from the South and West of Finland, through the Nanaimo coal mines, to the shores of Malcolm Island. Its importance in Sointula's story cannot be underestimated. The poem's idyllic rural vision and individualistic self-conception did not merely represent what the Finnish-Canadian

The Kalevala

Lemminkainen's mother said:
"Just don't, my offspring
go into Northland's cabin
to Sariola's buildings.
Men there have swords at their belts
fellows have weapons of war
men are mad from hops
bad from much drinking.'

1. Previous Page: Mural formerly hung in the Finnish Organization Hall in Sointula, now in the Sointula Museum

A heroic figure attempts to triumph in a far away land but is overcome by harsh nature and his own hubris. That this story could be an allegory for Matti Kurikka, one of the most important leaders in the formation of Sointula, and his attempts at utopia is fitting — "The Kalevala" is celebrated for capturing the multi-faceted nature of the Finnish people. Its influence in Finland is probably unparalleled.

Credit for this goes to the scholar Elias Lonnrot. Through the 1820s and 1830s, at a time when Swedish was the language of culture and refinement, Lonnrot discovered a Finnish treasure in Karelia (an area bordering Russia). There, local bards inheriting oral tales passed down through generations sang tales of a Finland rich in magic and beauty. Fascinated, Lonnrot joined these song/poems into one 12,000 line work, The Kalevala.

With its main focus on the struggle between Kalevala (the land of heroes) and Pohja (a northland ruled by an evil enchantress) The Kalevala was to serve as an archetypal example of the struggle between light and darkness, images Kurikka would explore in "Aika." This powerful imagery, coupled with dazzling stories (clouds pouring honey on the first crops of Man; the birth of a messiah figure in a sauna) was to inspire such notable Finnish artists as Jean Sibelius, Eino Leino, and Akseli Gallen-Kallela. Internationally, Longfellow would model his poem "The Song of Hiawatha" after it and J.R.R. Tolkein would use elements from it in his "Lord of the Rings." Translated into forty-five languages The Kalevala has been a source of pride and influence for the Finnish people, both at home and in the outside world.[1]

immigrants were attempting to create in Sointula — it was a vital ideological motivation behind the community's inception. The community named its founding company after this poem, calling it the Kalevan Kansa Colonization Co. ("The People of Kaleva"). They filled their newspaper and official voice, *Aika*, with references to *The Kalevala*.

The poem's impact, however, began much earlier than Malcolm Island. Helping engender a cultural pride within Finland's new cultural autonomy, it was in part responsible for triggering an educational reform movement that caused the Finnish language to grow once again. While the Lutheran Church, which enjoyed national jurisdiction over education in Finland, had promoted general literacy, it opposed universal education and supported instruction in only Swedish. But, on October 1, 1858, Finland's first Finnish-language secondary school opened. Nine years later, the removal of educational institutions from the jurisdiction of the Lutheran Church was cemented in a bill of separation. The Finns had opened the doors for increased educational opportunities in their own language.

However, government policy seemed to remain particularly hostile to the desire of the Finnish-speaking majority, requiring public pressure and dedicated liberal legislators to help Finns utilize these increased educational opportunities. Historian L. A. Puntila notes that in the 1880s, "efforts by the bureaucracy to stifle the development of the Finnish-language secondary school led to a rapid growth in the desire to learn and encouraged a great deal of volunteer work and self-sacrifice for the sake of these schools. The growth of interest in learning among the peasantry was striking."[2]

The spirit behind this growth of educational fervour in the face of official obstruction found its way to Sointula, manifesting itself in several attitudes that became characteristic of the Sointula community. In a very direct way, it resulted in the immigrants' stress on the importance of formal education in the Finnish language. By the early 1900s Sointula had the largest Finnish language library in Canada. In a less direct but equally important way, it resulted in a distrust of authority, a characteristic that would be emphasized and re-emphasized throughout Sointula's existence.

Much of this distrust was aimed at the power of the Lutheran Church. *Aika's* constant tirades against the Church (as notably distinct from Christian spirituality) speak of the dominant role that this institution had in nineteenth-century Finland. Not only had this institution attempted to stifle advanced educational possibilities for the common Finnish people, but, as the official church of Finland, it had been granted taxing privileges. "The priest's sack is bottomless," runs an old Finnish adage, referring to the extent of Church taxation and the days of labour that tenant farmers owed to the local parsonage.[3] Despite the liberal reforms regarding language and education that had occurred in this period, the nation remained under the control of a hierarchy, of which the Church was a central part. In the words of one historian, the Lutheran Church "was the Church of the Establishment, and the nation was of the Establishment."[4]

This national hierarchy also included factory owners and rural landholders, typically a Swedish speaking elite removed from the concerns of the Finnish majority. Industrialization had stirred unrest and encouraged Finnish nationalism as rural Finns moved to the cities and larger towns, only to find themselves struggling to survive in

Minna
Canth

an crowded, unhealthy urban sprawl. In the 1860s a devastating famine deepened this discontent, as it drove even more Finns to the cities and off their land. Life was no more certain for the majority of Finns who remained on their farms. As the descendent of an original Sointula colonist noted, "In the 1880s, Finland was like a dictatorship. You had to do what you were told, it was hard to own land, and you had to pay a lot of taxes to the government."[5] Puntila adds, "those who owned the land could turn out the tenants whenever they saw fit; often from fields the crofters had cleared themselves."[6]

Conditions such as these helped engender socialist activity, particularly in southern Finland, which had the largest number of peasant farmers. The socialist leaders emerging from this area included playwright and feminist Minna Canth and two of her acolytes:

Minna Canth, feminist, playwright, social activist, Tolstoy disciple, sometime journalist—it is not difficult to see the shared interests that this dynamic woman and the future leaders of Sointula would have had. As a patron of Canth's salon in the city of Kuopio, young Matti Kurikka was exposed to a personality and ideas that would greatly influence his thoughts and writings. But while the future leader of Sointula would never be able to turn this ideology into a workable reality, his mentor, through a zeal tempered with commitment, would become a lasting symbol for the Finnish people.

Canth would use the social discrimination she experienced in her working class childhood, along with a sense of nationalism gained at a teacher's seminary, to fuel her desire to educate the Finnish people. Together with her husband and fellow teacher Johan Canth, she proceeded to do just that, co-editing two newspapers ('Keski-Suomi' and 'Paijanne'), and contributing articles on feminism and social issues. When Johan died in 1879, Canth took her seven children and moved to the city of Kuopio.

Finding her niche in play-wrighting, Canth shocked audiences with inflammatory works, pointing out the hypocrisy, sexism, and social bigotry existing in Finnish society. Like Kurikka's 'The Tower of Babel,' Canth's works were attacked and her career threatened. However, unlike Kurikka, she knew when to pull back, following a controversial play with something more generally acceptable.

Canth was also active as a short-story writer and journalist throughout her life. In 1889-1890 she co-edited the journal 'Vapaita Aatteita' (Free Ideas) with another future Sointula leader, Austin Makela. She died of a heart attack in 1897. Since then, she has become a legend in Finland, celebrated as a nurturing mother, tireless reformer, and literary artisan.[1, 2]

the writers, journalists, and soon to be utopian leaders, Matti Kurikka, and Austin Makela. These future leaders of Sointula would spend hours in Minna Canth's salon discussing not only socialist and nationalist thought, but also the religious and intellectual ideas that were arising throughout Europe and America. Many of the ideas formed by Matti Kurikka in the comfort of Minna Canth's salon were controversial views that ultimately served not only to establish and inform Malcolm Island's unique ideology but also to divide it.

These ideas, however, had little time to take root in Finland. As the Industrial revolution continued, the already subsistent lives of the common Finnish people became even grimmer under the oppressive rule of the Russian Tsar Alexander III (1881-1894). Taking steps to curb Finland's special status, Alexander lessened the power of the Finnish Senate and placed the Finnish postal service under the control of the Russian Ministry of Internal Affairs. Russian oppression became even worse during the reign of Alexander's successor, Nicholas II (1894-1917) when he extended the Russian autocracy to Finland with the February manifesto of 1899. The edict effectively annulled the Finnish constitution and transformed the laws of the Finnish Diet into simple advice that the Tsar could take or leave as he saw fit.[7] It also allowed for the conscription of Finns into the Russian army, a development many saw as placing Finland on the same footing as any other Russian province.

It was all too much for many Finns. This increased Russian autocracy, together with the urban economic turmoil, unstable rural tenant system, and Church hierarchy, led to a grand scale exodus of Finns in the late nineteenth century – hoping to find a better life elsewhere.

Tens of thousands of these Finns settled in Canada, including a sizeable proportion of Finns who had initially emmigrated to the United States. Having become dissapointed at their prospects there, these Finns moved on to Canada for the opportunities that a young, quickly developing nation seemed to offer. However, Canada posed its own challenges and difficulties, and, becoming frustrated, many Finns began to search for some other place to fulfill their dream – a place apart from the rules, regulations, and confines that had held them in the past. A place of harmony.

2. Above: Minna Canth's Collected Works

What a life was yours
on these farms of your father's!
You grew in the lanes of a flower
a strawberry in the glades...
Now you are leaving this house
going to a different house
to a different mother's rule
to a strange household.

- 'Laments' from **The Kaleva**

2.   Forming the Dream

For many Finnish immigrants in the late nineteenth century, Queen Victoria was to become their "different mother" and Canada their "strange household." It has been estimated that by 1911, the Finnish-Canadian population had reached 15,000. While not large compared with many other ethnic groups in Canada, the Finns made their presence felt through their hard work, political activities, and a marked ability to form a united front – a tendancy that would earn many Finnish-Canadians a reputation for being 'clannish.' However, it was an understandable response to the insecurities they faced in a new country, one that, while seeming to offer so much, withheld the prosperity Finnish immigrants longed for.

Starting in the Dark

The Finns search for prosperity and a sense of community is perhaps best captured by the first-hand account of original settler Matti Halminen, *The History of Sointula and the Kalevan Kansa*. Halminen notes that Finns did not start arriving in Canada in any real numbers until the 1880s, when the Canadian Pacific Railway, aided by the Canadian government, attempted to secure workers for the construction and maintenance of its transcontinental line. These first Finns, many of whom were from the poor south-western Lapua region of Finland, found work on the BC section of the CPR, several of them securing coveted section boss positions. Though hardly joining the ranks of the province's business elite, this first wave of Lapua Finns continued to hold important positions on the railroad for decades to come, affording them the chance of advancement and a better life in British Columbia.

The same cannot be said for the second wave of Finnish workers, who, upon arriving in B.C., started work in the Vancouver Island mines. Halminen recalls how Vancouver Island coalmines had found themselves in need of labourers when, due to frequent gas explosions and deaths, a large number of workers left on account of the risk. Finns, who were making their way to Nanaimo from the United States in Canada, saw these job openings as an opportunity and were quickly snatched up by eager mine owners. Writing to others back home and in the US of the favourable job prospects, they paved the way for an influx of Finnish migrant miners to the area.

In many ways, the initial experience of Finnish migrants in the mining communities of Nanaimo, Ladysmith, and Extension was only a magnification of the problems they had experienced back home. With little chance of being able to secure farmland at an affordable price, the new immigrants were relatively dependent on the whims of the industrial bosses, just as they had been in Finland. In relating the abuse that occurred, Halminen highlights the practical reasoning behind Sointula's ideological core:

> As the [Nanaimo] coal seams became depleted around the turn of the century, the owner of the mines,…James Dunsmuir, began to mine for coal at a place twelve miles away known as the Extension mines. The workers who sought employment there dismantled their board-constructed homes and carried the materials with them to rebuild on lots rented from a private

3. Previous Page
An early Malcolm Island
homestead, with potatoe crop.

4. Opposite Page:
Early Malcolm Island homestaeders,
Matti Halminen in centre.

landowner. Soon after, that same millionaire decided to form a new town on the shores of Oyster Harbour where the Extension coal was loaded onto ships. As a result, he decreed that all the Extension miners who wished to continue working for him must move to live in the new town that he named Ladysmith...Once again, the miners were obliged to dismantle their homes as directed and to purchase lots from Mr. Dunsmuir at high prices. If anything can teach a thinking man to despise subservience and to escape from beneath despotic conditions, it is recollections about events like those.[1]

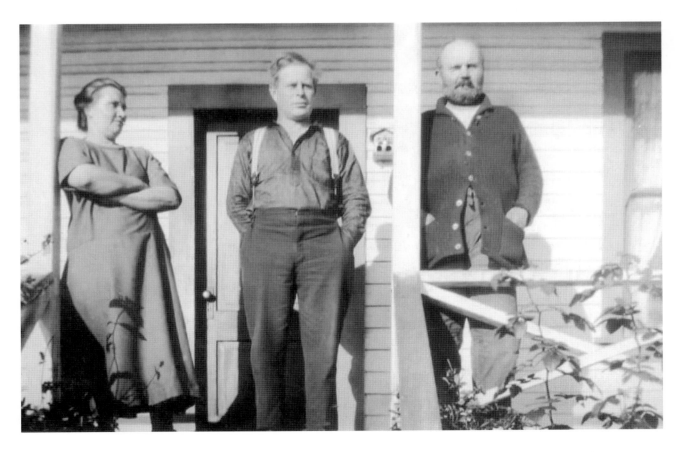

Low wages and forced relocation were by no means the only hardships faced by these workers. Far from the support and social stability of home, and isolated by their lack of English, many Finnish miners turned to alcohol for comfort, earning them the derogatory moniker of "bad Russian Finns."[2] Recalling the unhealthy atmosphere of this time, Halminen notes that "gang fights and drunkenness were everyday fare during holidays as well as during the working week."[3] Historian Allan H. Salo relates that the mine owners of the time were all too happy to encourage this debauched lifestyle, arranging to have alcohol delivered to the miners, keeping them disunited and in debt.[4] With little hope for advancement and lacking a sense of community, the freedom that many Finns had come to Canada to find was in reality becoming a trap of poverty, shame, and booze.

A Reawakening

It was at this low point in the early 1890s that two temperance organizations were formed near Nanaimo, *Lannen Rusko* ("Western Glow") on Feb. 5, 1890, and *Allotar* ("Water Nymph") on Oct. 11, 1891 – the former being the first Finnish temperance organization in Canada. These two groups had an enormous impact upon the Finns of Vancouver Island, and led, by direct and indirect means, to the formation of the Sointula experiment. Though not a founding member of *Lannen Rusko*, Halminen joined soon after and found it an uplifting experience;

> [When] a person grasps hold of the proper perspective of life's higher virtues he will most often direct to his new undertakings the same vigour which he had formerly applied to less constructive activities... this became very evident within the temperance movement and later that enthusiasm showed itself in union labour participation.[5]

This vigour was dramatically accelerated with the founding of *Allotar*, an organization that did far more than promote temperance. It helped establish a Finnish language library, gave rise to a Finnish brass band that played prominently in English temperance marches, and served as a forum through which Finnish immigrants could begin to discuss their place in the English-speaking society. Such efforts seemed to powerfully transform a dispirited group of foreign speaking migrant workers into a purposeful unit, one with hope for the future. Halminen, who was a founding member of *Allotar*, describes this point of his life as a "spiritual awakening."[6]

But if *Allotar* and *Lannen Rusko* had given the Finns in and around Nanaimo spiritual hope, they were still searching for an economic foundation on which to base that hope. In his *History of Sointula*, Halminen makes clear that in the 1890s the Finns around Nanaimo had already discussed the possibility of a co-operative enterprise to fill that gap. This was quite a natural development as the Finns had a long history of co-operative dealings. Historian W. R. Mead notes that rural Finland had a tradition of *talkoot*, collective house and barn building, harvesting and fishing, that went back centuries.[7] Further, the modern co-operative movement in Finland had gained momentum in the late 1870s and dairy co-ops, consumer co-ops, and workers' joint-stock companies arose throughout the 1880s and 1890s. The Finns of Vancouver Island would either have had direct experience of them, heard about them from relatives, or read about them in Finnish publications, such as those brought in through the activities of *Allotar*. This communitarian history, coupled with the lack of opportunity for individual advancement for Finns in an English-dominated society, made co-operative ventures a decidedly practical choice.

Dreaming Out Loud: The Kalevan Kansa Co.

Yet, something was missing. While the reasons for a co-operative were there, the co-operative movement needed a spark to set it off. That spark was to take the form of the charismatic and controversial journalist/playwright Matti Kurikka. Halminen and his fellow miners had heard of Kurikka, of course; what literate Finn hadn't? He had been the mercurial editor of the Helsinki working class newspaper *Tyomies* in the 1880s; had scandalized Finnish society in 1899 by deriding its political and religious hierarchy with his play *The Tower of Babel*; and had run for leadership of the Finnish Socialist Federation political party that same year. Having narrowly lost his campaign for leadership, Kurikka immediately left for Australia to form a utopian commune in Queensland, an attempt that failed by 1900.

While Kurikka was pondering his next move, three ex-members of his attempted commune had arrived in Extension, BC, looking for work. There, they happened upon

Halminen, who was naturally curious to hear more of this somewhat infamous man. Halminen, who had been given some pamphlets that Kurikka had written concerning workers rights, was impressed. He exchanged letters with Kurikka, the miners raised money for passage, and in the fall of 1900 Kurikka arrived in Nanaimo.

For the next year, Matti Kurikka did what he did best: dreamed out loud. In doing so, he prompted others to share his dreams. Though Halminen noted that many of his early ideas would later be regarded as impossible, Kurikka had the gift of making them seem "practical and imaginative" when he presented them.[8] Kurikka's vision centred around the idea of forming a joint stock company, the Kalevan Kansa Co. – a vision that resonated with the co-operative hopes that Halminen and others had previously discussed. To promote this vision, Kurikka founded the newspaper *Aika*, a forum in which he connected the stock company to notions of socialism, Christian love, and women's rights. Then, through lecture tours, he carried his campaign for the Kalevan Kansa Company throughout BC and the West Coast of the United States.

Classically good looking with long dark hair and a captivating voice, Kurikka's meetings drew in crowds of potential investors and settlers. Starting softly in his talks, he would gather momentum until he charmed his audience with a "frantic speech" that denounced organized religion, capitalism, and the evils of western society, all of which he promised the Kalevan Kansa would avoid. Though much of what he was saying merely echoed ideas already formed by Halminen and his fellow workers, Kurikka provided the inspiration to make these miners' dreams a reality. As Halminen himself admits, "without Kurikka's assistance we did not have the needed faith to make it come about. We needed his eloquence and sharp pen for our assistance."[9]

Halminen makes clear, however, that "In practical matters we could have depended on ourselves."[10] He tells how he himself was to find the colony's future home. Having travelled to the legislature buildings in Victoria in the spring of 1901, Halminen was given a handful of maps by the Ministry of Lands and Labour. Malcolm Island, located between the north part of Vancouver Island and mainland British Columbia, seemed perfect. It was close to shipping lanes, was an appropriate size, had a sizable forest area, and, most importantly, was designated as a prime agricultural area. This last part was particularly attractive. Whatever the varied ideological reasons people had for coming

5. Right:
Early Portrait of
Matti Kurikka

6. Far Right:
1904 Edition of Aika

I   No 10

AIKA

Huhtikuun 1 p. 1904.

TOIMITTAJAT:
MATTI KURIKKA.   AUSTIN MÄKELÄ.

Kirjoitukset vastaamaan tekijäinsä kinnoilt, onnistuneet, eitä he — yhteen — ovat vastuunalaiset omien valtuoyrunä mielipiteissä.

TILAUS-HINNOISTA J. M. Austin Consulatta teko-aivulla.

Ilmoitukaila ei ohota mukaan vastaan.

OSOTE: AIKA
                  SOINTULA B.C.
                      CANADA.

Sointula, B. C., Malcovan Kasawa C. Oien Kirjapaino.

to Sointula, the desire to farm was paramount. Long-time Sointula resident Arvo Tynjala relates how his father travelled from North Dakota to Sointula with four or five families, all of them bent on farming.[11] This hope was even stronger amongst the disillusioned miners of Vancouver Island. Halminen's reaction to the possibilities of Malcolm Island was immediate and direct: "That island we must attain for our settlers I immediately thought – we must try to get it right away."[12]

Though not yet formally registered as a company, by 1901 the Kalevan Kansa was a working unit, with a board of directors and an acting President (Kurikka). They shared Halminen's enthusiasm for the possibilities of Malcolm Island, but two problems existed. First, as many of the potential settlers did not have the necessary $200 to buy a share in the Kalevan Kansa Co., it was arranged that settlers could pledge to work off their share in labour. However, while this allowed the company to get off the ground, it left it cash poor. Second, the Industrial Power Company of British Columbia had recently received Malcolm Island as part of a timber lease. Resourcefully, the Kalevan Kansa Co. used the second problem to help solve the first, negotiating a contract with Industrial Power to log the timber on the island. In theory, everything seemed to be in place for the Kalevan Kansa company to take possession of the island.

Unexpectedly, the provincial government, which had previously been supportive of granting the company possession of the island, seemed to have last minute doubts and began to drag its feet. Perhaps it was remnants of old popular opinion that made the government question the wisdom of handing over an island to a group of "bad Russian Finns." But, at just the right time, the group began receiving unprecedented favourable press supporting its position. Through the activities of *Allotar* and *Lannen Rusko*, public perception of Vancouver Island Finns had become quite positive – a reputation that was rienforced though publicity of their plight of living under the harshness of Russian rule. *The Nanaimo Daily Herald* noted that the Finns promoted "industry, refinement, and a belief in realistic idealism,"[13] while the *Victoria Daily Colonist* noted that the future settlers of Malcolm Island were "an industrious, frugal, and easily contented people willing to work hard to secure peaceful homes."[14] The combined force of this public opinion and the Finns persistent inquiries had its effect. On November 29, 1901, the Kalevan Kansa signed an agreement with the government for possession of Malcolm Island.

7. Right:
Early Photo of Sointula's
Hall, down First Street

On the surface, the agreement seemed hugely favourable to the Finns. The settlers were given seven years to bring 350 people to the island and to make improvements worth $2.50 an acre. If successful, not only would Malcolm Island be granted to them, the government would also pledge them an additional property the same size as Malcolm Island. The stipulation that the Finns build a school and have their children educated in English seemed to be but a small matter. As Kurikka noted, "I feel the language and nationality of a truly vital, civilized nation will not disappear — even if it is in constant contact with other languages."[15] Kurikka was overcome with enthusiasm: "We will be self sufficient and produce everything we need. Unemployment and sickness will evaporate into the past and strikes and poverty will become unknown. It only depends on us to break free from the feet of the capitalists."[16]

Yet, despite this optimism, Kurikka was not without doubt. His original utopia in Australia had foundered largely due to a lack of capital, and, fearing the same possibility in Canada, he made a deal with the king of capitalism himself – James Dunsmuir. Attempting to secure employment for Malcolm Island settlers and sufficient capital for the Kalevan Kansa Co., Kurikka agreed to provide up to 200 miners for Dunsmuir at a rate of $2.50 a day, fifty cents below the standard daily wage of $3.00 a day. Further, in exchange for receiving their job, each worker would have to agree to pay at least five dollars a month towards their membership in the Kalevan Kansa. Though this scheme could have brought in a much needed one thousand dollars a month to the company coffers, the board of directors was outraged: "The Kalevan Kansa will not be founded by trampling the wages of other workers, injuring them and thereby irritating them to be against us!"[17] Ironically, this plan was to be nullified by Dunsmuir himself, who shut down the proposed mining site upon hearing that some of the miners were attempting to unionize.

While nothing ever came of the incident, it revealed a problem that the island would continue to have to deal with over the next century: how should a leader of a communitarian enterprise lead? It was a problem that was perhaps most accutely felt in Kurikka, whose charisma included the tendency to leap boldly into a project without properly considerning all the factors unique to this community.

In truth, Kurikka's ability to get carried away with his own ideas, seemingly caught up in his own fiery rhetoric should not have been a surprise. His striking out against political and religious elites in *The Tower of Babel* had cast him out of the upper echelon of Finnish society; his deriding of Marxism as hate-oriented 'stomach' socialism had set him at odds with both Finnish and Canadian socialist groups that were potential allies; and his fiery lectures against the church in North America caused a backlash against not only himself, but against the Malcolm Island community which he represented. His attacks on religion were so notorious that when describing a lecture by Kurikka, a reporter in Worchester, Massachusetts, noted that "word spread among our citizens that the devil himself has now arrived."[18]

Kurikka himself admitted that he needed a counterweight to his fiery personality, and recommended his old university friend, Austin Makela, for the role. Cool-minded and methodical, Makela had helped temper Kurikka's extreme nature in the late 1890s when the two wrote for the workers' daily paper, *Tyomies*, in Helsinki. At least one observer has noted that the direct and thoughtful Makela was "much more danger-ous to his opposition than the shifting and inconsistent Kurikka."[19] Makela responded to Kurikka's request almost immediately, arriving on Malcolm Island in January of 1902. In his memoirs Makela suggested that he left Finland one step ahead of the Russian secret police, who were set to arrest him for his role in directing underground Marxist literature into Russia; others suggested that he left Finland one step ahead of his alcohol, a personal demon that was ruining both his journalistic career and his strong influence with the Finnish Labour Party. Whichever the real reason, both alcoholism and Marxism followed him to Malcolm Island, tempering his own development as he attempted to temper Kurikka.

Yet, despite the fact that Makela's 'stomach' Marxism was anathema to Kurikka and his alcoholism offensive to the temperance-minded community, his presence on the island had the desired calming effect right from the beginning. The government, in reaching an agreement for Malcolm Island, had insisted that the Kalevan Kansa require all prospective settlers to swear an oath of allegiance to the King and commit to take up arms in defense of Canada should the need arise. For the Finns, these clauses brought up the ghosts of both government interference in their homeland and the conscription of Finns into the Russian army. Yet Makela was able to dispel these fears before they could begin to create a problem. While agreeing with his fellow settlers that it would have been best to dispense with any oath of allegiance, he made light of any great need that the King of England would have for remote Malcolm Island; he likewise deftly defused conscription fears by noting that the only nearby enemies of Canada were Russia and China, and who would not take up arms if those "barbarians" attacked?[20] In a similar vein of strategic com-promise, Makela soon changed his name to Austin Mckela, explaining, "I just took things from a practical point of view. I spelled my name in a way that enables the English speaker to read it and write it."[21] The name Mckela may also have enabled the Finn to more easily carry out Kalevan Kansa business in a British Columbia dominated by an Anglo-Saxon hierarchy. Where Kurikka moved boldly and often earned criticism, Makela moved sub-tly and earned respect. In the end, his ability to strike compromises and work practically within the larger society set the standard by which Sointula would continue to develop.

Austin Makela

8. Left:
   Early Photo of
   Austin Makela

"If Makela was here he'd straighten it out." As Justice of the Peace, community judge, and link between the developing community and its utopian roots, Makela provided a steadying influence on Malcolm Island, one that was missed after his death in 1932.

Ironically, he himself led a far from steady life. Within a one-year period in 1907-1908, he resigned his position as lighthouse keeper on Malcolm Island, edited a socialist newspaper in Massachusetts, and returned to political activism in Finland. Perceiving a lack of socialist values in his birthplace, he derided Finland as "a land of spies and cordwood dealers," and returned to Sointula.

Continuing as lighthouse keeper, while writing occasional plays and stories, Makela remained unsteady in Canada. Alcohol was an ongoing destabling factor. A lack of empathy with his adopted country was another. In 1913 he wrote, "What do I know about Canada? What do I care about Canadian affairs?"[12] He was a poor English speaker in a country more conservative than socialist in nature. He had left Finland in his past, and could see no place for Canada in his future.

Sointula, however, had certainly held a place for him during his lifetime. At his funeral on February 28, 1932, most of the community walked in a procession from the FO hall to the cemetery, the Soviet flag waving at front. Makela was honoured for his socialist beliefs, and for being a strong leader during difficult times — for being "the one who stayed on Malcolm Island."[13]

And the need for a practical mindset on Malcolm Island became clear. The Kalevan Kansa's first annual report in June of 1902 noted an outstanding debt of $1300. By November of the same year, the island had 200 residents, many of whom were living in tents, not only trying to make ends meet, but needing to work off their $200 membership fee. The farmland that had been so coveted by these settlers remained covered with forest and dense brush, and the Kalevan Kansa's business dealings were not doing well. After having negotiated what he felt was a shrewd contract with a Rivers Inlet salmon canning company, Kurikka set out with a Malcolm Island fishing expedition, only to be told he had arrived too late and someone else had been hired.

Even the news that the Industrial Power lease of Malcolm Island timber had been cancelled did not turn out to be as good as had been hoped: while Malcolm Islanders could now reap complete profit from their logging efforts, they did not have the infastructure needed to overcome the prohibitive costs of marketing and transporting their wood. With the completion of a sawmill near the end of 1902, the community hoped that these setbacks could be overcome and the Kalevan Kansa would be put back on the right financial track. However, even this accomplishment was of dubious worth, as the inexperienced Sointula workers had been unable to get the sawmill up to an acceptably profitable speed.

While exploring on a remote beach early in 1902, the first Finnish Malcolm Island settlers discovered a rough wooden shack and rusted pipes from an abandoned steam plant. It was learned that they were all that was left of a previous utopian commune established by Joseph Spenser, a penitential clergyman who had arrived on Malcolm Island with his own group of settlers in 1895.[22] Given the events of 1902, it would not have been unduly pessimistic of Kurikka's settlers to forecast their own futures in these rusted remains. That they did not do so speaks to the command of the shared dream that captured the majority of the colony. Even the moderate and cool-headed Makela noted in his memoirs that his reaction upon arriving on Malcolm Island was that "there would have been room for the whole Finnish working class."[23] Makela's words reveal that the colony's vision was a large as the history they carried with them; "I thought of building a big ocean vessel which could bring the whole Finnish nation to that free land."[24] Like Kurikka and Halminen, Makela seemed overcome by the possibilities offered – a response shared by leaders and community members alike.

9. Left: Steam donkey on Malcolm Island in 1920s .

10. Right: Steam donkey on Malcolm Island, date unknown.

A Spiritual Light

The vast majority of the first Finnish settlers on Malcolm Island were in their twenties and thirties. One long-term Sointula resident, Irene Michelson, recalls elders of the island discussing the start of the colony: "they were all so happy, young, healthy, ambitious to make everything to turn good."[25] Clearly there was something beyond simply material gain driving these settlers. Sointula resident Mrs. L. E. Guthrie notes that her father was a successful businessman in Oregon who moved to Malcolm Island after becoming intrigued by the thought of establishing a more socially just society.[26] The colony's first doctor, Oswald Beckman, had likewise been brought over from Astoria Oregon, convinced by Matti Kurikka to leave a successful private practice in pursuit of a dream. The settlers of Malcolm Island were not just seeking an escape from economic and political oppression; they had a sense of creating something new.

This creation, at times, took on a decidedly mythic quality. *Allotar*, the temperance society from which the original idea of a co-operative venture sprang, is the name of a water goddess in Finnish mythology. The boat that brought the first settlers to the island, the *Aino*, is the name of a heroine of the Kalevala epic. In the March 1902 issue of *Aika*, Kurikka wrote of creating a place of peace, *Rauhala*, in an island bay – where no living creature shall be hurt. Kurika wrote that a duck had waddled unharmed through a group of armed settlers, flying away to spread the word to others of the good people to be found there.[27] Inspired by the *Kalevala's* theme of the bond between nature and humanity, Kurikka had a wonderful ability to wed these elements of Finnish myth with a strong theosophic belief, learned in part at the salon of Minna Canth.

Theosophy is described as being based on claims of a "mystic insight into the nature of God and the laws of the universe,"[28] whereby the true theosophist relies on his or her "insights" as more valid than pure reason. Kurikka not only uses this philosophy to deride symbols of structure and reason in European society (at one point pairing science with organized religion as two symbols of false authority), but to promote a true Christianity based on simple love. Issu (Finnish for Jesus) is written of consistently throughout the pages of *Aika*, Kurikka noting that the colony on Malcolm Island was to be "a Nazarene's light in Europe's darkness." This light was to be evoked through literature, music, and the sharing of philosophical ideals.[29]

It is difficult to know how deeply the other settlers believed in Kurikka's vision for the island as a theosophic utopia. Makela, for one, categorized theosophy as merely "the seventeenth form of religion that they have tried to force upon me in my lifetime."[30] Yet, though Makela's common sense views of life were respected from the beginning, it was Kurikka's passion and vision for the island that brought the community to life. Kurikka's choice for the colony's name, Sointula (place of harmony), easily won out over Makela's less colourful choice of Kodiksi (home place). When the first board of directors was elected at the first annual meeting, Kurikka was made President, receiving every one of the cast votes. Even the practical Matti Halminen wrote in his memoirs that at this starting point, "it truly seemed possible that we could build a utopia."[31]

Early and practical application of the shared ideals of this utopic vision helped keep this dream living as long as it did. As a direct reflection of the exploitive working conditions in Finland and in Dunsmuir's mines, the colony set out certain standard working conditions: an eight hour work day; one dollar a day in wage; leaders for each work group chosen by that work group; and, at the end of the year, each stock holder would receive a five percent dividend on their stock – half of which would go back into the company for recreational and intellectual benefits.[32] All stockholders, women as well as men, were to be entitled to vote on the affairs of the colony. As well, in keeping with both the educational and linguistic reforms that had begun in Finland, Sointula developed a 2000-book Finnish language library, run by settler Katri Riksman. Even the cultural desires of the colony were largely met through the production of its own plays, and the creation of its own music. By 1904, an assortment of the colonists' poems were even published in two volumes entitled *Kansan Sointuja I and II* (Kalevan Kansa Songs of Harmony); Kurikka, having set some of them to traditional Finnish hymn music, read and sang them on his lecture tours, eventually selling 2500 copies off the island.[33] These practices and achievements gave the colonists of Sointula a degree of optimism and pride in their utopia; times might be hard, but look at what was being accomplished!

So much seemed possible that it may have been difficult for the colonists to separate the achievable from the fantastical, as evidenced by the board of directors meeting of July 8, 1902. As would later occur at the Sointula Co-op store's semi-annual meetings, the Kalevan Kansa board concerned themselves with matters beyond business, including community concerns and celebrations. At this particular meeting the matter of beginning English lessons for the community was discussed and agreed on, after which *The Tower of Babel* was performed, and a song by Kurikka sung. The colonists also agreed upon the less practical idea of creating an entirely new calendar, based on a six-day week, and a five-week month, after which brother Martin Henrikson gave a lecture on the duty of the colonists to become model citizens who would 'spread the light' wherever they went in the world.[34]

12. Right:
Sointula actors in FO
Hall play, date unknown.

From the start there was an inner battle in the hearts of the colonists: on one side, the desire to fit in with the rest of society while still proudly promoting Finnish heritage and socialist thought; on the other side, the hope of creating a new society apart from the capitalist world, one which would influence Western civilization with the power of its example. In the end, only one of the ideas would prove practical enough to survive.

Discord and Devotion

The demise of the hope of creating a new society may very well be seen to have begun on the night of January 30, 1903. True, many holes had already been shot through the utopian ideal before this point: unsuccessful financial ventures, including a recent attempt to raise dairy cattle on the island that failed because of the lack of fodder; an exodus of many settlers disappointed with the colony's lack of comforts; and the grumbling of many who remained at having to live in communal dwellings. But, as Halminen notes in his memoirs, Kurikka was tireless in combatting these problems. Just when it looked like the money was running out, Kurikka would return from Vancouver with money from a log shipment; as old settlers left, Kurikka would convince more settlers to take their place: and if the recently completed three-story log house nicknamed *Melula* (noisy) was not any colonists' idea of utopia, it was at least a temporary housing solution until individual cabins could be built.[35] As Halminen wrote, without Kurikka, the colonists did not have the necessary faith to make this venture a success, the faith to believe that the dream of making something new was in fact happening.

When the *Melula* was destroyed in a fire that claimed eleven lives, faith in this dream of creation was severely shaken. "I will not try to present a description of the effect of that blow," Halminen writes, "I will simply say that the strength was gone from my feet...Eleven people, who were to me like brothers and sisters have been killed."[36] Though paling in comparison to the loss of friends and loved ones, the loss of colony goods was great as well; it is estimated that thirteen tons of supplies, as well as passports and the company ledger, were destroyed.

At perhaps no other time was the strength and example of the colony's leader needed more. Yet, at just the time when the community needed to pull together, the figure of their leader became a dividing point. People began to find curious goings-on regarding Kurikka's conduct in this affair. Even before the fire, some disgruntled ex-settlers had sent letters to various newspapers questioning their leader's honesty and competence. The financial affairs of the Kalevan Kansa that winter were grim, and Kurikka had himself admitted to Halminen that at times it was necessary for him to "lie a little," just to keep the colony afloat.[37] The creditors of the Kalevan Kansa Co. had sent a representative named Bell to Malcolm Island to see if it was worthwhile to give the colony any

13. Left:
Sointula Band,
date unknown.

more credit; by coincidence, the fire occurred while Bell was staying in *Melula*. Rumours spread that Bell was an auditor sent by the government, and that Kurikka himself had started the fire to get rid of evidence that he had been embezzling funds. This speculation was fueled by the fact that Kurikka was among the very first out of the burning building, his hands having apparently grabbed only his important poems on the way out. In light of these circumstances, the rumours were almost impossible to combat; nearly a year past the event, Kurikka was still defending his actions in *Aika*.[38]

The fact that these rumors persisted despite there being no credible evidence of arson by Kurikka is significant. Bell was not a government inspector, and it seems unreasonable that the leader of a fragile colony would desire a blow like this. What is clear is that a portion of the Kalevan Kansa was beginning to doubt the character of its leader and to perhaps question whether such a man could create a new and just society on Malcolm Island.

Many settlers had reached their breaking point, including the irreplaceable doctor Beckman, who left to start a new life in the United States. Other settlers were driven away when they persisted in their rumours against Kurikka. Though he had decided not to formally prosecute those who had besmirched his name, Kurikka insisted that two of the worst offenders be tossed from the island, threatening to resign if they were not. Makela, who had received his own share of unsubstantiated accusations regarding the fire, unexpectedly opposed this motion. While Kurikka won, the first truly open split between Kurikka and Makela had begun.

Remarkably, though surrounded by signs indicating that the dream of creating a new society had begun to die, many of the settlers clung to the vision which had brought them there. Three weeks after the fire, an annual meeting of the Kalevan Kansa was held, at which it was disclosed that the company had debts totaling nearly $61,000, and had made a grand total of $32.38 profit the previous year. Yet the *sisu* (grit, or determination) of the colony was not destroyed: individual log cabins were built to replace *Melula*; $1,000 was raised to improve the printing press; a bigger engine for the sawmill was purchased through a settler's $2,000 donation; and the attendees even considered the feasibility of forming a bank to lend money to others coming to the island (the dream of an island-based bank would come to be realized in 1940, with the formation of the Sointula Credit Union, as discussed later).[39]

Even more incredible was the creation of the 'settlers' agreement.' Drafted by Makela at the request of the board of directors, the agreement stated that members of the Kalevan Kansa were to look upon their work, money, shares, or other donations to the company, not as outside society would see it, but as part of the co-operative venture of the utopia. Accordingly, any disagreement over private property was to be settled by the company rather than by an outside court.[40] Thus, members were prohibited from leaving the colony with their goods and money, and thereby threatening the colony with bankruptcy.

While the agreement was an attempt to stabilize the company's economy, it helped cement an idea that was to remain on the island for generations: interference by outside authorities is unnecessary, the community can take care of its own affairs. And, generally speaking, the outside world did not care to interfere. Despite assurances in *Aika*

14. Upper Left:
Kalevela School with Paul
Salo in front, date unknown.

15. Lower Left:
Sointula Schoolhouse,
date unkown.

that capitalists such as Dunsmuir were distraught at losing their Finnish workers to the Sointula utopia, the activities of the Malcolm Islanders were viewed as a private affair.

Matti Kurikka: A Beginning and An End

The outside world's view changed, however, as Kurikka began to write more and more about what came to be known as "free love." Tying in socialist ideals with notions of the purity of nature and women's equality, Kurikka wrote that "once private ownership is abolished, the family becomes unnecessary and marriage recognized as fornication, what could be purer than what is already seen in uncorrupted nature."[41] Uncorrupted nature, Kurikka noted, meant that it is fine for a woman to have different fathers for her children. Kurikka defended his belief by noting that traditional marriage placed women in a subordinate position to men, and that it was this inequality that he was attempting to fight.

The world outside the island saw Kurikka's views somewhat differently. Jhan Lundell, a Lutheran preacher at Extension, wrote to the provincial government that "Matti Kurikka is the leader of a socialist and atheist element and he personally advocates free love."[42] It is uncertain what Lundell expected the provincial government to do with this information, but, as Halminen relates, many settlers feared this scandal would cause the authorities to become involved in the colony's affairs. While this did not occur, Lundell's depiction of Sointula was not easily shaken. Sointula resident Laila Butcher recalls how years after the initial accusation, a passenger ship passed by the island, its loudspeaker noting the "free love commune" to be seen on the left-hand side.[43]

Some have viewed Kurikka's championing of this cause, at least in part, as a way to encourage single men to stay on the island; an island with a male-female ratio of about three to one. Makela, however, went further, stating that "as a single man Kurikka is interested in all women and would like to see every marriage dissolve."[44] As Makela's own marriage began to fall apart, he eventually even came to accuse Kurikka of seducing his wife. Opposed vocally by many women on the island, attacked by his former best friend, and lacking any visible support, the free love debate initiated by Kurikka seems to have been a typically bold yet unthinking gesture on his part. Whether or not the claim that Kurikka was ahead of his time in his views on women and marriage is correct, it is certainly accurate to say that he was taking the communalism of Sointula to a degree that few in the community then, or today, would agree was appropriate.

The same may be said of his desire to have the children of Sointula raised in a communal manner. In March, 1904, the Kalevan Kansa opened a communal home that was to educate and raise the children of the community. Parents were encouraged to leave their children there either full time or for the work day. Once again, Kurikka was willing to explain to women what would be best for them, using the pages of *Aika* to tout the freedom to engage in meaningful work and to ponder meaningful ideas that would come as a result of loosening the bonds of motherhood. That the majority of women resisted the idea did not bother Kurikka: "If a chicken has made its nest in a dangerous place…and you try to bring it and its young ones to a safer place, what does the chicken do? It screams and pecks and does everything to resist the change."[45] Not only had Kurikka once again pushed the community's communalism beyond its comfort level, he did so in brash, insulting language that might just as well have been designed to alienate a large segment of the population.

Kurikka, it seems, became lost in his own vision. His signature bold schemes and great dreams were becoming painful in their exaggeration. The president of an obscure company continually on the brink of bankruptcy saw himself as being in the same league as some of the era's elite businessmen. In the March 1904 issue of *Aika*, he announced that, "the design of our company is so vast that already now BC's biggest capitalists could take its place. With a few dollar's incorporation expenses to the United States even Rockefeller and his companions could join."[46]

It was perhaps this self-delusion that led Kurikka to the business venture that effectively put an end to the utopian experiment. In the spring of 1904, Kurikka put a three thousand dollar bid on the construction of the Seymour and Capilano Bridges in North Vancouver. When other colonists suggested that the bid was too low, Kurikka responded that the important thing was the "possibility of future contracts in the Vancouver area worth tens of thousands of dollars."[47] The result was a debacle: Halminen estimates that, when all the tallying was finished, one hundred men contributed eight to nine thousand dollars worth of free labour to the municipality of North Vancouver and some of Malcolm Island's best timber was effectively given away.[48] No additional building contracts were forthcoming.

The litmus test for any leader is, perhaps, how he reacts during a moment of crisis. As the first one out the door during the *Melula* fire, Kurikka had not been a shining example. Now, during a financial crisis that he had caused, Kurikka decided to focus his energies on ideological rather than mere practical matters. During June and July of 1904, while the other men of Sointula were building free bridges in Vancouver, Kurikka was busy deriding the Ten Commandments as having been "brought down from Mount Sinai by a Semetic robber chief."[49] Noting that the commandments were based on control rather than love, Kurikka offered as a counterpoint his own twenty-one *Guiding Principles for the People of Kaleva*. In its many pages describing "right living," Kurikka advises, "Let us play, but let us not romp...Let us lose our temper, but let us not get angry."[50]

It is not recorded how the people of Sointula reacted to receiving platitudes from their self-styled Moses at the very moment of a financial disaster perpetrated by the same. It is clear, however, that much of the colony was weary of Kurikka's high flown ideas and lack of practical knowledge. Sensing this, and fearing that he would lose his position as president in an upcoming special meeting, Kurikka resigned from the Kalevan Kansa on October 10, 1904, taking his leave of the colony. It is a sign of his strong personality and vision that approximately half of the colonists left with him, twenty-four of them even starting a new utopia with him in the community of Webster's Corners later that year. It is a sign of his lack of practicality that six weeks later this new colony evicted him. For the BC Finns, Kurikka's dream had run its course.

Makela and the remaining settlers attempted to carry on, but the utopia lacked vision without Kurikka. Missing his eloquence and quick tongue, Sointula also lacked new settlers and investors. Makela, for all his calm rationality, could not inspire people the way that Kurikka did. On May 27, 1905, the last meeting of the Kalevan Kansa was held and the few remaining assets divided. A company called Dominion Trust took over the dairy herd, the sawmill, and the forests of Malcolm Island, which it sold in 1907.

The dream of utopia was gone, but not the dream of a better life. "Slightly more than 100 people remained at Sointula. They now had their own parcels of land, for which they had paid $1 an acre, some basic foodstuffs such as flour and meat that were evenly distributed from the colony's stock of food, and very little else. At least there were no more debts to pay; they were making a fresh start, and they had their own resourcefulness."[51] No Russian autocracy, no bosses, no dominating church, and no impediments to owning their own land – despite the apparent economic poverty of their situation, the people of Sointula had gained many of their goals. In the coming century, through the avenue of the Co-op Store and other joint activities, Sointula would achieve much more. It would never reach Kurikka's vision of utopia, but it would remain a unique community, following a practical dream of its own.

3.

Utopia to Community, Dream to Reality

The period of thirty-four years, from the Kalevan Kansa's end to the start of World War II, can best be described as a growing up period – Sointula's young adulthood. The somewhat scattered socialist thoughts of Kurikka's utopia were maturing into practical socialist and co-operative ideals, displayed through institutions such as the Co-op Store and the FO Hall, and through union activity in the logging and fishing industry. It was a process of discovering not only who they were, but who they wanted to become.

Birth of the Co-op

17. Previous Page:
Pulteney lighthouse on
Malcolm Island.,
date unknown.

18. Right:
First Co-op Store, 1909.

With the dream of the Kalevan Kansa utopia having failed them, the people of Sointula were forced to place their immediate focus on making a living on a rather remote B.C. island. Through the next several decades they would not only succeed in this struggle, but would also find a way to bring their ideologies and communitarian values into their workplaces, into the community's cultural and political endeavours, and into practically every aspect of daily life. This mix of the practical and ideal would reach its high point in the creation and elevation of Malcolm Island's centrepiece: the Sointula Co-op Store.

To someone who hasn't grown up in Sointula, it is difficult to understand both the enormity of the role that the Co-op Store played in the community and the corresponding depth of feeling that many people have had for this institution. "The Co-op was the heart of the community," Dave Siider remembers, "it did everything."[1] Sally Peterson, whose father Theodore Tanner was the first president of the Sointula Co-op, recalls the Co-op Store as a unifying force. "I think that the Co-op held the people together, you know, because they were all working for the same thing there. Trying to make the Co-op grow and go."[2] The secret of the Co-op's hold on Sointula stems from the leadership role it assumed in the community and the circumstances in which it was formed.

The Sointula Co-operative Store was begun out of simple necessity – the need for a stable supply of groceries and goods for the community. As an isolated community in early nineteenth century British Columbia, it was not easy for Malcolm Island to keep its settlers supplied with the necessities of life. As Wayne Homer recounts, "Up to 1909, Peter Hilton kept a private store in his living room. But his stock was very small; it didn't go very far. He didn't have money to begin with. So the community got together and decided they should buy Hilton out and move his store into a larger building and establish the Co-op Store."[3]

The Co-op Store's initial attempts to supply the community's needs can best be described as a modest success. In a 1959 article celebrating the fiftieth anniversary of the Sointula Co-op Store, *The Fisherman* newspaper recalls the humble beginning of the Co-op: initially formed by just 26 members, the first store opened on December 4, 1909, and did $2,000 worth of business in its first month with a net loss of $50. The report on

the first month's business ends on a note reminiscent of the false optimism seen in the Kalevan Kansa days: "We look to the future with hope."[4]

This time, however, that hope and optimism would prove to be well founded. As *The Fisherman* goes on to relate, by 1959 the Sointula Co-op had 341 members (a few even from neighbouring communities) and had sales of $425,000 per annum. However, the store had become more than just a purveyor of goods. It focused on meeting the community's needs in a number of ways. This included installing a doctor's and dentist's office in the store to accommodate the periodic visits of both in the community.[5]

Importantly, in focusing on the needs of the community, the Co-op was not driven by the bottom line. "They managed to keep the prices way down, way below other private stores because they bought in quantity. Then it was agreed by the membership that the store should not charge more than five percent mark-up over the landed cost here. Well, that kept the price way, way down."[6] In her 1927 account of Malcolm Island, Virginia Johnson recalls that the Co-op Store's prices were actually lower than those of many stores in much more accessible communities in the south.[7] A more capitalist outlook might well have seen the people of Sointula as a captive market, and a community store as a potential money-making source for one or two entrepreneurs; but on Malcolm Island group security trumped individual gain.

That group security prevailed over individual profit was not simply a matter of ideals, but of practical business operations. Individually, Malcolm Islanders were vulnerable in the outside world. As Malcolm Island farmers attempted to market their produce to the rest of British Columbia, they recognized that the cost of individually shipping eggs, butter, and other products was too great to ensure a decent profit. Arvo Tynjala notes that the Co-op, able to ship goods in large quantities, was able to ensure better rates; and so the farmers sold their produce to the store, and the store collectively sold and shipped the island's goods to the outside world.[8] It was a solution that not only allowed individual farmers to make an acceptable living, but as Wayne Homer recounts, it also ensured the success of the store:

> It was the marketing which really built up the store. There were numerous people with small farms and they had enough land cleared so they could support three or four cows and a couple hundred chickens...This guy in Prince Rupert, he came here to buy furs and he discovered that there's something else to be bought here: the farm produce. So he made a contract with the store that he'd take everything they had to give and he sent it to the various villages, mines and logging camps and fish canneries around Prince Rupert...It sold very well.[9]

The Co-op Store also helped mitigate the problems caused by the lack of grain and fodder to be found on the island. Resident Tauno Salo, a Co-op Store employee in his youth, recalled the Co-op ordering huge lots of feed for the farming community, and even ordering in hay during poor growing seasons.[10] The previously outlined difficulties with large scale farming on Malcolm Island were not erased by these measures; however, they did serve to promote some economic stability on the island, giving both individual farmers and the Co-op Store a much needed boost during their first few decades of existence. It was a symbiotic relationship between the Co-op and the farmers that has continued throughout the Co-op's existence.

The relationship's mutual benificiality was secured through the Co-op's fifty-two *Rules and By-laws of the Sointula Co-operative Store Limited*, which spelled out in detail the obligations the store and its members had to each other. These included:

- The store was obligated to disburse profits to its members at a set rate, which was dependent on the value of the member's purchases (rule 30);

- As the store was set up to aid Malcolm Islanders, no non-residents would be taken as members (rule 4 - though this was later amended so that non-residents could be accepted);

- Applicants for membership could be rejected by the five-member board of store trustees (later known as the board of directors), but this decision could be overturned by a two-thirds majority vote at the yearly general meeting (rules 5 and 6);

- Members had to purchase as exclusively as possible from the Co-op and no member could carry on a similar business (rules 7 and 8).[11]

It was give-and-take for both sides. Members would profit based on their commitment to the store, and, though no one was forced to become a member, those who were accepted upon application had an obligation to shop at and support the store, and could be expelled for not doing so.

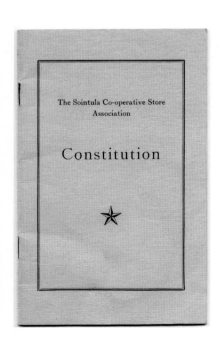

The Sointula Co-operative Store
Association

Constitution

Members' commitment to the store was further strengthened by the democratic nature of the arrangement. The two-thirds majority needed to overturn the rejection of an applicant was relatively unusual; in almost all cases, a simple majority vote on a matter raised at a general meeting prevailed (rule 40). As both owners and customers, the members of the Co-op had control over their institution – an arrangement that satisfied the Malcolm Islander's general socialist ideology of giving power to the people. The Co-op was designed to operate according to the needs and desires of the community that it served.

21. Left:
Group meeting in
fromt of the FO Hall,
circa 1930s.

As the years went on, more and more members of the community became members of the Co-op Store. This success in attracting people was – practical and ideological considerations aside – largely a result of the broader community role that the Co-op undertook. In a community with no mayor and no real local government (to this day Sointula has not incorporated) local groups and organizations invariably fill the gaps. One such organization was the Finnish Organization (FO), which provided entertainment, taught languages, and promoted the community's socialist ideals. The Sointula Co-operative Store undertook similar necessary activities. It funded the local library, a source of pride in the community;[12] it used the Co-op truck to haul gravel out to fix the roads;[13] and it allowed community members to use its vault as a bank, with the Co-op manager writing up makeshift bankbooks for depositors.[14] In a gesture sure to please a future co-operative generation, children 16 and under received a present from the Co-op every year at the annual Christmas celebration at the FO Hall.[15] The Co-op became ensconced in the lives of Malcolm Islanders.

In no way was that more obvious than in the general meetings held by the Co-op twice every year in the FO Hall. While these meetings were initiated to deal with the business of the Co-op Store, as more and more of the community became involved with the Co-op, they began to deal more and more with general community issues. "I guess it was almost a town holiday," Lennie Pohto remembers, "everybody, all the adults, or a good portion of them would be at the meeting. They'd debate things that weren't maybe involved with the Co-op at all, just sort of other community…[he trails off and begins to laugh]…Maybe some woman's cow was in the neighbour's garden, for all you know that would get on the agenda, looking for ways to solve those kinds of problems."[16] Co-op meetings became a type of town forum, a chance for the community to air and hopefully solve some of their concerns.

The Co-op meetings were also social gatherings, and were celebrated as such by the children of Sointula, who eagerly looked forward to their "mulligans," a special soup filled with meat and vegetables. Lennie remembers:

> Come lunchtime, the women there, they'd have a committee set to prepare
> the food. And they used to make these big mulligans – meat, beef mulligans
> – sort of a Finnish traditional dish, I guess, on the island here. And us school

kids, the school was just below the hall...come lunchtime I guess all the kids would...they'd go up to the hall and we'd have our lunch up there too. They used to call them eating meetings, you know, you'd have the meeting then you'd eat there, and then we'd go back to school and the adults, they'd go back to their debating the rest of the day.[17]

A mainstay of the community from the 1910s to the 1950s, there is probably not a resident of Sointula who lived on Malcolm Island during that time and does not recall the Co-op "eating meetings." The debates, the food, the all-day nature of the event – all marked it as a special occasion, or as Lennie Pohto noted, as almost a town holiday. The Co-op Store had become the centre-piece of the community.

Initial Struggles

As a centre-piece, the Co-op had to shift its focus to meet the needs of a community whose livelihood was changing from farming to fishing and logging (as discussed below). Co-op reports indicated a need for the Co-op Store to adapt its efforts towards the needs of the fishing community; however, as farming still played a vital, if lessening, role in Sointula, the Co-op could not abandon its role as a supporter of the farming community. The Co-op had to be tremendously versatile.

Demonstrating this versatility, the Co-op maintained an indispensable role in the comunity through expanding its activities to meet individuals needs. Tauno Salo recalls working at the Co-op Store in 1936. He relates how he would deliver groceries to isolated parts of the community twice a week, and how fishermen could make special orders through the Co-op that would arrive on the very next ferry. From its humble beginning of maintaining a meager supply of groceries in December of 1909, the 1936 Co-op had developed a hardware store, a dry goods department, a meat counter, and a separate warehouse for lumber, gas, and oil.[18] This ability to provide flexible goods and services for the community, help support farming on the island, and keep its prices low, was in large part responsible for helping keep the community going through its rough times, particularly the Depression of the 1930s.

The Great Depression had its effect on the Co-op. From 120 members in 1927, the Co-op bottomed out at 96 members by 1938, most likely as a result of residents leaving the island in search of work.[19] And, from a net profit of over $4,600 in 1928, the store incurred a net loss of close to $4,000 in 1931, its first loss since 1910.[20] The Co-op continued to bounce between profit and loss throughout the 1930s, creating a situation that, while not desperate, was highly unstable.

This instability was, in part, created through the inexperienced and limited human resources that the community could offer the Co-op. While the managers, directors, and members of the Co-op in later decades would be able to draw on past practice to guide them in their endeavours, much of the Co-op business in these formative decades was run by simple trial and error.

The Co-op's first audit in 1910 demonstrated this somewhat haphazard organization: "The whole of the business has been managed with care and in a businesslike

22. Above:
Co-op Store delivery truck, date unknown.

23. Left:
Arial Photo of Sointula, in 1927.
(A) indicates the FO Hall,
(B) indicates the Co-op Store.

manner, especially when taken into consideration that those concerned have been compelled to sell goods before they received the bills, and before they were properly marked and priced, and other obstacles in the way of bookkeeping."[21] The audit was carried out by Felix Myntti and George Kangas, two respected members of the community who, like everyone involved in the Sointula Co-op at that point, were not professionals. In fact, a professional auditing firm would not be used until the 1930s. Predictably, this left the Co-op prone to making mistakes that more experienced personnel might have avoided.

24. Left:
Co-op Store Directors, circa 1930, from left:
John Fredrikson, Gus Savola, Teodor
Tanner, John Tynjala, John Malm,
Willie Ahola, Ouno Salmi.

25. Above:
Second Sointula Store, 1934.

26. Above Right:
Co-op Store, 1940s.

This lack of qualified personnel was perhaps most acutely felt within the management of the store. As a director of the Co-op in the 1950s and 60s, Dave Siider notes that it was very difficult to find suitable managers for a store that handled everything.[22] This same problem seems to have been true of the Co-op's first thirty years. Though the exact backgrounds are not available for every Co-op manager during this period, by 1939 the store went through seventeen of them.[23] To be fair, the turnover rate for managers in the first thirty years may also reflect the difficulty in managing a co-operative that was in the process of adapting. As will be discussed below, the community's livelihood was changing. Whereas every director in 1917 had listed their occupation as farming, by 1926 four of the five directors were fishermen, and the fifth, a carpenter. Not only was the Co-op compelled to adapt its services, but between 1909 and 1932, at least thirty-two rule changes were made to the fifty-two original Co-op rules.[24]

Demonstrating their *sisu* (grit and determination), the Sointula community not only navigated through operational difficulties, but they succeeded in overcoming two events that shook the Co-op's stability in 1933. The store had reached a fair size by this time, as it had been added onto in fits and starts to meet the increasing need for greater and varied supplies. Dramatically, in an accidental fire in October of that year, it was almost completely destroyed. But, as *The Fisherman* notes, this setback did not long deter Malcolm Islanders: "the people demonstrated their loyalty to the store. Volunteer workers not only repaired the damage, but soon other improvements were added and a larger and better store was the result."[25]

A less outwardly spectacular, but potentially more serious crisis arose when the Co-op was struck off of the Register of Companies for failure to file its Annual Reports for three consecutive years. Quickly employing the skills of its notary public, Adam Hilton, and securing the services of a law firm, the directorship of the Co-op attempted to correct the error. Through a petition to the Supreme Court of British Columbia, Co-op secretary Bruno Kaario made his plea to have the Co-op reinstated, noting "that the failure to file the said Annual Reports was due to inadvertence and the Directors were not aware that the Association had been dissolved until they were advised of the matter on the 27th day of September, 1933, by the solicitor for the Association" – nearly eight months after the Co-op had been officially dissolved.[26] Kaario's petition succeeded, and the Co-op was restored to the register on January 3, 1934.[27]

Though the co-operative's efforts in this matter were successful, the incident raised serious questions: why, after more than twenty years in operation, did the Co-op fail to fulfill what would appear to be a fairly straightforward and necessary administrative duty? Whose job was it to make certain that this task was carried out? The manager's? Kaario's? The board of directors as a whole? Perhaps it was simply that those involved with running the Co-op at this time were more knowledgeable of co-operative ideals than of required business practices. While the Co-op's democratic, grass-roots operation was crucial to the community's survival, it clearly created challenges which would have to be better met.

The Co-op, it turns out, was up for the challenge and was able to learn from the first thirty years of its development. Not only did the end of the Depression in 1939 bring better economic times, but the Co-op wisely chose to hire Hannes Myntti as its manager. Myntti, who went on to manage the store for 29 years, gave the Co-op the stability and experience it needed. He established a set routine through which both local store business and provincial administrative business would be done. While there would still be rough patches for the Co-op in the future, the growing pains of the first thirty years would largely be left as memories.

A Changing Livelihood

Just as the Co-op had to adapt to the last thirty years, so too did the community itself. At first, Malcolm Islanders had hoped that the practical and the ideal might coalesce around an original community dream: farming. Indeed, with each settler able to work his or her own parcel of land there was some success, especially among the most enterprising. Theodore Tanner's apple, plum and cherry trees thrived, and the indefatigable Matti Halminen, his coal mining days forever behind him, became "a farmer once and for all. He cleared about eight acres of farmland out of the green timber with his own bare hands. He had a beautiful orchard; he had cows and sold milk and butter with all the other peoples."[28] Other settlers' eggs, chickens, and butter exports were moderately successful, and even as late as 1917 the majority of the community members identified their primary occupation as that of "farmer."[29]

However, though some success would come from agriculture, three factors were working against it in the long run: one, the heavily wooded soil of Malcolm Island was just not conducive to large scale crops; two, Malcolm Island was relatively isolated, making the export of farm produce and the import of farm supplies difficult; and three, as was witnessed in the Kalevan Kansa days, lack of fodder for farm animals made raising a herd of beef or dairy cattle problematic. An objective look at the overall farming potential of Malcolm Island did not reveal a promising future. As people began to realize that farming was not going to provide most people the livelihood they needed, more and more settlers turned to the two obvious alternatives on the British Columbia coast: logging and fishing. Both of these activities would take men away from the security and relative comfort of the Malcolm Island community.

The Life of a Lumberjack

Settler Arvo Tynjala relates how in the years following the break-up of the Kalevan Kansa, small groups of Sointula men would be forced by necessity to travel to logging camps, the best English-speaker among them stepping forward to ask for work:

> We used to go from Sointula with rowboats all the way down to Seymour
> Narrows on this side and into the different inlets and islands, sometimes

27. Previous Page:
Raking Hay at the
Malm Farm, 1930.

28. Upper Far Left:
Laurie Pohto combining, 1936.

29. Upper Left:
Halminen and Pohto farms, 1930s.

30. Bottom Left:
Teodore Tanner working on farm, date
unknown.

hundreds of miles looking for jobs…The [logging camp] conditions in those days were awful as far as living quarters go. The loggers carried their own blankets and bedclothes, and there was nothing in the bunkhouses but the mattresses and the bedbugs. There were plenty of them![30]

Tynjala goes on to note that the loggers would usually arrange for a little time off to go home and have a good cleaning in their saunas. As the Finns were noted as hard workers, the logging companies would usually accommodate them in these requests. However, the Sointula Finns were also noted for another quality that sometimes made it difficult to even secure a logging job: "In many cases they [the logging companies] would prefer the men who came from town, because they had no boat to row away in if they got into trouble. We were kind of independent you know."[31]

Yet this independence did not preclude a commitment to co-operative and social- ist ventures; the lessons of the past had been well learned. Each resident of Malcolm Island was aware that individually, as in Finland or in Dunsmuir's mines, he or she held no real power, and might easily be exploited by the logging companies. One of the ways

The Sauna

The Sauna speaks to king and peasant
To low and upper classes,
And blows away the hate of men
As the rocks give heat that pleases,
As wounds fade and soul it cleanses.

- Onni Pouttu

31. Left:
Pioneer Timber Company,
on Malcolm Island, 1936.

"All Finns have to have their sauna," Norma Williams laughs, "that's the only way we cleaned ourselves." Seen as a necessary utility, a sauna was one of the first buildings made in the Kalevan Kansa days. When people starting building their own homes a sauna would often be automatically included. Consisting of a cedar room heated by wood in an enclosed firebox with hot rocks on top, the sauna would let out all the "dirty muck" inside. So hygienic were these early saunas that Sointula midwife Edla Malm delivered over 200 babies in her birthing house sauna.

The sauna was also of cultural significance. Alfred Williams compares past attempts to take steam baths away from Finns to attempts to take away potlatches from First Nations people — a cultural desecration. On the island the sauna was often a family affair, mothers and daughters, grandfathers and grandsons bathing together. Sometimes a group of neighbourhood men or women would get together to talk over the week's events. Soothing and meditative, the sauna served to relax the mind as it cleaned the body. Though often electric today, saunas are still common place on Malcolm Island, a comfortable cultural icon from the past.

in which to fight possible exploitation and to secure some group security was through union support. Tynjala remembers transporting Lumber Workers Industrial Union (LWIU) organizers to a deserted beach at night, then sneaking them into a logging camp where they would attempt to organize the men. He notes that this tradition would continue in later years, with Sointula fishermen transporting International Woodworkers of America (IWA) organizers (the LWIU's successors) from camp to camp, sometimes even taking them to rest in the safety of Sointula.[32] As major logging companies could blackball those suspected of union activity, there was some risk involved in aiding the unions. However, doing so was in line with the socialist ideals that had been such an important part of the Finn's original vision of utopia.

While bedbugs and blackballing might, ironically, have strengthened the loggers' resolve, giving them an enemy to fight and a cause to rally around, the isolation of logging life was not so easy to combat. Sointula singer and poet Laulaja Mies recalls his early days as a migrant worker in a poem that captures the sense of loneliness and eroded values he saw occurring among these young lumberjacks:

In my wanderings, I stopped at a hotel
I went to see how the lumberjacks were celebrating
When I entered the doorway
My shoes got wet with vomit.

Oh the poor young man,
Who drinks the poison there.
One of the loggers sat at the door,
Another was thrashing near the wall,

The others tried to dance
when Frank the mandolin was playing,
They shouted: "Our money will never run out."
They promised drinks for all.
They said: "Bring, girl, some drink,

So we don't die of thirst."
The hostess' face shone like the sun,
When for a dollar's drink she charged fifteen.
She put her arm around the boys' necks
And bid the boys to sing.

The joy only lasted about a week,
When the pockets of the loggers contained no dollars.
The boys don't feel like singing,
When they wake up by themselves.[33]

Depicting the fear that arose in these loggers, who, through alcohol abuse and lack of community support, were robbed of their self-respect, this song could just as easily have been about the Finnish coal miners of the late 1880s.

Though many Sointula men had no choice but to leave their homes to earn a living, the community was concerned about how the capitalist world would influence them. This concern proved justifiable. In the decades to come, the influence of the outside world would be a factor that would make its presence felt more and more upon the people of Sointula.

Fishing: Co-operative Inroads With Others

In the short run, however, it was the Finns who, while working away from Malcolm Island, would influence the capitalist world. Though this occurred to some extent through the union activities they helped initiate in logging camps, Sointula Finns would most actively change the industry that would become their mainstay: fishing. Their drive to do so can be traced to the great importance that fishing had in their lives. As fisherman Alfred Williams states, "Without fishing we would have been practically starving, we wouldn't have anything. Everything we have here comes from fish."[34] Driven by both practical and ideological concerns, Malcolm Islanders helped transform the industry through ingenuity, hard work, and the application of socialist and co-operative ideals.

The first fishermen of Sointula had operated locally, catching enough to supply the needs of their own families and the community at large. However, as their utopia began to break up and the limits of farming became felt, making a living required finding more fertile fishing ground. Rivers Inlet, located on the central British Columbia coast, became perhaps the most important salmon fishing grounds for Malcolm Islanders. It was relatively close to home and, especially in the first part of the twentieth century, had large runs of the commercially valuable sockeye salmon – the fish choice for the canning companies.[35] However, the rowboats owned by most Sointulans were of little use in salmon fishing. As a result, they were forced to purchase their equipment from the same large canneries they fished for: "It was all company owned gear. You went up to the cannery. You got this skiff; most of the time it was sunk, tied to the float...You'd bail it out...the rent for the season was $10 for that boat."[36]

Sointulans found themselves in an uncomfortable position: forced to sell to the big canneries, dependent on them for their equipment, and having to accept the prices that they set. As costs rose and the companies kept their prices at 15 cents a fish, the Rivers

32. Left:
Pioneer Timber Company, spar tree and hay rack for loading trucks, on logging road made of flattenned trees.

Inlet fishermen decided to fight back. In 1917 these fishermen met in Sointula to form the United Fishermen of British Columbia (UFBC) union, going out on strike that same year.[37] Though the canning companies tried to divide the strikers by pitting one group against the other, the union held firm and negotiated a raise to 22.5 cents a fish.[38] More important than the actual increase in price or the future of the newly formed union (the UFBC folded in 1924) may have been the example set: united, the fishermen had won out against the powerful companies. It was an example that the Sointula fishermen in particular would use in upcoming battles.

They would also use their individual drive. Paula Wild recounts how throughout the 1920s more and more Sointula fishermen began to build their own boats in an effort to free themselves from the grips of the canning companies. Boat builder John Anderson led the way in 1918, setting up the first boat yard in Sointula, one that by 1951 had built over 600 vessels.[39] Though much smaller in scale, eight other boat yards would come into existence on the island through the years, making the community known as a boat-building centre. Such efforts also helped make Malcolm Island a more self-sufficient community.

Wild also notes how this drive to succeed had its inventive side. Fisherman Laurie Jarvis was a gill-netter, tired of hauling in nets by hand. Using the rear end system from a Model A Ford, Jarvis invented a gillnet drum that would reel in the fishing nets, an

33. Above Left:
Hand Canning Sockeye
Salmon, 1965.

34. Above:
Fishing Skiffs tied
together at Rivers Inlet,
early 1920s.

35: Right:
Early fishing
boat with gillnet.

36: Far Right:
Flshing skiffs outside
Anderson Boat Ways.

invention that came to be employed by fisherman worldwide. Unfortunately, it would prove too easy to make for Jarvis to maintain an effective patent.[40] While activities such as Anderson's boat yard and Jarvis' drum did not make their proprietors rich, they demonstrated Malcolm Islanders' strong independent streak and passion to excel at their chosen livelihood.

This individual drive for a better life, coupled with a co-operative instinct, took its fullest form in the creation of the British Columbia Fishermen's Co-operative Association (BCFCA, 1929-1932), the first fishermen's co-op in BC. In *Tides of Change: A Story Of Fishermen's Co-operatives In British Columbia*, fisherman and author A. V. Hill recounts how Sointula fishermen, debating in their community hall and unwinding in their saunas, started to explore the idea of a co-operative fishery, free of big cannery control.[41] Initiated by such Sointula Co-op Store alumni as Bruno Kaario, Victor Macki, and father and son John and Felix Myntti, this fishing co-operative grew to have over 2,000 members, and became the proverbial "thorn in the side" of several big canning companies.

The BCFCA ran on a new concept in British Columbia fishing: collectively marketing members' fish and returning these profits to the fishermen. For example, while private companies were offering fifteen cents per fish for blue back salmon, the co-op would offer an initial payment of ten cents per fish – with a probable final payment of greater than five cents to the fishermen when the fish were sold. Though it entailed an act of

faith on the fishermen's part, the idea took hold, aided by an effective public relations campaign. A yellow 'flag' was hung from the masthead of every co-op member, giving rise to the recruiting slogan: "A yellow flag or a yellow streak."[42] In the first month of the 1929 fishing season, 90 per cent of marketed BC blue back salmon had gone through the co-op.

37. Left:
The "Klanche" - the first
boat by Anderson Boat Ways,
a steam boat for Nimpkish
Timber Company.

Over the next few years, the success of the BCFCA would both frighten and anger the private canning companies, undercutting the monopoly they had held, as well as their control over certain groups. At this time Japanese-Canadians comprised a large percentage of BC fishermen. Living predominately along the Fraser River in houses rented from the large canning companies, they had been required to deal exclusively with these companies. However, in 1930 the BCFCA had appealed to the Department of Fisheries to abolish a recent 10 per cent cut in fishing licenses issued to Japanese fishermen. Partially in thanks, many Japanese fishermen decided to deliver fifty per cent of their catch to the co-op from then on. Though incidents of racial conflict between European and Japanese-Canadian fishermen were hardly uncommon along the coast, the memories of such co-operation across racial divides helped foster a more accepting attitude in places such as Sointula. Fisherman Dave Siider, though too young to have had direct experience in the matter, recalls older Sointula fishermen speaking very highly of their Japanese counterparts of this period.[43] As with later union activities, bonds formed in shared co-operative ideals crossed over divisive lines.

Though the large canning companies had been unable to stop defections to the co-op camp, the BCFCA still faced many factors working against its success. One was the Co-op's lack of a large bank loan. Many companies and organizations would face bankruptcy in the Depression as it hit at the end of 1929; banks were more likely to give loans to those it had already loaned money, protecting their initial investment. Operating on capital generated from the $25 shares it was selling to its members, the BCFCA would find itself *persona non grata* in most banking circles.

The second obstacle was a split within the co-op, gravitating around one man – Francis Millerd. A recent provincial law, championed by the large canning companies, had forbidden the issue of any new salmon cannery licenses, forcing the BCFCA to buy an existing cannery that had recently gone bankrupt: Millerd's Cannery. As part of the sale's terms, Millerd insisted on being kept on as manager. While he seems to have been an active and honest manager for the co-op, his behind the scenes deal making and general top down management style went against the co-operative nature that the BCFCA stood for. The co-op president, Bruno Kaario, and secretary Otto Ottava, led a faction pushing for a more co-operative approach to decision making. Millerd, in turn, had the support of many non-Sointulans who felt that Kaario and Ottava's consensus approach was interfering with Millerd's effective company management. Far outnumbered, Kaario and Ottava were forced out of their leadership roles.[44] The co-op was weakened with distrust, and its Sointula members felt excluded from the very organization they had built.

The third force working against the Fisheries Co-op was simple bad luck, which, compounded by poor judgment, spelled its end. On one occasion, rushing to buy a load of bulk salmon gillnets for their members, the BCFCA found itself with $3,000 of sub-par nets that proved of little use. It was also discovered that two BCFCA directors (non-Sointulans) turned out to be secretly employed by large canneries – creating, at best, a conflict of interest, at worst, spies in the house.[45] Finally, in a case of bad timing shared by many other companies, the co-op needed funds in the onset of the Depression. At the beginning of 1932, the BCFCA leadership estimated that it could start the 1932 season if it could secure a mere $10,000 loan.[46] But, as no effective credit union system was yet in place, and as no bank would agree to float a loan, the BCFCA was forced to fold in the spring of 1932.

The $93,000 worth of assets were sold off over the next three years. But the collapse of one co-op did nothing to deter people from the idea of co-operation. Trollers, seiners, and gillnetters alike had experienced the benifits of working with each other, and had become inspired by the relief it provided from the exploitative practices of the fishing companies. As the economic conditions of the great depression set in, the co-op model became a common solution, with the idea behind the BC Fishermen's Co-op sparking a movement of fishing co-ops and fishermen's credit unions that has continued to this day.

As for Sointulans, they would try again in 1946 to create a fishing co-op, the Sointula Fishermen's Co-operative Association (SFCA). Much smaller in scale, it succeeded until it decided to merge with the larger Fishermen's Co-operative Association (FCA) in 1950. The FCA, apparently a victim of infighting and competition from private companies, went under a few years later. Through the FCA, Sointula fishermen again experienced the power of being united with others in challenging the control exerted by large commercial fishing companies. However, they also learned that being part of a

38. Right:
Docked gillnet boats.

39. Far Right:
Demonstrating solidarity,
boats raft together at
Rough Bay during strike.

large democratic movement sometimes meant losing their point of view to a majority not their own. Aware of these benifits and difficulties, Malcolm Islanders continued to play an active role in large co-operative, socialist, and union activities in years to come – but they made sure they were the ones steering the boat whenever possible.

A prime example of Sointula leading the way was the 1936 strike in Rivers Inlet. Fish prices had been rising fairly steadily since the 1917 strike, reaching forty-five cents a fish by the beginning of the Depression. With hard economic times, however, the canning companies began to cut back. By 1936, they were offering only thirty-five cents a fish.[47] What is more, the prices were not based on a poundage system and thus it did not matter how big the particular fish was. Eighty-three year old Victor Wirkki recalls the 1936 fishing season as a particularly memorable one in his career: "The very first year that I went out fishing alone we didn't fish only a week in Rivers Inlet, then we went on a strike...The companies, they didn't get the fish; that's the only way that you could figure that the fishermen won. But then the following year [the prices] were up all right!"[48] As Sointula fisherman Lester Peterson recalls, this was a turning point in the BC fishing industry:

> Never previously had there been a completely solid front of the fishermen...
> The Japanese fishermen ceased fishing, the Indian fishermen, although they
> had great discussions with the Indian Agents, stopped fishing. The next year

40. Right:
Logging turntable, unloading
logging trucks in Mitchell Bay.

the fish were bought by the pound and on the average it probably was around 45 to 47 cents a fish…But the leaders in the strike, who held us together, were Sointula fishermen.[49]

Equally important may have been the behind the scenes work of the Sointula Co-op Store, as well as the efforts of the women of Sointula. Fisherman Scotty Neish, a future leader in the BC fishing unions, recalls the strikers running low on necessary groceries and denied credit by the company stores: "It was mainly fresh stuff that we were short of. We were all tied up in Alert Bay, but the Sointula Co-op store offered us credit over there, so we used the *La Paloma* [Neish's boat] to go and pick up the groceries for the whole fleet. The women in Sointula were cooking fresh bread and buns for the whole fleet."[50]

It is, of course, true that Malcolm Island as a whole had a vested interest in supporting the strike; increased fish prices would benefit almost everyone on the island. It is also true that by leading the strike, Malcolm Island fishermen ensured themselves a say in how it would unfold. However, the leadership of the Sointula fisherman, and the support by the Sointula Co-op Store and the women of the island, can also be traced to ideology. Concern for the average worker was a belief that went back to the original utopia, and in many cases beyond.

During the formative years of the Malcolm Island community, the fishing and logging industries were instrumental in bringing the community closer to their vision. The freedom that the Finnish settlers had sought through farming on their own land, began to be achieved in the forests and on the ocean. Though Malcolm Island loggers predominately worked for others in this period, the reputation they enjoyed as good workers, the proximity of a home community to return to, and the existence of an alternate livelihood (fishing) gave them leverage in achieving decent working conditions. In fishing, the increase in self-owned boats, coupled with the growing power of union activity (and to a lesser extent co-operative ventures), gave Malcolm Islander fishermen much freedom in their chosen livelihood. Thus, through the two industries, a contrasting mix of independent living, economic success, and communitarian ideology were realized. All combined to create a stronger, more close-knit Malcolm Island community.

The Socialist Ideal

Given the adherence of Malcolm Islanders to both the practical and the ideal, to independent living and to working class support, it was not always easy for outsiders to understand or categorize Sointulans. A classic blunder in this regard was perpetrated by a non-resident entrepreneur, Andrew Anderson, who had a colonization scheme in mind. In a May 25, 1909, letter to Premier Richard McBride, Anderson described how optimistic he and his fellow "joint capitalists" were to see the good people of Sointula ridding themselves of their "foolish notions" of the past: "They have stuck individually to their lands - built beautiful, neat houses and all have more or less cultivated lands around their houses. They are anxious to make good for themselves."[51] Anderson went on to promote himself as a business link between Sointula and the province, suggesting that the people of Malcolm Island were looking to investors and the government for help in developing their community.

Anderson's belief that Malcolm Islanders could be capitalists-in-waiting is in some ways understandable; even within the original utopia, Kurikka had remarked upon members holding what he deemed to be the decadent beliefs of the capitalist West: "They think of getting butter for their children's meals, while their neighbour's children do without milk."[52] In describing the actions of the settlers upon the break-up of the utopia, Arvo Tynjala noted that those families with means bought up the best farm land, leaving the less desirable areas for the poorer members of the community.[53] These actions, coupled with Anderson's observations regarding the great enthusiasm with which the Finns of Sointula built up their own property, might well have fooled any casual observer. The socialist idealism of Sointula was, from the start, tempered by a drive for individual success that did resemble aspects of capitalism.

However, as seen in their fishing and logging efforts in the first forty years of the twentieth century, individual strength and a desire for success does not rule out a concern for the welfare of others. Anderson might have done well to look around and take note of the enthusiasm with which the people of Sointula had already embraced socialist politics in his time. In 1907, Malcolm Islanders formed the Sointula Socialist Club (SSC), joining with the Socialist Party of Canada (SPC), which had translated its platform and constitution into Finnish to entice just such spirited socialist Finnish communities.

Two years later, in the 1909 provincial election, every single Sointula vote was cast for the Socialist candidate in their riding.[54] A few years later the devoutly Marxist Austin Makela, unofficial leader of the community until his death in 1932, wrote an article denouncing the provincial government as "bandits" who had joined with capitalist "robbers" to pillage the people.[55]

The commitment of Sointula to socialist parties throughout the twentieth century is a perfect example of idealism steered by practical concerns. From the beginning, as long as the people of Malcolm Island felt that a political movement was fulfilling their needs, they were model activists. The Sointula local of the SPC raised funds for campaigns and held community meetings regularly, which, as at the Kalevan Kansa meetings, was attended by whole families. Extolling the enthusiasm of the Sointula local, the socialist newspaper *The Western Clarion* lamented, "If only our Anglo-Saxon members had half the zeal of the Sointula Finns!"[56] This zeal could sometimes take on a rather draconian form. When it was discovered that three Malcolm Island men had not voted for the SPC, the community immediately expelled them from the local. Independence was highly valued in Sointula, but residents were expected to fulfill an obligation to support the community.

Yet, it would not be long before Sointula, and indeed the Finnish-Canadian community as a whole, would turn away from the SPC. The signs of a potential rift were woven into the makeup of the organization. Historian Alan Neil Kuitunen notes that as early as 1908, Finnish-Canadians made up a sizable portion of the SPC membership; however, English-Canadians dominated at the executive level, seemingly hesitant about sharing their power.[57] At a 1908 inter-provincial party convention in Fernie BC, John Rivers, a Sointula logger who had co-founded the Sointula SPC local with Austin Makela, made a motion to run a Sointula resident as an SPC candidate in the upcoming federal election; he was told that the provincial executive committee of the SPC could not help financially.[58] Though it may truly have been a matter of lack of funds, the Finns of the SPC were beginning to get the idea that they were valued solely for their numbers and enthusiasm, not for any ideas or leadership potential.

This notion was cemented when Sointulans began challenging the SPC's impossibilist ideology. The party's platform could be summarized in three principles: one, that capitalism could not be reformed; two, that trade unions benefitted few workers in the short run and no workers in the long run; and three, that the workers as a class must rise up and destroy the wage system.[59] Sointulans were not interested in a philosophy that, far from addressing practical ways in which to improve the lives of working people, seemed bent on achieving the same sort of idealistic society that the people of Sointula had already seen fail on Malcolm Island. To make things worse, when the Sointula local started to argue for changes to this stance, they were denigrated as "clannish foreigners."[60] It was an unacceptable relationship for Malcolm Islanders; reminiscent of their early days as new immigrants, they were once again under the authority of an English-speaking elite that discounted their opinion. The situation between the Finnish locals and the rest of the SPC reached such an unbearable level of distrust and acrimony that by 1911 the entire Finnish membership had either been expelled or had left the party.

The FSOC: Celebrating Finnish-Socialist Community

Though Sointula's first foray into politics had failed in some respects, it remained a positive endeavour for several reasons. If nothing else, through their joint participation in the Sointula Socialist Club, the people of Sointula had united. Just as they had done with the Kalevan Kansa, the community banded together to fight for an organization that promised a better future for all, and in doing so returned a sense of unity to the community – a unity that would be displayed in future socialist and co-operative ventures.

However, their experience with the SPC not only united the Finnish community on Malcolm Island, it also served to increased its interaction with other like-minded Finnish-Canadian communities. Sointula was already well known outside of British Columbia because of its unique beginnings; as author and former Malcolm Island resident Paula Wild notes, in the early twentieth century, Finns everywhere had heard about the Kalevan Kansa experiment.[61] However, while this familiarity had resulted in some interaction between Sointula and other Canadian Finns, the SPC was the first organization in Canada to bring socialist-minded Finns together in one body. And, though the SPC failed to fulfill Finnish expectations, the unity it had temporarily provided proved to be the stimulus needed for the formation of a national Finnish organization. In 1911 socialist-minded Finns in Ontario joined to create the Finnish Socialist Organization of Canada (FSOC), with a Sointula local being formed later that same year. It would grow to be an inseparable part of the community for decades to come.

While it would be misleading to state that the majority of Finnish-Canadians during this time period were socialists, the numbers were much higher than for the general population. Kuitunen estimates that by the end of 1914, roughly thirty per cent of Canada's twenty thousand Finns were members of the FSOC.[62] Sointula, then, found themselves ideologically united with approximately six thousand other Canaidan Finns in the FSOC. The ties that united these Finns were clearly spelled out in the party's purpose statement:

The purpose of the Organization is:

1. To assimilate the Finnish-speaking people of Canada with the native population by instilling in their minds the benefits of Canadian citizenship [and] by the teaching of the English language…;

2. To advance the standard of life of the Finnish-speaking people of Canada by encouraging and developing co-operative enterprises tending to secure their material interests;

42. Below: Mural and Banner in FO Hall, 1932.

43. Below Right: Mural in FO Hall, date unknown.

3. To develop the mental faculties of the Finnish-speaking people of Canada by the holding of educational lectures, by furthering artistic endeavours such as singing, music, theatricals, gymnastics, and by maintaining libraries and reading rooms;

4. To own such buildings and other properties, and to carry on such businesses as are necessary...in particular (1) To publish a newspaper and other publications; (2) To maintain bookstores...

> Taken from: *The Rules of Foundation of the Finnish Organization of Canada*, Chapter I, "Names and Purposes"[63]

In many ways, the FSOC merely provided national support for the same activities and beliefs that Sointula had formed back in its Kalevan Kansa days. The Sointula library, created during the original utopia, was still in existence (the collection is now in the Sointula museum, having been replaced by the regional library). English language lessons, having initially been encouraged by Kurikka, were now carried on through the FSOC by such Sointula residents as Aina Tynjala.[64] The FSOC paper, *Vapaus* (Freedom), was modelled on the Kalevan Kansa's *Aika*, and continued to employ the skills of Austin Makela and Katri Riksman as editor and contributing writer, respectively.[65] And the new FO Hall, which housed musical, theatrical, intellectual, and athletic activities, was not new at all; it had existed in Sointula since 1903, but was now renamed the Finnish Organization Hall, FO Hall for short. The local FSOC provided a new unifying identity and strength to the Sointula vision.

In addition to strengthening its own local interests, the FSOC also allowed Sointula an opportunity to have an impact on national socialist and working class activities. When the FSOC threw its support behind the Marxist Social Democratic Party of Canada (SDPC), Sointula made sure to secure a voice for itself in the party by purchasing shares in *Cotton's Weekly*, the SDPC organ.[66] Sointula boat-maker Ole Anderson recalled the strong union support given by the residents of Sointula: "Say there was a strike of the miners back east; well they would come through the Finnish Organization. You had to take up a collection or you could even put up a show or something and the proceeds would go towards the aid of the strike."[67]

More than mere political manouvering, Sointula's engagement in national issues was born out of a genuine concern for the well-being of others. Resident Alfred Williams recalls how Sointula residents were taught to take an interest in both local and national social issues at a young age, and did so largely through the Finnish Organization: "In the old days, the FSOC was for the working class. There were meetings every Sunday night, and kids age ten and older were expected to attend. Someone would read the news from the FO in Toronto and we would discuss what needed to be done around the community."[68] While other BC communities of the time often celebrated their shared life philosophy through Sunday church services, the Sointula Finns would do so through

44. Right:
FO Hall from water,
centre, 1935.

these Sunday FO meetings. It is a comparison not lost on Sally Peterson, who equates the Sunday meetings as, "a kind of religion…you learned the values."[69]

This religion was not the earlier Theosophy of Kurikka's, but rather seemed to resemble Makela's simple humanism. As outside observer Virginia Johnson noted in a 1927 article, "98% of the people on Malcolm Island do not profess any religion - but each Sunday have classes where the younger generation are taught physical drill, nature study, and Esperanto." Johnson went on to note that the community's focus on their cultural and material growth left them with "no spiritual hopes for the future and no fears for the present."[70]

It would be misleading to say that socialism and the FO Hall operated as direct substitutes for religion in Sointula. The community remained suspicious of any one organization that purported to control their community as the Lutheran Church had done in Finland; commitment to individual independence, diversity of thought, and the importance of other institutions, such as the Co-op Store, prevented Malcolm Island from

succumbing to hegemony. However, the Finnish Organization, through such efforts as supplying striking workers with food and promoting physical and cultural activity, had a tremendous ability to transport the "spirit" of Sointulans in a very real way. If the FO's blend of socialism and cultural promotion was a religion, it was a practical and active one. As Ole Anderson recalls;

> [We] just had to make our own fun. I don't think there was a night of the week that there wasn't something doing at that hall. There was athletic practice or song practice or show rehearsals; you name it. There was a show there just about every Saturday....they were mostly Finnish plays, pertaining to the Finnish Organization and the labour movement and so on.[71]

It would be equally misleading to view the FO's activities as typical small town ways to keep active. There was an importance attached to them not generally seen in other communities. Sointula fisherman Wayne Homer's recounts the Saturday plays: "Everybody had to take a part in the show; they couldn't say no. The committee in charge of the play, they decided who they were going to shanghai for the parts and that was it."[72] With the only organized form of entertainment on Saturday nights, and with the ability to conscript their cast, the Finnish Organization in Sointula had a perfect venue for promoting its ideals. It was "fun" served with a healthy dose of "idealism."

Persistence of Values

Many Sointula residents have commented throughout the years on the security they felt while living in Sointula. Unlike FO members in mining towns, who had to combat strike breakers and the RCMP, or those in cities, who had to deal with a conservative English-speaking population suspicious of Finnish accents and politics, Sointula was a place filled with generally like-minded people. Rather, while never encountering the opposition that many in such other communities faced, the people of Malcolm Island found their isolated harmony disrupted by remote national and international events.

The first of these events was set in motion by the Russian revolution. In 1917, as the Bolsheviks gained control of Russia, they made peace with Germany, resulting in

Soviet Karelia

In the early 1930s, the Soviet Union began its first 'Five Year Plan' of economic recovery, an important part of which included forest industry exports. Karelia, a region of the Soviet Union bordering Finland and one of the Soviet's most important forested areas, needed many more experienced loggers than they had available. Meanwhile, in Canada, the Great Depression was throwing many such men out of work. Karelia sent out a siren call to left leaning North American Finns.

Spurred by the FO's Vapaus newspaper, which trumpeted the success of the Soviet plan, some two to three thousand Finnish Canadians emigrated, including Sointulans Eric Pouttu, Albert Maki, and John Anderson and family. But, instead of discovering a socialist utopia these Finns found "a place of exile and forced labor on a gigantic scale." By the mid 1930s, Finns in Karelia were singled out for supposed 'anti-Soviet' tendencies, victims of a Stalinist purge. Maki and Pouttu disappeared; Anderson and his family, by hiding money away in the shoe of their youngest son, were able to buy their way out. The example of Karelia may have done as much as anything to weaken commitment to hard-line socialism in Sointula.[1, 2]

suspicion being cast on socialist groups. On September 25, 1918, the Canadian government responded by declaring the FSOC, along with other socialist organizations, illegal. After over a year of negotiations with the government, the FSOC was allowed to reorganize as the Finnish Organization of Canada (FOC) – with the understanding that it would no longer associate with socialist organizations. By 1922, however, the FO had become a foreign language member of the Worker's Party of Canada, later renamed the Communist Party of Canada (CPC).[73] As Paula Wild notes, "Almost everyone in Sointula was a member of the FOC, and since the FOC requires its members to carry a CPC card, almost everyone in Sointula was also a member of the Communist Party."[74] Although this attempt at government control had failed, it served as a reminder to the people of Malcolm Island that despite their isolation, they were not immune from government interference in their lives.

A second incident also stemmed from events occurring during WWI. In 1917, growing conservative forces in Finland, known as the Whites, fought a civil war against the country's socialists, known as the Reds. Finnish-Canaidan communities found themselves likewise divided between Whites and Reds, as their ideological differences compelled them to support warring factions in their homeland.

Calling themselves loyalists, the Whites were generally conservative, church-going Finns, hostile to the socialist cause. Accordingly, they erected White Halls in competition with the socialist FO Halls. While no White Hall immediately sprung up in Sointula, by the beginning of the 1930s a confrontation was developing. As Wayne Homer relates, with the advent of the Depression, a space was needed for the newly formed Unemployed Worker's Organization to meet; however, according to Homer the FO Hall was under the control of hard-line communists who would not let the new organization use the hall, perhaps judging the newly formed organization to be too concerned with capitalist matters, such as wages and employment. Not to be deterred, Homer and others of his organization built their own hall, which would come to be known as the White Hall.[75]

There is no suggestion that this Unemployed Worker's Organization was in any way a conservative body; resident Tauno Salo recalls the "White Hall being built and run by the Canadian Commonwealth Federation (CCF) group."[76] That the most conservative organization in town was composed of CCF supporters is perhaps the best indication of how deep socialist values ran in the community. While this situation might strike us as oddly amusing today, it signalled a very real divide at the time. Located within fifty yards of one another, the two halls each had their own members and activities, with virtually no crossover. Like the members of the FO Hall, the 'syrup gang' (as the White Hall members became known) put on regular Saturday night plays, and almost always had a dance to follow. Norma Williams recalls how, as a child, she was one of the few people who could easily move between both camps: "I had two sets of grandparents, one were the Whites and one were the Reds. But I was lucky because I could go to both halls."[77] Her husband was not so lucky: "Albert could only go to *one* hall!" Perhaps because the members of both halls shared much of the same ideology, the split never seems to have led to any serious confrontations. In fact, the split did not last long, as the White Hall closed a few years later, going on to become a restaurant, a butcher's shop, and currently, a net loft.

If the White Hall and the syrup gang did not soften hard-line socialism in Sointula, time and technology did. Victor Wirkki recalls that when the FO Hall started showing motion pictures in the 1930s, the frequency of plays became less and less.[78] Though the FO would continue trying to instill its ideals to the audiences of the largely commercial movies, by the mid 1940s people seemed more interested in the hall's entertainment than its messages. As Dave Siider remembers: "There used to be an old guy here, he was always advocating the communist system at the community hall...There used to be a show every Saturday night and sometimes he'd take to the floor and have a big speech. Us young kids especially, and even older people, would just shake their heads...They were getting very tired of it."[79] Movies eventually replaced the socialist plays and Sunday FO meetings that had helped foster these ideals in the younger generation.

However, the FOC remained the centre of political and cultural action in Sointula for many decades, occupying a prime role in keeping the initial socialist values of Sointula alive, as well as fostering cultural, social, and physical activities that would keep the community united.

45. Left:
Music in the FO Hall, 1940s.

Sointula at Play

While Malcolm Island's socialist and co-operative ideals had matured as it tried to hammer out its dreams, to reduce the life of Sointula Finns during this period as being merely practical or idealistic would be undeservedly simplistic. Much of what bound the community together during its youth can perhaps be best described as play. Like almost every small Canadian town, regular recreational and social activities helped create the bonds that held Sointula together. Yet even Sointula's play, structured around community ideals and institutions, carried a distinctive socialist quality.

May Day, a socialist holiday not generally given much prominence in Canadian communities, was a huge event in Sointula:

> **Ole Anderson**: …May Day was the biggest celebration Sointula had. Everything was closed on May Day. It was the Labour Day here. That was the big celebration. Most of the women even got a new dress for that day. If they didn't get one any other time of the year they had a new one on May Day. It was the same as sports day is today. You'd have different outdoor races, but you also had the indoor programs of recitations and songs and different things. Each one had a prize for the kids…

> **Gloria Williams**: I remember the tree where they used to have that speaker's platform, it was what you called a 'schoolmarm.'

> **Alfred Williams**: …It was split like a 'Y' in the middle, in the crotch; they had the platform with a little fence around it. Whoever wanted to hold a speech, well he would get up on there and the people used to sit on the grass in a circle and listen to the guy. The political speeches lasted forever.[80]

Socialism and sack races were a definitive part of a Sointula childhood in the 1930s. May Day was only once a year, but it was still an occasion where the community could join together, not only around a political ideal, but in a sense of fun as well.

This combination of fun and politics was also, as already mentioned, provided frequently by the Finnish Organization through its plays and Sunday meetings. However, the FO also had a specific program for youth recreation in the form of the Young Pioneers. This group acted as a Boy Scouts and Girl Guides on Malcolm Island, keeping island boys and girls amused and active. Albert and Norma Williams recall this organization as being an integral part of growing up on Malcolm Island. On Sundays, some adults from the FO would organize dances at the hall for the children, some of the older kids playing accordion and piano. In the summer, they would have picnics and camp at a huge house out by the lighthouse. Chaperons such as Elma Kaario would tell "wonderful stories" of

WE DEMAND BETTE
LIVING CONDITIONS FOR
WORKERS CHILDREN
FREE FOOD AND CLOTHIN
THE SCHOOLS WITH
MONEY NOW USED F
CADET TRAINING!

WORK
JOI
YOUNG PIONEERS

Finland, so real that "you lived in there."[81] These activities not only gave the children of Sointula something to do, but also connected them, through Finnish music and stories, to the heritage of their homeland.

One significant part of Finnish heritage maintained on Malcolm Island was a commitment to exercise and physical fitness – traditional rural Finnish life emphasized physical rigour. Arvo Tynjala tells that Finnish people are generally athletic and that athletic programs are well organized in Finland.[82] Although logging, fishing, and farming all contributed to maintaining physical hardiness on Sointula, to boost fitness levels even higher, exercise classes were also held throughout the week.[83]

As the FO Hall was usually abuzz with a number of activities, the exercise classes were generally outdoor and thus dependent on co-operation from west-coast weather, which was not always forthcoming. Judging that their physical needs were not being adequately met, the Young Pioneers approached the FO in 1930 and requested an Athletic Hall in which to exercise. The way in which events unfolded from that point demonstrates not only the importance of physical fitness to the community, but also the intricacies and interconnected nature of Sointula's institutions:

> [The] Finnish Organization mortgaged its building, the old hall, to this Co-op Store and borrowed the money. The Co-op Store borrowed the money from individual people. You see, they wanted the security. But the way it was worked...the Finnish Organization had no authority...anybody wouldn't have trusted them, you know, for a loan or anything because they are not

a financial organization anyway. It might die all of a sudden without anybody knowing it's dead. But the Co-op Store was in a different position and everybody could lend money to them.[84]

Working together, Sointula's two most important institutions of this time helped bring the Athletic Hall into being in 1931. In typical Sointula fashion, the hall served a number of functions: the first floor consisted of a large gymnasium, while the top floor became the new home for the library; Theodore Tanner taught exercises and debating techniques to the Young Pioneers every Sunday morning; and when the children were not using the gym, the adults of the community would take over, undertaking such activities as creating human pyramids up to the ceiling.[85] Everyone got involved in the formation of the Athletic Hall; everyone received some benefit from it. Even in its recreational activities, the majority needs of the community were served.

Not all of the recreation was communal or regulated. Part of the joy of growing up on Malcolm Island in this time period seems to have been the independence that residents enjoyed. A typical summer activity for teenage boys in Sointula was to take a rowboat and a friend and camp their way around the island.[86] The journey usually took two or three days, the teens living off their provisions, wild berries, and whatever fish they could catch. The older teens and the men of the island would take part in hunting expeditions for deer and game-birds, the rugged nature of the island providing a natural habitat for this wildlife.[87]

Even in their work, Sointulans found time for some unstructured play. Fisherman Dickie Michelson recalls teenage memories of going to the dances at Beaver Cannery, for which many Sointula men fished, and many Sointula women canned: "There was a float with a bootlegger down the coast a way. Sometimes the old folks would disappear for a while and leave us kids paddling around the rowboats or fishing, getting into mischief really, I think…One dance, a couple of guys were dancing too lively and they fell off the dock and damn near drowned."[88]

While such incidents might recall the debauchery of Dunsmuir's mines or the isolation of the loggers in Laulaja Mies' song, it would be innaccurate to draw similarities. Kids getting into mischief for a few hours, dancing too lively, men sidestepping temperance ideals the occasional Saturday night – these speak to the independent spirit of Malcolm

Islanders who were celebrating their youth and relative freedom, not debauchery or isolation. After each celebration, Malcolm Islanders had the stability of their home community to return to. As has been noted, "co-operation and independence were the twin poles of life in Sointula."[89] The sense of security gained through their co-operative efforts at home gave Malcolm Islanders the opportunity to exercise their independence, in their work, and in their play.

The bonds formed in these first thirty-some years of life after the Kalevan Kansa, helped create a united community in Sointula. As Ole Anderson recalls, "everybody

51. Left:
Harold Malm, rowing Doris and Harriet Malm, 1930.

52. Below:
Sointula first Street, 1930s.

knew everybody – knew what everyone was thinking about."[90] Irene Michelson, who arrived in Sointula in 1905 at age five months, relates that with the picnics, trout fishing, Saturday night dances, and other activities she "never felt isolated" on Malcolm Island.[91] Even those who were able to get away to the big city did not always relish the chance. Resident L. E. Guthrie recalls that the young women who went to Vancouver to earn money for new clothes and such were always eager to return, unused to the rules and regulations of the outside world.[92] Life on Malcolm Island in this time period was secure; neighbours knew and trusted one another and institutions such as the Co-op and the FO looked after the needs of the community. Life was also free, with fishing and logging offering the chance of an independent livelihood, and with a beautiful, semi-wild island offering a wonderful home in which to pursue that independence. Sointula had succeeded in becoming a co-operative community.

4.   Growth and Change

The year 1939 marked a transition for Canada. It was the end of the Depression and its economic hardships, and the beginning of new economic and cultural growth during the war effort. As wartime production kickstarted the economy and large numbers of enlisted youth experienced foreign countries for the first time, an energetic patriotism birthed a new Canadian self-assurance. Sointula, having been an isolated and homogeneous group of socialist Finnish immigrants, shared in this growth, maturing into a more diverse community. While its core socialist and co-operative beliefs would not disappear, their survival required adjustments, as they would now have to share a stage with new ideas. Whereas Sointula's first thirty-nine years were characterized by creating freedom and security, its next thirty- some years would be marked by fluctuation and adaptation – practical responses to a changing world.

The War Years

One of the most immediate practical responses occurred during the war years, with the outward "Canadianization" of much of the island. The Finnish organization Hall, long the bastion of socialist, anti-imperialist sentiment, hung photographs of the King, Queen, and Winston Churchhill on its walls. A recording of "God Save the Queen" was even played before and after special events.[1] By 1944 the Sointula Co-op had purchased $26,700 worth of Victory Loans;[2] in April that same year, the *Vapaus* newspaper reported a $300 donation by the first unit of the Sointula Red Cross. and in November, *Vapaus* reported that the Sointula Ladies Aid Society had donated forty care parcels to the boys in the Armed Forces.[3] For perhaps the first time in its history, the activities of Sointuila's institutions were in step with those of the surrounding communities, and indeed, the Canadian norm.

Some have suggested that the patriotism displayed through these institutions reflected a growing sense of nationalism among the young adults of Sointula. Arguing that the children of original Sointula immigrants had become increasingly Canadian, Paula Wild notes that, in contrast to their Finnish parents' tepid response to World War I, a number of these young adults volunteered for the armed forces in the 1940s.[4] Albert and Norma Williams, who joined the service in 1942 and 1943 respectively, recall that quite a few Sointula women volunteered to serve, either in the forces or as nurses.[5] Further, the Island became host to the Armed Forces as they were stationed along the coast. Longtime resident Diane Hufnagel notes that Army, Navy, and Air Force personnel stationed along the coast during the war would end up at the FO Hall dances.[6] The isolation that had perhaps been most responsible for keeping Sointula out of Canada proper was starting to erode.

This increased contact with the outside world also seems to have sped up the anglicising of Malcolm Island. This trend had already been underway for some time; children had previously begun learning English at school, and English films had already begun to nudge local plays off the stage at the FO Hall. The war years, however, helped fast-forward the process. As one Sointula resident recalls, "during the war, some Sointula girls wouldn't speak Finnish. If you talked to them in Finn, they would answer you in English. Some of them had boyfriends in the Air Force, and it wasn't fashionable for them to

53. Previous Page: Fishing Boats at Sointula Wharf, 370.

54: Below: Sointulans in uniform, 1940s.

55: Below Right: Arne Johnson's Defence Certificate, from WWII.

56: Below Far Right: Alfred Williams in Uniform, 1940s.

speak Finn."[7] Finnish names underwent a change as well. The Honkala brothers are three examples, among several, of those who anglicized their names during World War II. Vaino, Henry and William Honkala became Wayne and Henry Homer, and William Williams.[8] Whether these name changes had any connection with the Sointula girls' preference for English isn't clear; what was clear was that the Finnish-Canadian community of Sointula was starting to lose a little of its Finnishness.

This Canadianization, however, should not be overemphasized. While the outside face of patriotism in Sointula undoubtedly reflected changing values, there is some question as to the overall depth and strength of these changes. Albert and Norma Williams indicate that many of the men who served in the Second World War were probably conscripted after the enactment of the 1944 Conscription Act.[9] Echoing that sentiment, Victor Wirkki believes that most men were called into service, very few joining out of any sense of patriotism. Wirkki notes that Sointula fishermen were, in fact, much more likely to avoid enlisting by joining the Fisherman's Reserves, or "Gumboot Navy":

> [The Gumboot Navy] was a bunch of fishermen with these seine type boats, bigger boats. They were controlling this...BC coast during the war years, [looking for] submarines, or anything that shouldn't be around...For

the Gumboot Navy, that section, they wanted to get in there so that they wouldn't be called into the regular navy or army or something of that sort.[10]

The original settlers of Malcolm Island had fled a regime that had wanted to conscript their men into its army, sending them away from home to fight foreign wars. The Gumboot Navy allowed these settlers' sons to put their knowledge of the sea to use in the defense of Canada, while still avoiding conscription. Patriotism may well have been on the rise in Sointula, but it was a patriotism steered by both practical concerns and a general wariness of outside control.

Conflicting Loyalties

Sointula's growing patriotism was also mitigated by influences that many Canadian communities did not face: loyalty to a foreign country (Finland), and loyalty to a worldwide movement (socialism). These two competing concerns were highlighted through an event that was to have a far-reaching effect on the community of Sointula: the Finnish-Russian Winter War of 1939-1940. Finland had always had to contend with the security concerns of its great Russian neighbour to the east. As noted in chapter one, in order to create a buffer zone between itself and the growing power of France under Napoleon Bonaparte, Russia had persuaded Finland to cede it its territory in 1809. Now, in 1939, the Soviet Union tried to persuade Finland to cede it part of its territory in order to create a buffer zone between itself and the growing power of Germany under Adolph Hitler. This time, however, a more independent and right-wing Finland refused to bow to the pressure of its giant neighbour. As a result, while most of the rest of the Western world was focusing on the threat of Germany, from December of 1939 to March of 1940, Finland was fighting a David and Goliath war with the forces of the Soviet Union.

Despite an increasing bond with the rest of Canada, Sointulans' reaction to this Winter War indicated that Finland was still largely regarded as the homeland. As Alfred Williams recalls, "the whole town got pretty hot under the collar during the Russian-Finnish War. There were two groups: the anti-Russians and those that sympathized. So there was a little 'war' here too!"[11] While not violent, the disagreements between residents disrupted the usual calm that pervaded the island. Before the war, the Co-op Store had placed seats inside its doors that had traditionally been used by members to sit and discuss local and international events, but after several disruptive arguments broke out over the merits of the Winter War, the Co-op was forced to have these seats removed.[12]

Of course, Malcolm Islanders had a history of fiery political debates, and with the settling of this war in March of 1940 (marked by the ceding of some Finnish territory to the Soviet Union), the whole Winter War argument might well have gone down as one of the island's more vocal disagreements, and nothing more. Other factors, however, intervened.

57. Above:
Gumboot Navy members, 1940s.

58. Left:
Gumboot Navy dragging for mines, 1940s.

The first factor was the broader national perception of the war. The Canadian government, together with public opinion, viewed the war as a drama, with Finland cast as the little independent hero struggling against an aggressive giant. Food, funds and supplies were gathered to support the hero's cause. Finnish-Canadian historian Varpu Lindstrom notes that the popularity of the Winter War in the Canadian imagination of the time lay in the fear and suspicion Canadians felt towards communism. And so, while Canadians supported the newly conservative Finland in its fight against communism, they grew to once again fear a vestige of Finland's socialist past, the Finnish Organization of Canada – an organization which openly hoped for a Soviet victory. As had happened in the First World War, in August of 1940, the FO was banned.[13]

As mentioned earlier, largely due to its geographic isolation, Sointula had enjoyed relatively little opposition to its socialism compared to socialists elsewhere in Canada. During the 1930s, Finnish socialists in Ontario described living in constant fear of an RCMP knock on the door. However, with the FO's banishment, some measure of this fear now became a reality for Sointulans as well. Following a visit by the RCMP in October of 1940, the *Alert Bay Bulletin* announced that the Sointula FO Hall was now under the administration of a local committee, in accordance with the Defense of Canada regulations.[14]

While the Sointula FO was able to get its hall back when the Finnish Organization was taken off the government's list of illegal organizations in October of 1943, as Lindstrom makes clear, the Finnish Organization never fully recovered from the banning:

> During the period of illegality [the FO] lost many of its members...Many objected to the FOC's stance during the Winter War and its open desire for a Soviet victory over Finland. After the ban was lifted, halls were in poor condition: two had been sold and two, one in Nipigon, and one in Sudbury, had burned down...Other smaller communities decided that they were unable to pay the taxes in arrears owed on the properties.[15]

Not only was the FO now a weaker organization, but, with the anglicisation of Sointula Finns and the disquiet over the FO's hard-line communist stance on such issues as Soviet Karelia and the Winter War, the importance of the organization to the island waned. A secret RCMP report on Sointula from 1944 indicates that the Sointula FO's

Community Justice

latest meetings had not been well attended.[16] Subsequent RCMP reports in 1948, 1952, and 1956, indicated financial troubles within the organization and a disinclination of young Malcolm Islanders to become involved in it. While the Sointula branch of the Finnish Organization did not quickly or easily disappear, its glory days in the community were fading.

Ironically, a second factor that increased the Winter War debate's impact in Sointula was government suspicion regarding supposed right-wing sympathies on the island. When the Winter War ended with Finland ceding territory to the Soviet Union, the conservative Finnish government had turned to the only ally who could help them fight the might of the Soviets: Germany. In June of 1941, Finland and Germany joined forces in an attack upon the Soviet Union. While right wing Finland had been the darling of the

Wary of outside authority, Malcolm Islanders did without an RCMP presence on the island until the mid 1960s. In a small, stable community, problems regarding law and order were few, and when such problems did arise they were handled locally.

Public meetings were held to decide the fate of lawbreakers, with Austin Makela and a Justice of the Peace from Alert Bay usually acting as judges. Even the fate of a mother who had killed her newborn baby was decided in this fashion; only women judged this case, decreeing the mother not mentally responsible for her act. The liberal sensibility displayed in the Malcolm Island "court" was well ahead of its time.

Occasionally, matters would be handled without the benefit of a public forum. Dave Süder recalls escorting two miscreants off the island; a third, a bootlegger who had drawn a gun on Dave's son, left the island upon hearing that Dave wanted to talk with him. "We policed ourselves," Süder remembers.[1]

For matters not serious enough to warrant banishment, the "Dave Davidson Dungeon" would suffice. Named after the first man put into it, this dungeon was a room in the basement of the FO Hall, a holding cell for people causing trouble in the town.

Though community justice has lessened in Sointula, its survival for so many years is a testament to both its independence and communitarianism.[2, 3]

Western media during the Winter War, it soon became demonized as a Nazi ally on the eastern front of the Second World War. Perhaps due to the vocality of the Winter War debate on Malcolm Island, as compared to other western Finnish-Canadian communities, Sointula was singled out by the RCMP as a possible zone of pro-Axis sympathy: "It is ascertained that a new political philosophy appeared and is being agitated among the members of the Finnish settlement of Sointula, Malcolm Island, B.C. This new philosophy may eventually develop into fifth column activities unless checked in time."[18] No specific government action appears to have followed from this report, and indeed, no evidence of any pro-German activity on Malcolm Island during World War II was ever discovered. But the community experienced a new level of RCMP presence – a presence that secretly continued for some time (though it would soon return to socialist suspicions).

While this RCMP surveillance may have had no real effect beyond reminding Malcolm Islanders that Canadian authorities could be very suspicious of groups and ideologies outside the Canadian mainstream, the incident is significant on a symbolic level: that the community associated with Matti Kurikka, Austin Makela, and long-standing socialist ideals could ever be considered a haven for pro-Nazis sympathy seems to defy all logic. Even with a gradual softening of socialist ideals on the island, what would explain an emerging viewpoint that seemed far enough to the right to alarm the Canadian authorities?

Part of the answer may lay in the influx of new Finns who came to Sointula before, during, and after the Winter War. Muriel Lowry, the granddaughter of Matti Halminen, recalls well the debates that occurred in the community and in the Co-op Store over the Winter War and the merits of socialism. She notes that it was predominately the new Finnish immigrants who would question and dispute the socialist ideals that had been so ubiquitous on the island. Having fled Finland due to the threat of the socialist Soviets, and having been raised in a 'loyalist' tradition since the defeat of Finnish socialism in the civil war of 1917, these newcomers had a different perspective than what had been formed on Malcolm Island; undeterred by the removal of the Co-op Store seats, they sat on nail kegs and argued with their socialist neighbours.[19] As far removed from reality as the idea may appear now, it seems more than likely that it was members of the new wave of conservative Finnish immigrants who, with recent ties to a pro-Nazi Finland and vocal in their anti-socialist views, set themselves apart from the community enough to come under the RCMP's suspicion.

This added conservative element on the island seems to have aided in weakening the hard-line socialism of the Sointula Finns, a view that had previously almost unanimously supported communism. Tula Lewis (nee Tula Jarvinen) was one of the new Finns who had been part of the small wave of Finnish immigrants who came to the island in the early 1950s. While insisting that there were no real political battles between the new and old Finns at this time, Lewis does agree that there was an ideological divide: "All the ones that came when we came were certainly not [communist or socialist]."[20] New blood and new ideas had arrived in Sointula.

Another factor in the community's move away from hard-line socialism, however, may have been an emerging political realism. As the years went by, it must have become obvious to the original socialist Sointulans that the Communist Party was unlikely to ever be a political force, either provincially or federally. However, the more mainstream Co-operative Commonwealth Federation Party (CCF), established in 1933, and its successor, the New Democratic Party (NDP), established in 1961, would be. Norma Williams (for many years a provincial elections return officer) notes that many, if not most, of the Sointula old time communists found their way to the CCF and then to the NDP as the years went by.[21]

And so, with the arrival of new conservative Finns, the weakening of the FO due to its war-time ban, and an emerging political realism, the Finnish Organization in Sointula became more and more a recreational and cultural entity. In name, at least, the organization lasted until 1978, when the FO Hall was taken over by a non-political Recreational Society, as discussed below. However, the decline of hard-line socialism did not give way to the capitalism the island had struggled against, but to a new commitment to communitarianism.

Religion Returns

The new Finns also seem to have helped instigate a new view of religion on the island. Though there were undoubtedly some long time residents in Sointula who had some religious leanings, as noted earlier, most viewed organized religion with the same suspicion as their predecessors had. Lennie Pohto notes, "the majority of the people that were here, they just had no need for a church...I guess if the Finns would've wanted a church they would have built one in two days."[22] Yet, in the early 1940s, informal religious gatherings began taking place in the buildings that the earlier Finnish immigrants had built in an attempt to construct a community without religion. In 1941, a chaplain from the ship MS Columbia conducted a service in the FO Hall, and in 1948, missionaries Alf and Margaret Barnes began semi-regular bible classes at the Sointula school.[23]

As documented in a 1952 article in the *Alert Bay Pioneer Journal*, the island experienced a real divide between a pro- and anti-church movement. Covering the funeral of a Sointula Finn who had recently migrated from Finland, and noting that a Lutheran minister had to be brought from Vancouver for the ceremony, the *Pioneer Journal* ran a headline reading, "Prayers for Church at Sointula." John Anderson, in a subsequent edition, heatedly retorted, "that article may express the opinions of the newcomers who arrived here a year or so ago from Finland but it does not correspond with the feelings of our pioneers."[24] The rift would continue through the 1950s.

However, it would be oversimplistic to describe the division as occurring only between the newcomers and the old guard. Recalling the eventual establishment of the Sointula Community Church in 1961, one anti-church resident noted that some of those who started the church had been long-time residents.[25] Norma Williams, further recalling the religious path taken by both her and her husband's grandmothers, suggests that this emergence of religion in Sointula may have re-awakened some long dormant feelings:

> The oddest thing about this whole deal about religion, like with Albert's grandmother and my grandmother from the Tynjala side -they were brought up with religion in Finland. Very religious. And then as they got out of it altogether, they almost condemned religion...She [Norma's grandmother] was in her 90s when she died, she did nothing but read...her Finnish Bible.

59. Right:
Sointula Community Church, 2004.

And Albert's grandmother really shocked me because when her time was up she wanted a Finnish pastor from Vancouver to come and see her.[26]

While it is certainly not uncommon for people nearing death to turn to religion for comfort, it is also quite possible that religious beliefs had always existed in some form among a number of Malcolm Islanders – beliefs that had been suppressed amid the more dominant anti-church and socialist atmosphere of the island. Either way, the newcomers, who had not been raised in such an environment and certainly felt at ease in displaying religious feelings, set an example that helped bring about a new acceptance (if far from unanimous support) for religion on the Island.

Malcolm Island Meets British Columbia

In the gradual erosion of its hard-line socialist principles, and in the grudging acceptance of organized religion on the island, Sointula was following a path similar to other Finnish-Canadian communities. As historian Edward W. Laine notes, unlike Finns in the United States, the majority of Canadians Finns came to this country in the twentieth century after socialism had already taken root in Finland (Matti Halminen and his fellow miners being obvious exceptions). It was not until the post World War II period that conservative, church-minded Finnish immigrants began to change the nature of Finnish-Canadian communities.[27] As this happened, the bonds of socialism that had tied Sointula to other like-minded Finns throughout Canada were being lessened, and Finnish-Canadian communities started to more closely resemble other Canadian communities.

This transformation on Malcolm Island was further aided by the emigration of several long time Sointula residents. Through a detailed study of the history of Malcolm Island houses, Wanda Laughlin, a Malcolm Island "newcomer" (she moved to the island with her parents in 1961) has noted that the biggest disappearance of original owners occurred in the 1950s.[28] Laughlin has two explanations for why this occurred: one, people began to do well enough financially through fishing that they could afford to purchase a home in Vancouver or Surrey; and two, for the first time enough people were coming into the community that it was possible to actually sell your Malcolm Island home.[29] Though Laughlin does credit the influx of new Finns in Sointula for some of the change, she notes that there is an entire group of people who are often overlooked in the settlement accounts of the island: the loggers.

While logging often took men away from Malcolm Island to find work, it also provided employment and entrepreneurial opportunities on the island. During the 1940s and 1950s, names such as Belveal, Shiels, Wooldridge, and Laughlin entered the Malcolm Island lexicon – as English speaking loggers first moved to, then married into, the Sointula community. Shiels Logging ran its operations out of Rough Bay by Elgin Shiels (and his father before him), employing six to eight workers in its best seasons; Malcolm Island Logging ran from 1950 to 1960, a much bigger operator than his own, as Shiels recalls;[30] and the ever active Delmare Laughlin was responsible for starting three different logging camps on the island, as well as a sawmill that shipped lumber as far as Burnaby, and even into the United States.[31]

Though Laughlin himself admits that Sointula was first and foremost a fishing community, the loggers played an important role in the development of Malcolm Island's post-war economy. These new immigrants also helped to promote the communitarian ideals of the island, largely through its major institutions. Though it is doubtful that many English names ever appeared in the Sointula FO register, these names became increasingly frequent in the Co-op and credit union reports as not only members, but directors and committee heads; the loggers who had moved to Sointula became a part of the social and co-operative fabric of the community. There is no doubt that the replacement of long-time Finnish speaking settlers with new English-speaking immigrants helped speed along the island's anglicisation. However, by marrying Sointula women, by engaging in a typical and respected Malcolm Island occupation, and by being willing to give back to the community through support of its institutions, the loggers who came to the island did not so much alter the community as strengthen it by their presence.

The Alert Bay Connection

Part of the transformation of Sointula into a more typical Canadian community seems to have been an increased connection with other BC communities, most particularly nearby Alert Bay. However, this connection had existed long before the social changes brought about by the war. Ever since the Aboriginal people of that community had helped ferry some of the first settlers to Malcolm Island, the two communities had maintained a practical association with one another. As Victor Wirkki explains, "We used to be more or less connected between Alert Bay. They had the doctor and the hospital there, and the police were there, and the beer parlours were there."[32] For the people of Alert Bay, Sointula was a source of both needed supplies from the Co-op Store, and of entertainment at the weekly FO Hall dances. Alfred Williams, in a 1979 interview, relates that so many Alert Bay people were coming to Sointula's Saturday night dances in the 1930s that its start times were changed to accommodate Sunday laws against dancing.[33] Albert and Norma Williams note that Alert Bay had just one, smaller grocery store, and so used to come to Sointula to stock up.[34]

However, while it is difficult to measure, ideological differences did create a divide between the two communities. Alfred Williams notes that Alert Bay residents, having held strong loyalties to the Commonwealth, were royalists, whereas Sointulans were socialists.[35] A survey of the *Alert Bay Bulletin* during the early 1940s confirms the community's royalist nature, particularly in its reports of the enthusiasm with which Alert Bay organizations greeted Empire Day celebrations (a day commemorating the British Empire, notable by its absence in Sointula). Seemingly recognizing such a divide, the March 15, 1940, edition of *The Bulletin* noted that there was a need for more unity in the district.

It is difficult to ascribe a particular cause, but it appears as if the war years helped bring about some of that unity. While May of 1939 saw no mention of May Day in the *Bulletin*, the May 1, 1940 edition of the paper was devoted to Sointula and her May Day celebrations. The same edition of the paper went on to note how the Sointula Athletic Club was putting on a play at the Parish Hall in Alert Bay to aid the Canadian Red Cross.[36] With an Alert Bay newspaper commemorating a socialist holiday, and with a Sointula club previously associated with the FO and socialism, raising money for Canada at a church hall, it seemed that there was at least an effort being made towards bridging the ideological boundaries dividing the two islands in the war period.

This period also saw the two communities meet in the realm of co-operative development. In May of 1939 the BC Credit Union Association was formed; Sointula would form its own credit union a year later, Alert Bay the year after that.[37] The timing of these new credit unions seems to have been auspicious, for with the booming economy of the war, people were placing their building savings in these institutions at a quick rate.[38] Though the importance of the credit union over the decades in Sointula will be more fully examined in later chapters, it is noteworthy that it began side by side with the neighbouring Alert Bay CU; as the war years progressed, the ideologies of the two islands seem to have become increasingly similar.

These ideologies were, of course, helped along by further practical interactions between the two communities in the coming years. While most of the buildings put up in Sointula's first fifty years were erected with volunteer community labour, when the time came to build a new Co-op Store in 1950, probably the most important structure in town, the community entrusted the task to Alert Bay father and son Alfred and Tage Westerlund. Malcolm Islanders would also entrust Alert Bay's Dr. Harold Pickup with their most important commodity, their health. Dr. Pickup would begin coming to the Co-op Store office to give checkups in the early 1950s, making house calls to invalids, and making himself a welcome addition to Malcolm Island life.[39] Before neighbouring Port McNeill started to grow in the late 1950s and early 1960s, and before the ferry service improved at roughly the same time, the connection between Alert Bay and Sointula was important, and generally quite friendly.

However, while the connection between Sointula and the white people of Alert Bay appears to have been generally amicable, the relationship between Malcolm Islanders and Alert Bay's First Nations people – the KwaKwaKa'waKw – is more difficult to categorize. Certainly some families and residents seem to have been on good terms. Before working in the Alert Bay hospital, Muriel Lowry had developed close relationships with some Alert Bay natives while accompanying her father, Oiva Halminen, over to that island. Oiva, like his father Matti before him, brought farm produce such as butter and eggs to sell to the natives at Alert Bay, building friendly relations in the process.[40] Muriel recalls an opportunity she had to encourage the work of a young native carver, a patient who was a member of the renowned BC carving family, the Hunts.[41] Tauno Salo recalls a similarly amicable relationship with natives coming to the Saturday night dances, some bringing saxophones and drums in order to jam with the Sointula band.[42] In a 1982 interview, long time resident Wayne Homer affirmed that Malcolm Islanders and Alert Bay First Nations had a unique and respectful relationship; "Oh, between the Indians and the Finns it's been friendly neighbours from the very beginning. We never had a quarrel with the Indians, but the Alert Bay whites, they had several quarrels with the Indians."[43]

But others in the community question the validity of this "unique" relationship, noting some real tensions between the two groups. Muriel Lowry relates that the teenage boys of Sointula during the late 1930s and early 1940s were against any Alert Bay natives dating Sointula girls, feeling that they were not good enough for their ladies (though that did not stop an independent-minded Muriel Lowry).[44] Victor Wirkki recalls incidents of natives turning up drunk at Saturday night dances, at a time when drinking was still frowned upon by older temperance-minded residents (though hardly unpracticed in Sointula).[45] Dave Siider sums up the relationship quite simply: "There was a difference between the natives and the white men on Malcolm Island."[46]

This mixed view of the native population seems to have existed since the colony's beginnings, demonstrated between the different views of Sointula's two early leaders, Makela and Kurikka. Describing the native population of Alert Bay in 1904, Makela depicted the native people as natural socialists, giving away their excess belongings to others, presumably through potlatches. He noted that they often came to Sointula's dances and communal dinners, and were better neighbours than those most of the settlers had in Finland.[47] Makela's view is one that is present later in the Halminen family's interactions, in Alfred Williams' remembrances of native participation in the dances, in approval of native participation in the great strike of 1936 (as mentioned in chapter three), and in Wayne Homer's belief in a mutually respectful relationship. It is an inclusive view, finding common ground in shared socialist values and in a desire for economic security, and then building bonds from that.

Matti Kurikka, however, expressed an alternate view as early as 1902. Coming upon a boat of drunken Finns consorting with native women, he described the people as "repulsive losers with the half-animal females."[48] Though the drunkenness of these Finns is part of what disgusted Kurikka, he was clearly disparaging an association with people he viewed as less human. It is a view of Alert Bay natives as something innately different than Malcolm Island whites, a view Muriel Lowry described as present in the 1930s and 1940s.

It is, of course, difficult to say whether an inclusive or exclusive view dominated on Malcolm Island, or even whether such a complex relationship can be defined in such simple terms. Like Malcolm Islanders' relationships with other outside groups, such as the new Finns, Alert Bay royalists, or simply the rest of the country, Sointulans' connection to Alert Bay natives differed between different members of the community, and changed over time. As with these other groups, Malcolm Islanders seem to have found areas of common interest, perhaps building on shared socialist/working class interests; but, at the same time, Malcolm Islanders also seem to have attempted to distinguish their own community through pinpointing differences between themselves and the First Nations. The only safe generalization regarding the relationship between Sointula

60. Right:
"Car Race" between Sointula,
Alert Bay, and Port McNeill.

Finns and Alert Bay Aboriginals over the twentieth century, would appear to be that it was multi-faceted and deserves further study.

A Community at Odds with Itself

During the 1940s, it became increasingly difficult for Malcolm Islanders to distinguish themselves by pointing out their differences from other communities. Some of the big changes, such as the decline of the Finnish Organization, the influence of conservative Finns, and the increased patriotism inspired by the war, have already been noted. But many of the changes in Sointula involved subtle, gradual alterations in social norms. Victor Wirkki recalls a large wooden sign that used to hang in the FO Hall: "Man be a man - don't come here drunk!" Wirkki notes that even in his generation, coming of age in the mid to late 1930s, the sign's advice was being ignored more and more.[49] Lennie Pohto notes that by the early to mid 1950s the rules against drinking had pretty much "fallen by the wayside."[50] The community did not, of course, descend into the debauchery and alcoholism of the nineteenth century mining towns whose example had inspired Sointula's temperance, but one more distinguishing feature of this community was disappearing.

The change in spirit and community feeling was not immediate. Growing up in the 1940s and 1950s, resident Loretta Rihtamo recalls playing badminton at the FO Hall at least once a week, and seeing Sointula-produced plays in both English and Finnish. She also recalls, however, wishing there was more to do in the community, a sentiment not expressed by earlier generations.[51] Certainly, the Saturday night movies at the FO Hall were an attempt to cater to this new sentiment. Lennie Pohto, like many Malcolm Island residents, has fond memories of the Saturday night movies. Describing them as the teenagers' "event of the week," Pohto notes that the youth of the community would have fun getting into mischief up in the balcony, while the adults were watching the show down below.[52]

Malcolm Islanders' mobility changed too. Paula Wild notes that in the past people would walk wherever they needed to go, visiting their neighbours along the way. Starting with a surge in automobile purchases in the 1940s, however, people began to drive more.[53] A faster-paced lifestyle was developing, one that did not place as much emphasis on community ties. Resident Alfred Williams saw this change as emanating from the effects of the war, and the resulting economic boom: "After World War II things changed - people got too much money - didn't need the same spirit. You can go to Vancouver and go see a movie, and go to night clubs, etc."[54]

Accompanying these new desires for modern recreation and mobility were aspirations for adventure and new careers, particularly among the women of Sointula. There were an increasing number of young women in the 1940s and 1950s who completed their grade 12, only to find few career options on the island. While young men were much more likely to drop out to begin fishing or logging, several young women felt the need to leave the island and find jobs or careers elsewhere.[55] Muriel Lowry left the island at age 17 in 1946 to see what Victoria had to offer.[56]

Though hardly an exodus at this time, this changing attitude to the outside world, coupled with economic motivations, slowly altered Malcolm Island society. In 1958 the Union Steamships, which only ran twice a week, was replaced by the Island Princess, a vehicle ferry that ran once a day. The fact that each vehicle had to be lifted on to this ferry by crane (a cumbersome process), together with the sorry state of the Vancouver Island highway system at the time, limited the number of excursions from Sointula. Slowly but

61. Left:
FO Hall sign, now in the Sointula Museum.

steadily, however, Malcolm Islanders were getting more and more opportunity to experience the rest of the province. Economic changes, transportation improvements, and an increased curiosity about the outside world were changing life on the island.

Despite this new openness to the outside world, an important ingredient was added to the community in the war-time period that served to maintain the island's traditional identity. While the influx of the Finns during the war helped introduce new religious and political ideas to the community, it also contributed an element that supported Sointula tradition: language. At a time when English was beginning to overwhelm the island, the arrival of strictly Finnish-speaking immigrants was an important counterweight. Albert and Norma Williams credit these new Finns with preserving the Finnish language for at least a generation on the island – a living language that helped keep Sointulan's distinctive identity and community bonds alive.[57]

New Institution - Old Ideals: The Sointula Credit Union

The phenomenon of the new reinforcing the old in Sointula occurred not only through the influx of new people, but also through the creation of new institutions during the war and post-war period – organizations that would help solidify the island's communitarian traditions. One of the first of these new institutions was the Sointula Credit Union, first formed in March of 1940.

To some measure, the formation of the Credit Union was the result of efforts by the UBC Extension Department. Several educational meetings and study clubs had been organized in the community between 1940 and 1943 by the Department's province wide efforts to educate remote fishing communities regarding the role and operation of credit unions and other co-operative ventures.[58] Through these meetings, the Cambell River fishing community also incorporated a credit union in the same month.

In Sointula, though, the Credit Union found a unique home. Not only a practical solution, the credit union reflected the island's ideological commitment to communitarianism – operating as a safety net for average working people, but also for their co-operative organizations. Had it existed earlier, it may well have saved the British Columbia Fisherman's Co-operative Association during its credit crisis in 1932. And its

62. Upper Far Left:
Union Steam Ship "Catala" makes her last call to Sointula.

63. Upper Left:
Union Steam Ship "Camoson's" makes her last call to Sointula.

64: Lower Left:
Union Steam Ships "Catala" and "Cardena" docked in Sointula, 1930s.

members would, largely, be those who were also members of the Co-op store, persons practically and ideologically committed to its existence.

This continuity enabled the Credit Union to quickly become financially viable, gaining necessary funds through active investment by Sointula residents. Having ensured its creation, however, Malcolm Islanders did not then use the Credit Union for the practical purpose for which it had been established – borrowing money. It is likley that the relatively low point of the Malcolm Island economy in 1940 was largely responsible for this lack of use. Depositing money in the Credit Union was an acceptable risk since one could always get it back; the risk of borrowing money for a business venture or home improvements may have been too great. Whatever the reason, the Credit Union closed in the early 1940s. However, as the economy grew, it reopened in 1949, becoming an essential and much used institution to the present day.

Though never as vital to the running of Sointula as the Co-op Store, the Credit Union was recognized as an important part of the community; indeed, the organization's 1941 credit committee consisted of Hannes Myntti, Otto Luck, and Peter Hilton, three recognized leaders on the island and pillars of the Co-op Store as well.[59] Its primary importance, however, lay in the immediate use that Malcolm Islanders were able to make of it. Determined not to allow the new Credit Union to suffer the same fate as the first, board members such as Otto Luck took out loans that they did not really need so that the Credit Union could make needed interest, and, presumedly, so that the inspector of credit unions would not shut it down.[60]

Such acts of 'community spirit' would soon become unnecessary. From a meager $5,826 in personal loans in 1949, the Credit Union was loaning over $64,000 in 1960;[61] loan requests had grown so quickly by that point that the Credit Union contacted the chief inspector of credit unions in British Columbia for advice on how to keep up with demand (the inspector recommended using the "very large deposit account of $54,500" to cover these loans).[62] With the post-war boom, increased fishing prices, and the influx of new immigrants to Sointula, residents were investing their money in the Sointula Credit Union and community, taking out loans primarily for house mortgages.[63, 64] The Credit Union helped the people of Sointula take advantage of their increased economic prosperity.

The Credit Union was also important on an ideological level. Banks' poor reputation had only worsened in Sointula since Kurikka's tirades in *Aika*: they had pulled out of many communities in the Depression, were reluctant to extend credit to ordinary people, and had failed to back community endeavours such as the failed fishing co-ops. Here at last was a "bank" that was run by the people of Sointula, that was not driven by profit (the yearly profit for the CU didn't rise above $4000 a year until the 1960s), and that was responsive to the needs of the whole community (the CU even bent credit union rules by doing business with non-CU members, as a community service).[65] Housed for years in the Co-op Store, the Credit Union worked with Malcolm Island students to not only provide learning material, but to educate the school kids in the co-operative credit union tradition.[66]

The United Fishermen

Not only did economic advances in the war years help bring about the rise of the credit union system in British Columbia, but the war economy helped bring about the formation of an organization that would, arguably, play an even more pivotal role in Sointula: the United Fishermen and Allied Workers Union (UFAWU). However, though it was the economic and bureaucratic environment of World War II that helped cement union gains and the eventual formation of the UFAWU in 1945, much of the credit for the union's birth can be traced to the pre-war period.

As has previously been noted, BC fishermen in the 1930s and earlier often had a hard go of it; low fish prices, combined with control of the industry by large canning companies had left the average fisherman feeling alone against formidable odds. However, decades of increased co-operation between fishermen, as witnessed in the fishing co-ops and the 1917 and 1936 fishing strikes, had begun a process of change. The importance and example of the 1936 strike was brought home in the first ever edition of *The Fisherman*, a newspaper that was to become the voice of the UFAWU. On its first front page, the paper would cite a resolution passed during the "great Rivers Inlet salmon fishermen's strike the previous year," calling on existing unions and organizations to "take immediate steps to build one industrial union."[67] Inspired by the example of that strike, and by the spirit of this resolution, activists in the fishing industry began pushing for this one, all encompassing body.

In 1938, the Salmon Purse Seiner's Union (SPSU), supported by the Pacific Coast Fisherman's Union (PCFU), struck to demand an increase in fall chum salmon prices. The strike was successful, becoming the SPSU's first signed union agreement. Two disparate unions had been brought together, demonstrating the power of this strategic union of unions.[68]

At the same time, BC fishermen were showered with three war-time blessings: a huge demand from the Great Britain armed forces for herring and canned salmon; exceptional fish runs; and the creation of the Regional War Labour Relations Board (RWLRB) as a third party in labour negotiations.[69] The first two factors created an optimal fisheries market – a large supply of a product in large demand. The third factor gave fishermen an impartial body through which they could negotiate improved conditions, such as the union certification of shore workers (primarily cannery workers) and price increases for union members. Encouraged by their successes, and wishing to build on them, the SPSU, the PCFU and various other groups joined with the shore workers in 1945 to form the UFAWU.

The importance of the UFAWU in Sointula has been considerable over the years. Victor Wirkki, a member of the UFAWU from its inception up until 1978, notes that, especially in Sointula, most of the fishermen belonged to the union and profited well by it; "Most of the time they done good anyways. Sometimes the prices came up so much that it was hard to believe."[70] In 1951 alone, the union was able to secure a $35 to $50 a month raise for its shore workers and a twenty-five to thirty six per cent increase in salmon prices for its fishermen.[71]

Such early success helped make it a matter of common sense for Malcolm Islanders to support the union. Though adherence was never one hundred per cent – as with community supported initiatives in the past, such as the Co-op Store, the FO, and the SPC – considerable peer pressure was involved in ensuring as much union support as possible. Dave Siider, who started fishing at the end of the 1940s, notes that joining the UFAWU was expected of a Sointula fisherman in his time.[72]

65. Right:
Cannery Workers, 1946.

66: Far Right:
Ken Homer cartoon, published in *The Fisherman*, 1955.

Though Malcolm Islanders were not the leaders in what was to become the largest fishing union in British Columbia, their support was dedicated and well organized. In 1943, Sointula resident Harold Malm employed his boat, "The Mistral," as the official fishermen's and shore workers' union organizing boat, writing a column about his adventures in *The Fisherman*.[73] Ken Homer contributed many barbed political cartoons in support of the union, including one celebrating fellow Malcolm Islander Laurie Jarvis and the invention of his gillnet drum.[74] And Sointula representatives of the UFAWU Local faithfully attended union conventions in Vancouver, with delegate Lennie Pohto serving for a time on the executive council of the UFAWU.[75]

The Women's Auxiliary to the Sointula Local of the UFAWU became very active as well, discussing with UFAWU delegates the importance of voting in provincial and federal elections, exploring educational advancement possibilities, planning events in support of the union, and inviting the "womenfolk" of fishermen to come and be involved in the union.[76]

The UFAWU was not only a means through which Malcolm Islanders were able to achieve higher fish prices, it was also an organization that, with the waning of the FO, was able to provide a solid connection to socialist ideals. In form, it was reminiscent of both Malcolm Island's early Kalevan Kansa days, and its experiences of the initiatives of the Finnish Organization. Just as in the *Aika* and *Vapaus* newspapers, *The Fisherman* promoted international socialism (and quite often communism) and was openly critical of activity deemed to be capitalist and imperial; it also took great pains to attempt to integrate the co-operative movement with union activity.[77]

The Malcolm Island PTA

As discussed, though the exact purpose and form of these new institutions were different from past ones, they held many similarities: they promoted socialist and co-operative ideals and they were community supported and run. However there is another, and often overlooked, similarity: they were largely dominated by the men of the community. From the founding male members of the Credit Union to the very name of the United Fishermen and Allied Worker's Union, the continued predominance of male control was clear. In the late 1930s, however, an organization was formed that would change this standard. The Malcolm Island Parent Teacher Association, which was in existence until 1966 – except for a brief hiatus from 1943 to 1949 – was a vehicle through which women gained a strong voice in the community.

Though the PTA was by no means exclusively controlled by women, they filled over half of its various positions, including its executive council. This was in marked contrast to the low percentage of women officially involved in the Co-operative Store, the Credit Union, or the UFAWU during the same period. In fact, female activity in the UFAWU was almost exclusively through the auspices of the Women's Auxiliary to the UFAWU as opposed to the main body.[78]

The PTA, as a venue for women to influence their community, became a recognized cornerstone of the community. In her 1950 book on the history of Sointula, resident Aili Anderson listed the Malcolm Island PTA, along with the Co-op, Credit Union, FO, and United Fisherman and Allied Workers Union, as the five most important organizations on the island.[79] The influence of the PTA in Sointula has been noticable in three distinct areas: in its efforts to improve its community through various initiatives; in its efforts

67. Left:
Tea break, 1957.

to connect Sointula to the wider British Columbia community; and in its general social activism.

Many of the PTA's community efforts were aimed, naturally enough, at projects directly related to the school and its pupils: stage dramas and basketball games were organized; school film projectors, badminton sets, and encyclopedias were purchased – all paid for by an endless assortment of PTA bake sales, fashion shows, raffles, whist drives, bingo tournaments and other fund raisers.

When the PTA re-formed in October of 1949, however, it made a commitment to embrace a wider mandate than it had previously. Just as the Co-op Store took care of more than just supplying groceries to Malcolm Islanders, so the PTA would do more than provide pencils for school kids.

One aspect of this wider purpose was to not only look after the educational needs of the school and its children, but of the parents in the community as well.[80] Throughout the 1950s and 1960s, the PTA organized night classes in woodworking and sewing for community members, and arranged talks to parents on such subjects as "the Social Development of the Child" and "the Mental Health of Children";[81] the stress on education that had been present in the earliest days of the Kalevan Kansa continued in these later years through the PTA.

However, the PTA had always concerned itself with more than simply education, involving itself with general community concerns – particularly health. On October 2, 1937, the PTA sent a letter to the Board of Health & Hospital Services, requesting that a Hospital Unit be set up in Sointula, as Alert Bay was too far away in an emergency, and was too busy besides.[82] This health-care role increased after the PTA's regrouping in 1949. In the early 1950s, having worked to secure the services of a dentist on the island, the PTA agreed to cover the $2.50 fee for any pupil whose parents could not afford to pay.[83] With the very real danger of both polio and tuberculosis in this time period, the PTA looked into x-raying school kids for TB, and arranged a committee to take care of polio shots – all the while attempting to secure the services of a public health nurse for the island.

The PTA also helped create ties with other communities, providing opportunities for young Malcolm Islanders to expand their immediate horizons. Sointula students were given the opportunity to compete successfully in an annual musical festival held in Alert Bay.[84] The PTA assisted, either through direct donation or through soliciting funds, in regularly sending two students to the annual High School convention at the University of British Columbia.[85] It further created a scholarship fund to help one graduating student every year attend university.[86]

These new ties were not limited to academic relationships. Having briefly disbanded during the mid-1940s the re-formed Malcolm Island organization had turned to the Alert Bay PTA for advice on how a successful PTA worked.[87] Five years later, both the Port McNeill PTA and the Malcolm Island PTA agreed to share expenses for a planned students' sports day. Further, noting that Alert Bay had been unable to stage its musical festival that year, the Port McNeill and Malcolm Island PTAs drafted a letter pledging their support for any future Alert Bay music festivals.[88] The PTA also enabled Sointulans to form connections with other Parent Teacher Associations across the province, especially through the annual PTA convention in Vancouver.[89] The group gave the islanders an opportunity to form bonds with neighbours and to experience more of the province.

Malcolm Island PTA concerns included much of the activist agenda the community was known for. On November 11, 1938, a PTA member was assigned to say a few words promoting Peace Week before the weekly Saturday night movie at the FO Hall;[90] on May 19, 1939, the association decided that all children from Sointula should go to Alert Bay on the 24th of May to attend a sports day, and to hold a demonstration while they were there. Though not stated, it is likely that this demonstration was either against the approaching World War, or in support of pro-union activities.[91] Further afield, the PTA sent donations to the "Aid for Greece" fund to help the country recover from its bloody 1944-1949 civil war.[92] The Malcolm Island PTA was an activist organization, locally, provincially, and internationally.

The Malcolm Island PTA continued on until 1966/67, when membership began to decline and a feeling began to emerge that "perhaps our PTA has served its purpose."[93] And indeed it had, accomplishing much that was necessary for the students and for the community. It had not done so alone, however, but through working together with other community organizations. A May 9, 1952, PTA report notes that the Sointula

Credit Union had volunteered to pay for the showing of a film at the school (the same report noting the PTA's purchase of another share in the Credit Union).[94] The December 1949 minutes describe a plan to join with the Athletic Club to start gymnastics and basketball after the new year;[95] and in 1958, short on funds, they shared the expense of sending two students to the annual High School conference in Vancouver with the UFAWU and the Sointula Co-op Store.[96] The PTA was a vital part of the communitarianism that seemed to still thrive in this period.

Victoria Welcomes the Neishes

With the success of the new institutions on the island, Sointula still stood out in the post-war decades as a unique place, its residents connected around the basic ideals of the co-operative movement, working class support, and community activism. Just how different Malcolm Island's ideology stood in relation to other B.C. communities of the time may be seen in the reception one family received in Sointula, versus their reception in the provincial capital. Elgin "Scotty" Neish was a fisherman, a socialist, and a key participant in union activities since before the UFAWU was formed. His union duties, and a stint with the Gumboot Navy, had frequently brought him to Malcolm Island during the Second World War. While attending a Saturday night dance at the FO Hall, he met Gladys Halminen, granddaughter of Matti and Anna Halminen. Ideologically in tune, Scotty and Gladys were married after the war, moving to a house in Oak Bay, Victoria.

Though Scotty Neish would never live in Sointula, his ideals would continue to be embraced by the community. Mr. Neish had taken a trip to China in 1952 as part of the Peace Conference of the Asian and Pacific Regions. Scotty Neish's son, Kevin Neish, notes that this trip to China, taken at the height of the cold war, lost his father a contract job with the provincial government in Victoria, blacklisting him for life.[97] In contrast, Scotty Neish's activities were well received in Sointula, providing for an interesting talk at the FO Hall and approving coverage in the school newspaper, the *Sointula Scuttlebutt*. The article noted that in his talk on January of 1953 at the FO Hall, Mr. Neish had noted that he had found the lives of the Chinese to be improved greatly since the communists had taken power.[98] With the advent of the cold war, Sointula's socialist outlook, how-

Moving to Malcolm

Moving to Malcolm Island in the post war period required adaptation. Arriving from Vancouver in 1943, Delmare Laughlin first had to adapt to the roughhousing of the school ground before facing the unfamiliarity of the fishing grounds (attempting to please his Finnish father-in-law). As an English-speaking outsider Laughlin recognized one truth: "you pretty much had to fit in when you came to Sointula."

It was not only English speakers who had to adjust. Arriving in Sointula in 1952 as a teenager from Helsinki, Tula Lewis (nee Jarvinen) was forced to conform to a much less urban existence. Her family's more conservative and religious background also set them apart; all sides would learn to accommodate on these issues in the coming decades.

For Delmare Laughlin's future daughter-in-law, Wanda, it was the innocence of the island that was unique. Arriving in the early 1960s, she was amazed to see a girl her age (ten) pushing a doll carriage! From listening to the jukebox in the local restaurant, to the chaperoned teen dances, Wanda Laughlin remembers joyfully adapting to a community that allowed kids to be kids longer.

Decades later, these three individuals still live on Malcolm Island, having been vibrant contributors to both the economic and social life of the island, adapting themselves to an adapting community.

ever softened it had become from its earlier stance, remained relatively unique in British Columbia.

Equally unique was the unquestioned nature of the island's union support. In the same edition that Scotty Neish's speech was reported, the *Scuttlebutt* also included the latest UFAWU news, admonishing people to get out and support the union. In Victoria, supporting the UFAWU was not so straight forward. Kevin Neish grew up believing that all families tied a pillow around the phone at night, not realizing that his mother was being targeted by verbally abusive anti-unionists on the nights his father was away (Gladys Neish kept a shrill whistle by the phone as a "deterrent" to these callers).[99] The daily nature of abuse directed towards union activists, even into the 1970s, came home to Kevin as he accompanied his dad along Fisherman's Wharf in Victoria. Kevin describes how two large men came hustling down the gangplank, yelling at his father that they were going to tar and feather him. 300 pound Scotty Neish started to yell right back, scaring one of the men back up the gangplank and the other into a phone booth (whereupon the man quickly closed the door and pretended to make a phone call). Questioning his father about the incident as they walked on, Kevin recalls Scotty's nonchalant response: "'Oh that - just anti-union guys. I'm surprised they did that with a witness around, usually they don't.' If I hadn't have commented he would have just continued down to the boat. It would have been nothing to him."[100] Where union support was commonplace and expected in Sointula, anti-union trouble was also commonplace and expected in the larger society.

It was not only union activity, however, that was attacked in this period, but some of the general socialist notions that had been fostered in Sointula. A pacifist and anti-imperialist viewpoint had been prevalent on the remote island since the Kalevan Kansa days, forwarded through the FO, and later *The Fisherman* magazine. A 1952 RCMP secret report on Sointula FO activities, notes that 395 community signatures were added to an "Appeal for Peace Pact," which was to be sent to the five great powers.[101] Kevin Neish notes that the credit for both his own later work in the peace movement, and his mother's involvement, can be attributed to the Malcolm Island example.[102] This ideology, however, was not a widely accepted one outside of Sointula. In the early 1960s, Kevin and Gladys Neish attended a silent peace vigil against the Vietnam War, long before any real movement against the war had begun. Standing in front of the downtown Bay store, the peace protestors were spit on and yelled at by passers by, denigrated as "communists" out to destroy the country.[103] The English-speaking majority in Canada had a limited history of pacifism, and a deep distrust of any activity deemed to be pro-communist.

The same was true about expressing doubts about God. At about the same time that organized religion was starting to be tolerated in Sointula, Gladys Neish was attempting to prevent her young son Kevin from being indoctrinated at school in Victoria. Told that he would make his own choice later in life, Kevin was instructed by his mother to sit down when the other children rose for the daily recital of the Lord's Prayer at school. As Kevin recalls, "that made a big kerfuffle. They didn't know what the hell to do with me!"[104] The controversy over the Neishs' views continued into highschool. Well known as the son of left-wing atheists, Kevin was singled out for conversion by a right-wing, church-going guidance counsellor. Alerted to the fact that her son was undergoing weekly conversion sessions with this man, Gladys Neish went to the school, had the principal call in the counsellor, and in Kevin's words "jumped all over him"; it was the last year this particular guidance counsellor would teach, moving on to a career in real estate.[105]

Though this story can be seen as a successful stand for individual freedom, it also stands as a clear example of a difference in ideology. While religion had to struggle to make inroads in Sointula, the Neishes had to struggle against religion making inroads into their family in Victoria. On Malcolm Island, atheism, pacifism, and socialist/left-wing values were the norms; they would face challenges and changes as the years went by, but they were the set values through which people's actions were judged. In much of the rest of the province, religious faith, patriotism, and conservative/right-wing values held sway; if they were to be challenged or changed, it would be through the efforts of an active minority: people like Gladys Neish nee Halminen.

The Sointula Co-op: Boom and (Near) Bust

That the people of Sointula held on to their communitarianism as their community changed and became increasingly exposed to the outside world's mainstream ideals had a lot to do with the practical benefits that the philosophy afforded them. Union activity made sense to fishermen benefitting financially and otherwise from the strength of the UFAWU. The presence of a community-owned financial institution responsive to local needs made credit union sensibilities logical. And when it no longer made practical sense to support a certain ideology or institution, such as the hardline socialism of the Finnish Organization, support was effectively withdrawn. The island's strongly held beliefs were tied to the practical benefits attached; institutions that did not continue to meet both the ideological and practical needs of the community could not survive. The Sointula Co-op Store, through its post-war success and troubled existence in later years, acts as testament to that creed.

Despite the rise of several new and important institutions in Sointula, the Co-op Store remained the centre around which much of the island appeared to gravitate. As noted previously, despite the social and economic uncertainties of the Depression, the Co-op had attained an enviable status, not only on Malcolm Island, but all along the coast. As Alfred Williams recalls, "People came from all over to shop at the Co-op. It had a fine hardware store and fishermen from as far away as Port Hardy would come here to rig up their boats."[106] The war years added a welcome jolt of enthusiasm and funds to the Co-op. From a modest 96 members and $34,000 in assets in 1939, by 1945 the institution achieved a membership of 220 and assets exceeding $93,000 (including Victory Loans, increased stock, and rental properties).[107] Though World War II had brought mixed blessings to some aspects of Sointula life, it meant an economic boom time for the Co-op.

That economic good fortune continued into the post-war boom of the 1950s, largely due to money brought in through logging growth and increased fish prices. But the Co-op was prudent in its offering of new technology to its increasingly well-off members. In 1950, the Co-op Store arranged to bring electricity to the island, paying B.C. Electric and then collecting from the community members to pay the bill.[108] Norma Williams, whose husband Albert was on the Co-op board of directors in the late 1940s and early 1950s, recalls this as being the "heyday" of the Co-op: "When electricity came, well naturally everybody bought ranges, they bought TVs [television arrived in 1953]… that was big dealings when you could sell washing machines, dryers. So that's why the Co-op did really well."[109]

Another reason why the Co-op may have prospered during this time was due to the steady professional management of Hannes Myntti. Though born and raised in Sointula, Hannes had left the island as a young man to go to Port Arthur (part of present day Thunder Bay), Ontario, where he acquired experience in co-op management.[110] Moving back to assume management duties at the Sointula Co-op in 1939, Myntti became by far the longest serving manager the store had seen yet, guiding the store until his retirement in August 1967. Loretta Rhitamo, daughter of Hannes Myntti, recalls her father as not only a hard-working and effective manager, but as an outgoing and friendly presence, someone who made the atmosphere of the Co-op inviting. She notes that with her father it was "Co-op first, everything else second!"[111]

Under Myntti's leadership, the store thrived, with its assets steadily increasing and its membership rising to a high of 368 in1962.[112] Even the tax man couldn't impede the Co-op's success: a 1953 decision by the Income Tax Appeal Board ruled that the large

68. Right:
New Co-op Store, (background) and old Co-op Store (foreground), 1951.

69. Far Right:
Hannes Myntti in Co-op Store, 1950s.

sums of cash placed by Co-op members in the co-op "bank" could not be taxed, as the money was in the nature of a debt, not borrowed capital. Reporting the decision in a March 23, 1953 article, the *Vancouver Sun* led with the headline, "Little Fellow On Top: Sointula Co-op Beats Tax Czars."[113] Not only was the Co-op allowed to reduce hundreds of thousands of dollars from its calculations of working capital, thus saving it a considerable amount of tax, but it did so with an influential mainstream newspaper cheering it on. In light of past provincial media obsessions with "free love communes" and "communist states," Sointula's depiction as an underdog who had taken on the tax man and won must have been a welcome change.

However, not everyone in Canada viewed the Sointula Co-op as a spunky little fellow fighting the good fight. Though Canada may have avoided the worst excesses of U.S. McCarthyism during the cold war in the 1950s and 1960s, it still engaged in active surveillance of groups and individuals with known or suspected socialist ties, including the Sointula Co-operative Store (the community, apparently, was no longer suspected of right-wing Naziism). Throughout much of the 1950s, the Special Branch of the RCMP enagged in active and covert surveillance of both the Sointula chapter of the Finnish Organization and the Sointula Co-operative Store Association, maintaining a file on both.[114] Though the surveillance of a grocery and hardware store on a relatively isolated B.C. island might seem to be a questionable use of manpower, the RCMP felt more than justified in its suspicions. In a classified 1955 document, the Special Branch detailed the movements of an unnamed Malcolm Island subject (Hannes Myntti) who they were following, stating that: "he is still manager of the Sointula Co-operative Store Association in the town. This position subject holds indicates subject is a member of the Finnish Organization of Canada in Sointula, as this co-operative is virtually run by the Finnish Organization of Canada."[115] Though no evidence exists in any of the Co-op minutes to indicate that the FO had so much as a voice in the running of the store, much less a leadership role, in the mind of the Special Branch the connection between the Sointula Co-op and the subversive Finnish Organization was clear.

And so the RCMP kept busy compiling seemingly innocuous information regarding the Co-op's profits, the formal layout of Co-op meetings, and the contents of the Co-op's constitution. Though it is difficult to imagine that anything of importance could have been uncovered, to minds obsessed with subversive activity there were obvious connections to be explored: Sointula Co-op meetings were covered in the pages of the FO newspaper *Vapaus*, Sointula activist Katri Riksman (pen name - "Grandmother") acting as columnist.[116] As well, the UFAWU, an organization also deemed subversive by the RCMP,[117] occasionally covered the activities of the Co-op in its *Fisherman* newspaper, noting approvingly at one point that three newly elected members of the Co-op board of directors were members of the UFAWU.[118] In a small, close-knit community such as Sointula, there were bound to be connections between the prominent groups in the community, people who were members of the Co-op and the FO, or the UFAWU, and common areas of concern and interest (such as how the fishing industry was doing, or the aforementioned peace movement on the island). In that sense, the Co-op was as much a part of the so-called subversive activity occurring in Sointula, as any other group or individual on the island.

However, in as much as it aroused the RCMP suspicion, it was this same remote and close-knit nature of the Sointula community that prevented effective surveillance of the community. An October 6, 1955 RCMP Special Branch report noted that "very little information has been received in respect to subversive affairs at Sointula, B.C. during the

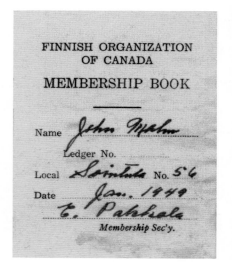

FINNISH ORGANIZATION
OF CANADA
MEMBERSHIP BOOK

Name *John Niemi*

Ledger No.

Local *Sointula* No. 56

Date *Jan. 1949*

E. Pakkala
Membership Sec'y.

past two or three years, due to the fact that we have no coverage of activities at that point."[119] The report ends with the hope that they will be able to procure a "new" informant to aid the police in their efforts, seemingly indicating that at one point there was an informant on or near the island. It is clear, however, that for several years no group or individual could be found who was willing to aid the RCMP in its surveillance. If Sointula had been located in the "outside world," it may well have faced greater surveillance and pressure from both a conservative minded public and conservative authorities. But the isolated communal bonds of Malcolm Island helped insulate the Co-op from such concerns, allowing it to all but ignore the ideological pressures of the cold war.

During the 1950s, and into the 1960s, the Co-op continued to demonstrate how its own success was tied to the community's development as a whole. Such major contributions as bringing electricity to the island and providing an office for the doctor have already been mentioned. However, many of the Co-op's accomplishments consisted of simple gestures – such as cash donations to organizations such as the Sointula women's softball team, the Sointula Library, and even to the Alert Bay Empire Day celebration. The Co-op supplied boxes of oranges for the UFAWU's children's Christmas party at the FO Hall and gave turkeys to the staff on most Christmases. There was also innovative thinking involved in customer accounts, one Co-op member being allowed to pay off his overdue bill in tomatoes, another to keep his overdue account open if he would at least make an effort to get some money by going fishing.[120] Despite the changes that had begun to develop on the island with the influx of new Finns and of new logging families, the Co-op Store still had a very close connection with the community – indeed, over half the adults in Sointula were members.

Ironically, the Co-op's communitarian activities and values may well have contributed to the organization's economic decline in the 1960s. An early example of this was the formation of a union at the Co-op in April of 1956 – Local 1518 of the Retail Food and Drug Clerks Union (RFDCU). Though no clear chain of events remains in the records, at least one informed voice believes that the union was in fact brought in by the 1956 board of directors themselves, presumably as an ideological gesture to recognize workers' rights.[121] Regardless, no initial reservation to the union was ever recorded in the Co-op minutes, and the RFDCU local was unanimously recognized by the mem-

71. Left:
Model A waiting in line for ferry,
Co-op Store in background , 1960s.

bers at the Co-op general meeting.[122, 123] While the shareholders and board of directors of a private, profit-driven company would undoubtedly have been less enthusiastic for unionization, on Malcolm Island it made sound ideological sense.

From a business viewpoint, however, it was a disruptive move. Relations between union and management began to get more and more rocky as the 1960s progressed, culminating in two narrowly averted strikes in 1968 and 1970.[124] Wages appear to have been the key stumbling block, major disagreements arising during times of economic hardship for the Co-op. It is difficult to judge whether increased union demands had any real detrimental effect on the Co-op's surpluses, or the extent to which the working atmosphere in the store suffered from the conflict. But the very presence of the union did have a measurable effect on decisions made outside of Malcolm Island. In 1969, during a time of financial crisis for the store, the Co-op was turned down for a loan by several banks and credit unions. One such bank, the Industrial Development Bank of Victoria, made its reasons for refusing the Co-op credit clear. First, the Co-op had a serious lack of operating capital. Second, and equally important in the bank's view, was the fact that the Co-op was unionized.[125] Feelings in the Co-op had changed so much that by 1970 the board of directors was seriously examining the option of terminating the union contract.[126] The socialist values of the past were running up against the economic problems of the present. Though the union remained, the ideological optimism that had welcomed its presence had become much more subdued.

Another example of the Co-op's non-capitalist ideology contributing to its decline may well have been the dissolution of the "customer savings bank" at the Co-op. As previously mentioned, the Co-op had maintained a makeshift bank on its premises before the appearance of the Credit Union – a practice continued long after the Credit Union was formed, lasting up until the mid 1960s. Though this practice had originated as a service to the community, attested to by the Income Tax Appeal Board's 1953 ruling that this money was a debt and not working capital, it had in reality developed into an integral part of the Co-op's finances. Dave Siider, Co-op board member in the 1960s, noted that at the time of Mr. Myntti's retirement in 1967, there was roughly $80,000 in customer savings, the money being used as working capital.[127] Perhaps alarmed by the prospect of theft (there had been an unsuccessful robbery of the Co-op in the early 1960s), perhaps feeling that acting as a bank fell outside the Co-op's mandate, manager Hannes Myntti began to encourage members to remove their savings from the store. Though Co-op records show that Myntti had secured agreement from the board for a gradual discontinuation of this service in 1965,[128] Dave Siider suggests that Myntti left the board "flabbergasted" when he encouraged members to withdraw their funds at a 1967 general meeting.

Whether the termination of this service took the board by surprise or not, there is no doubt that lack of working capital had a serious effect on the Co-op's finances (it being one of the two reasons given for being denied a loan in 1969). It is difficult to imagine a for-profit organization willingly forgoing $80,000 in finances; working with a different set of priorities the Co-op did what it felt was best for the community, even to its own financial detriment.

While acting in the interests of its members had placed the Co-op in a difficult financial position, the Co-op's most serious crisis came the following year in 1968 as it entrusted its interests to another co-operative. Appropriately, one of the guiding principles of the co-operative movement is co-operation amongst co-operatives themselves – a principle the Sointula Co-op seemed to generally accept throughout the 1950s and 1960s, attending provincial co-op meetings, negotiating loans with other co-ops, and advising potential co-ops on how best to get started.[129] In the latter part of the 1960s, however, the Sointula Co-op would take this co-operation to a new level, connecting itself more and more with the B.C. Co-op Wholesale, an organization that supplied goods, organized co-operative events, and provided financial assistance for many B.C. co-ops. The Sointula Co-op had already received advice on union negotiations from the Co-op Wholesale, and had attended some of its workshops for managers and store clerks; finding themselves without a manger upon Hannes Myntti's retirement in August of 1967, the Sointula Co-op requested the Co-op Wholesale to supply a temporary manager, and to undertake the accounting of the Sointula Co-op.[130] Though past experience in the fishing co-ops and in the left-wing political arena had taught Malcolm Islanders to be wary of outside control over their affairs, in this instance the Sointula Co-op decided to be guided by the Co-op Wholesale, a seemingly like-minded group adhering to the same co-operative principles as the store.

The new manager arrived from the B.C. Co-op Wholesale in October of 1967. A November 19, 1967, report by the Sointula Co-op noted that its account with the Wholesale was paid up to date, and that there were no outstanding bills;[131] by March 11 of the following year, the Sointula store had acquired an $80,000 debt with the Co-op Wholesale.[132] In a letter drafted at a July 20, 1968 Co-op meeting, the Sointula Board of Directors made clear who it blamed for the state of the Co-op's finances; the board accused the Co-op Wholesale of setting out to gain control of the Sointula Co-op by getting its manager to push the Wholesale's most expensive goods on the Sointula Co-op, thus running up the store's expenses. The Wholesale, having handled the Co-op Store's accounting, was also accused of deliberately not paying Sointula's bills to other suppliers, so that the Sointula Co-op's credit with these alternate sources would disappear, forcing a reliance on the Wholesale for supplies.[133] Importantly, the Co-op Store's board of directors was never able to present any proof of deliberate deception by the Wholesale. It is entirely possible that Malcolm Islanders' long standing distrust of authority and outsiders contributed to misinterpreting a case of simple mismanagement and inexperience.

Regardless, the financial impact of this debt made the next six years of operation perhaps the grimmest in the Co-op's entire existence. Ignoring the accusations made against it, B.C. Wholesale continued to firmly request its money (up to $84,000 at one point), while the banks, as mentioned above, would not provide the Co-op any loans. The scene was reminiscent of the earliest days of the Kalevan Kansa: the company badly in debt, outside help not forthcoming, Malcolm Islanders forced to rally to save a community institution.

This time, however, Malcolm Islanders did not rally. The role of the Co-op in people's lives had changed somewhat in the preceding decade, a change brought on by a closer connection with the outside world. In part, it was a connection that had been fostered by the Co-op itself. Responding to a request from the Sointula and Alert Bay Joint Board of Trade, the Co-op had agitated the Ministry of Highways in 1965 for improved ferry links between Sointula, Alert Bay, and Vancouver Island.[134] Whether influenced by the Co-op's actions or not, by the early 1970s, the government was running a regular vehicle ferry (one onto which cars could actually drive without the use of a crane) between Sointula and Vancouver Island. Even before this event, Malcolm Islanders were travelling off the island in increasing numbers. Records indicate that in 1966/67, passengers to and from the island had made nearly 17,000 trips; by the 1971/1972 period, that figure had more than doubled to almost 37,000.[135]

As communities such as Port McNeill began to develop in the 1960s, Malcolm Islanders found themselves with relatively easy access to other grocery and hardware stores. And, as the practical necessity of having the Co-op on Malcolm Island decreased, so did Sointulans' ideological commitment to the Co-op. Olga Landsdowne recalls how the Co-op board was forced to freeze the redemption of shares during the financially troubled times of the 1960s and early 1970s; though this was both legal and necessary under the circumstances, Landsdowne notes that this procedure shook many members' faith in the Co-op.[136]

On March 26, 1973, the Co-op board of directors met to discuss the fate of the Sointula Co-op Association, noting that members' interest in the Association was practically non-existent.[137] In December of that year, the board sent out a questionnaire to all Co-op members asking if they wished to sell the Co-op and all its properties; in February of 1974 they tallied the results: 90 Yes to 38 No – the Co-op Store was now for sale.[138]

That the Co-op did not dissolve at this point is a testament to good management, good luck, and good geography. On August 31, 1968, nearly six years earlier, Hugh Macmillan, responding to a newspaper advertisement, had arrived in Sointula as the new Co-op manager. Dave Siider describes Mr. Macmillan as "the man who put the Co-op on its feet."[139] During his six-year tenure, MacMillan was able to narrowly avoid two potentially disabling strikes, while slowly building up the store with solid management. In that endeavour, Macmillan was aided immeasurably by bookkeeper Phillip Au, described by board member Olga Landsdowne as a financial whiz who saved every penny he could for the store.[140]

Mr. Macmillan may also have been aided by a bit of good luck, in the form of an amalgamation between the B.C. Co-op Wholesale and the Federated Co-operatives of Saskatoon in May of 1970. By the end of the year, Federated Co-op agreed to turn Sointula's debt into a loan to be paid off monthly.[141] Though it is impossible to say whether the B.C. Wholesale would have offered a similar arrangement on its own, the fact that it hadn't in the two years leading up to the amalgamation makes Federated Co-op's entrance into the picture seem a fortunate one. The Co-op's economic position continued to advance over the next few years; an April 27, 1973 directors report to the Annual Co-op Meeting notes that 1972 saw "the first indication of the Co-op Store becoming a profitable operation again" with net income for the year reaching over $18,000, and the debt to Federated Co-op whittled down to $32,000;[142] by February, 1974, it was noted in the Co-op minutes that the store was now in a strong financial position (ironically this statement was made on the same day as the members' decision to sell the store was recorded).[143] Harold Macmillan resigned at this time, leaving the store in the capable hands of new manager Phillip Au.

Though strengthening the store's finances undoubtedly contributed to its continued longevity, in the end what kept the store going may have had more to do with simple geography. Though it is merely conjecture, it seems likely that a unionized store on an out of the way island may not have been the first choice for most prospective

buyers. As well, though getting on and off the island was becoming easier in this period, sheer proximity meant the Co-op was clearly the most convenient place for Malcolm Islanders to shop. As the Co-op minutes continued through the 1970s, all mention of selling the store and its properties simply disappeared. If the Co-op was no longer the *de facto* centre of the community, it was still an accepted and integral part of it.

5. New Paths, Old Ideals

While the post-war decades had been a period of adjustment for the Malcolm Island community, the basic communitarian concerns of the island remained. Olga Landsdowne notes that if you were going to so much as put up a fence on your property, you asked your neighbours if they had any objections.[1] Newcomers, up until this point, had either accepted or adapted to these ways. While subtle changes still occurred on the island, they were gradual changes, faced by a community akin in thought and manner. In the late 1960s and early 1970s a more abrupt change would occur, one that threatened to disrupt the close-knit nature of this society. Attracted for a number of reasons, young, socially-minded Americans began moving to this isolated British Columbia island. Though many monikers would be coined to describe the influx of these new settlers in this period, the most enduring has simply been, "the hippie movement." It was a movement which would precipitate a new wave of communitariansim on the island.

As author Paula Wild recounts in *Sointula: Island Utopia*, the immediate reaction of Malcolm Islanders to these newest arrivals to the community was akin to shock: "Sointula residents gawked at the newcomers' odd cars, baggy clothes and beads, and frowned at the long, dirty hair that was prevalent on both the men and women."[2] For many Malcolm Island residents the general appearance and upkeep of many of these new settlers immediately created a divide. As Norma Williams remembers, "It was the way they dressed and they weren't very clean, because I know that if there was a concert or something at the hall nobody wanted to sit too close to them because there was this odour. Cleanliness wasn't theirs."[3]

Whether real or perceived, other views of the newcomers also served to set them apart. After an American couple, Jane and John McClendon, bought a farm on Kaleva Road in 1969, they began to allow other new arrivals to camp out on the floor or in the barn. The false story that there was an active commune on Malcolm Island quickly spread.[4] Another practice, which resident Kelly Edwards describes as "disconcerting a lot of people," was a tendency of some hippies to squat in some of the abandoned farm buildings in the community.[5] The same was true of a common perception that these newcomers were involved in drugs. Wanda Laughlin notes that many in Sointula feared that these unknown people would influence the community with their drug culture.[6] Finally, there was a widespread belief, surviving to this day, that the newcomers were draft dodgers escaping the war in Vietnam.[7, 8] While there was likely little support on Malcolm Island for this war, the casting of these newcomers as "shirkers" likely added to the perception of these people as unreliable and unwelcome visitors. While the earlier post-war newcomers had seemed to fit in, and so quickly became a part of the close-knit nature of the island, the same was not true of the hippies. Cast as nomadic, drug-using, draft-dodging outsiders, it did not appear as if the hippies would be as good a fit.

Many of these newcomers must have likewise wondered how they would fit into a lifestyle that was so different from what they had known in the United States. Jenny and Jim Green came to Sointula in 1968, fresh from running an art gallery in America's "free love" capital, San Francisco. When the couple attended their first FO event a few weeks later, they began to realize how different life on Malcolm Island would be: "We opened the door and all this wonderful music came pouring out. At the top of the staircase

73. Previous Page:
Dick Hamill with his zucchini
and squash, circa 1975.

were a couple of drunks brawling, they fell down the stairs and landed at our feet. It felt like we had stepped back in time into the wild west."[9] Jenny Green's sense of alienation was compounded soon after when she was ostracized at the local café, the staff simply ignoring her until she left, unserved.[10]

While it should be noted that there is some dispute in the community around Jenny Green's cafe incident, there were other, not-so-subtle indications that the hippies were out of place. Logging trucks played chicken with approaching hippie cars; a newcomer's truck, having broken down on the road, was found torched when its owner returned; and an old cellar that was a suspected drug use site for a group of hippies was burned to the ground (the cellar was empty, as all occupants had been scared off in an RCMP drug raid a few weeks prior).[11]

Some incidents involving the American newcomers did nothing to facilitate matters. One was a seeming general increase in petty theft, possibly a result of an increasing number of transient persons on the island. Victor Wirkki recalls that it was no longer safe in this period to simply leave tools or timber lying around.[12] Another, and more serious incident, demonstrates that the divide between the newcomers and residents could not be solved through removing any debating seats, as previously possible. In 1968, a longtime Finnish resident got into an argument over money with a newcomer. One of the men grabbed a rifle and, as the argument escalated into a physical struggle, the gun went off, wounding the Finn – who later died of blood-loss.[13] In another incident, newcomer Roger Sommer closed an access road located on his property that served as a link between Sointula and the small community at Mitchell Bay (which was becoming a preferred location for the hippie community); despite some verbal abuse and some well-placed rocks thrown at the Sommer home, the road remained closed.[14]

The shooting of the Finn seems to have been treated as an isolated incident; and with the extending of an alternate road, one not located on the Sommer property, Mitchell Bay was soon readily connected to Sointula again. And so, neither incident precipitated an immediate fallout against the general population of newcomers. What the incidents did, however, was highlight and perhaps intensify an "us" and "them" feeling in the community. Jenny Green notes that while no one seemed to blame them as a group for the shooting, people in the community did look at them a bit more closely after that point.[14] And, while it is difficult to say if the community had associated the newcomers in general with the road closure, Sommer's anti-communitarian actions could only have widened the divide.

As real as that divide was, a number of the hippies' ideals eventually came to draw sympathy and even respect from the island's residents. The first was the hippies' sense of freedom from social conventions. Long-time resident Willie Olney noted that, "the hippie movement gave Sointula a complete freedom of fashion. They wore weird get-ups but they looked so comfortable. Pretty soon it seemed like everyone could wear whatever they wanted."[16] The hippies' seemingly communitarian values also began to be recognized, particularly by the old guard. Norma Williams recalls that the left-wing ideals of the hippies were greatly appealing to her uncle, an avowed communist.[17] Loretta Rhitamo believes that the ideals of the hippies were very like those of the Finnish forefathers of the island.[18]

One of the most obvious ideals that the newcomers shared with the earliest Finnish settlers was a desire to farm. Dick and Bette Geisreiter had arrived on the island in 1970, having bought the Halminen farm. Arriving with two sons and nineteen goats, the Geisreiters set out to work the land; soon they were growing most of their own food, selling vegetables and cheese to the Co-op Store, and selling milk, butter, and eggs in the community.[19] The Geisreiters' actions, indicative of the hippies' general desire to get back to the land, were reminiscent of the earliest days of the post-Kalevan Kansa era. Wanda Laughlin notes that at the end of the 1960s there were many abandoned farms and derelict houses outside of Sointula on Kaleva Road. In the early 1970s the American newcomers bought them, putting much time and effort into making their purchases successful.[20] While Laughlin admits that there was some trepidation about the "Americans buying up the island," the newcomers' attempts to "get back to the land" could not help but stir the memories of the old time Finnish residents of Malcolm Island.

The concrete steps of the so-called "hippies" to work the land and build permanent houses also helped dispel some myths about the newcomers. Clearly they were not all non-working drifters or draft dodgers looking for an easy life. As the longtime residents came to know their new American neighbours, friendships and mutual respect grew. Musically inclined, the Geisreiters found themselves hosting musical jam sessions with their Finnish neighbours, and being invited over for a sauna in return.[21] Newcomer Jane Field recalls an older Finnish neighbour coming over to see her house; the older lady's approval was quickly won when she discovered that Jane kept a well-maintained garden in back.[22]

Some of the differences between the newcomers and the older residents even became celebrated rather than divisive in the community. Norma Williams notes with approval that these were educated people settling on the island.[23] Echoing this sentiment, Wanda Laughlin estimates that 90 per cent of the so-called "hippies" came with university degrees, bringing a great deal of talent and skill to the community.[24] Though

76. Left:
Work crew bringing power
to Mitchell Bay in 1980.

Malcolm Island's economic focus had long been on the primary industries of fishing and logging rather than on "higher" learning, there was an appreciation for education on the island that went back to Makela, Kurikka and the original Kalevan Kansa library. The popularity of *Vapaus* and *The Fisherman* on Malcolm Island, with their many articles on socialist thought, economics, and international events, demonstrated a continued interest on the island for self-education. While BAs in History and English Literature may not have had immediate practical application in Sointula, the pursuit of knowledge was not unappreciated.

In the end, the element most responsible for bringing the newcomers and longer term residents together may simply have been time and lessons learned. The once strange and unknown faces in the community became familiar through contact. Those squatting or camping out in barns soon found that Malcolm Island's climate in the fall and winter (and often the spring) was not as inviting as the southern California many had previously called home. The newcomers had to make concrete decisions about committing to a rural community, or moving on to the urban centres many were more familiar with. Many of those who had committed by buying land and living off of it, soon had to face the same reality that the original Finnish settlers had faced: it was difficult to make a living just farming on Malcolm Island. Paula Wild recounts, as more and more of these newcomers realized this fact, they turned in the same direction as the original Finns had – to the logging and fishing industries.[25]

There were certain things that would continue to separate the newcomers from the old guard. The former would be more highly concentrated along Kaleva Road and especially in Mitchell Bay, creating a physical distance between themselves and the residents of Sointula. As well, distinctions would continue to be made in the community between descendants of the original settlers and the most recent newcomers. But as Loretta Rhitamo notes, "over the years they've got more like us and we've got more like them, maybe."[26] While the hippies brand of left-wing ideology initially found itself in some ways at odds with the isalnd's traditional left-wing socialism, through sharing a way of life the two paths have become less distinct. The hippies took jobs, built houses, raised children, grew gardens, and became good neighbours; and just as the Finnish newcomers of the post-war had helped preserve the traditional language of the island, so too had these newcomers of the 1960s and 1970s in fact helped preserve the island's left-wing approach to life. As the seventies turned into the eighties, the newcomers would, more or less, simply be part of a community that was facing wider changes.

All Fed Up

One of the main ideals from the past that the American newcomers of this time seemed to support was that of the co-operative movement. While this did not necessarily translate into support for the Co-op Store, these newcomers were key participants in other co-operative ventures, both on and off the island.

Ironically, participation in one of these other co-ops was sparked by a short-coming in the stock of the Co-op Store. When Ralph Harris, who had been working for a philanthropic organization in Fresno, California, moved to Malcolm Island in 1970, he discovered a growing community of about 50 to 60 Americans. Like many of his compatriots, Harris found that some foods he considered as basics (soya sauce and wheat germ, for example) simply weren't available at the Co-op Store. To compensate, Harris and some other like-minded newcomers joined the Fed Up Co-op in Vancouver, a federation of food buying clubs that ran a warehouse in that city. Through Fed Up, Harris and others were able to bulk buy items by catalogue at an affordable price; as the price of membership, someone from Malcolm island was required to work the equivalent of one week a year in the Vancouver warehouse. This was often broken down into several one or two day allotments, after which time the worker would haul the bulk order back to Malcolm Island. As time went by, the Co-op Store responded by bringing in more items that fitted the tastes of the newcomers.[27, 28]

Treesing: the Seeds of Equity

While this venture demonstrated the ingenuity and the idealism of many of the newcomers, its impact on the island was relatively minor. Of longer lasting, and more widespread effect was Treesing, a tree planting co-op formed by American newcomer Jane Field in 1974. Like the other newcomers, Field was adjusting to the task of making a living in Sointula. Though fishing and logging were the two main suppliers of employment on the island, both industries were traditionally reluctant to hire women. Field, who had a background in communal living, and was very sympathetic to co-operative ideals, responded by starting Treesing in an attempt to utilize co-operative ideals to solve the economic barriers many Malcolm Island women faced.[29]

In doing so, Treesing not only adopted co-operative methods familiar to the island, but introduced new ones. As the Co-op Store had done in 1909, Treesing began with a small core of members – the Co-op Store had started with 26 members, Treesing with 20 – each purchasing a share in the co-op. And, as with the original Co-op Store, to be a member of Treesing you had to be a resident of Malcolm Island.[30] However, unlike the Co-op Store, and unlike most co-operatives of that or perhaps any time, Treesing's policy was that half its membership had to be female. The policy was a very practical response to the lack of gainful jobs for women on the island, and fitted well with the ideals of the American newcomers who had been influenced by the feminist movement of the 1960s and early 1970s. Like a return to Kurikka and the days of utopia, Treesing centred on equality between the sexes through a co-operative venture; unlike the Kalevan Kansa days, however, Treesing would achieve it through practical application, not argue about it through divisive philosophical diatribes.

Soon after its formation, Jane Field received a contract to replant an area around the Malcolm Island dump that had been damaged by fire. Though of short duration, the job provided temporary employment for approximately forty-five people. Over the next twelve years, Treesing continued to thrive, offering the female members of the island a rare chance to make decent wages in the forest industry. The job also accomodated many of the needs of working women. It was intense work, but seasonal (primarily Fall and Spring) so that women with children could be away from home as little as possible; also, for the women who brought their children to camp, Treesing provided paid super-vision.[31] Again, this was reminiscent of the original utopia, and Kurikka's desire to "free women from the shackles of motherhood" by providing free daycare. The difference here was that the women of Treesing were making their own decisions regarding child rearing and work, not being dictated to.

The notion of equality was built into Treesing's operations in other ways as well. Regarding job performance, planters were paid according to the number of days they worked, not by trees planted. Though some planters were undoubtedly more produc-tive tree planters than others, this arrangement appears to have worked well for the co-operative. The same, however, cannot be said for the application of Treesing's equality principle in the realm of job sharing – giving each member a chance to not only plant, but to manage operations as well. While this arrangement helped create equitable opportunities within the company, it also resulted in a number of difficulties, most of which centred around the need for experience and continuity. First, while other companies often wanted to deal with the same manager, Treesing management was always changing. Moreover, unneeded conflict arose when those who didn't want to manage were required to do so, at the same time limiting the management role that those with the needed skills and initiative could offer.[32]

This job sharing got particularly troublesome as more and more core members left. Tree planting is gruelling work, and as the founders aged they took careers generally more conducive to their physical capability. The new members, largely transient workers, had neither the experience nor the permanence to be effective managers. The five core members who remained in the mid 1980s found themselves necessarily acting as management for the co-op, despite also being full-time planters. Understandably, they decided to compensate their exhaustive efforts through additional remuneration. Some dispute remains over what happened at this point: Paula Wild suggests that as receiving payment contravened co-operative policy, the co-op members decided to dissolve soon after rather than become just another business;[33] others suggest that the core members keeping the organization together were simply too exhausted to continue.[34] The task of continuing was made even more difficult by increased market competition. Treesing found themselves in a similar position as many other small reforestation companies – new, bigger companies were driving prices down and undercutting small companies' bids on contracts. In 1986, Treesing dissolved.

In its twelve-year history, Treesing played some very strong roles on the island. From an economic viewpoint, it was a constant source of seasonal employment; from a feminist viewpoint, it provided a way for women to earn a living in the forest industry, and was concerned with the welfare of its employees and their children; and from a communitarian viewpoint, it not only helped bring Malcolm Island newcomers into a traditional Sointula industry, it did so through a method close to Malcolm Islanders' hearts – a co-operative. Treesing was the first Malcolm Island co-operative that the American newcomers would be a central part of, and it would not be the last.

77. Right:
Various photos of Treesing members,
John Rosser pictured in toque, far left.

The Rec

Not all of the organizations that took root in the 1970s were initiated by the new American residents. In 1971 the Sointula Women's Auxiliary of the UFAWU asked a few community members to look into the possibility of getting an indoor swimming pool for Sointula. Wanda Laughlin and the others chosen soon realized that the upkeep of the pool would be more than the community could afford. These volunteers, however, also realized that there was a recreational need in the community that was not being met. Approaching the School Board they were able to purchase the old school (now the Senior's Centre and Museum) for one dollar and set up their Recreation Society there. Two big 'Sears' swimming pools were purchased, and over the next several summers, Summer Playground students from Victoria were hired to come and run recreation programs for the kids. The children of Sointula got swimming lessons and some structured activities for the summer; Malcolm Island got the Recreation Board, an organization that would, in many areas, act as the engine of the community for most of the next thirty years.[35]

The Rec. Board did so in the same way that organizations such as the Co-op and the Finnish Organization had so many years before: simply by being the group that got the necessary things done – necessary things that were, of course, largely recreational in nature. Kelly Edwards recalls the Rec. organizing roller-skating, volleyball, basketball, and badminton activities for the kids in the school gym.[36] With much more difficulty, the Rec. also organized the creation of a ball field on the island. Up to the mid-1990s, the community was stuck with what Wanda Laughlin describes as a "bog hole" of a ball field. Though many of the men of Malcolm Island wished to make a small softball field and then enlarge it at a later, unspecified date, The Rec. Board declined: "Uh uh, No!" Wanda Laughlin laughed, "We know you guys. We know men. No! Build the whole thing properly now or we're not doing it."[37] Laughlin estimates that the Rec. raised $300,000 through fund-raiser after fund-raiser. Along the way, they were aided by C1 contractors from Victoria (who, while in Sointula to build a sewer, helped provide fill for the ball field), a $21,000 grant from the government, and strong community support. Upon its completion in 1996, the community had a ball field that, in Laughlin's estimation, was bigger than anything north of Nanaimo.[38]

78. Right:
Treesing members haviong fun in spring snow.

The Rec. was also instrumental in organizing Salmon Days, a community-wide cel-ebration held in August throughout the 1970s and into the 1980s. Largely serving as a non-ideological substitute for the now defunct May Day celebrations, Salmon Days had some of the same outdoor games, as well as a huge salmon cook-off, the fish being donated by the local fishermen. Wanda Laughlin recalls Salmon Days as being a huge event, with fishermen flying home from wherever else they were fishing on the island to celebrate. Though the event ended in the early to mid-1980s due to a disruptive fishing strike and the increasing difficulty of fishermen getting home, in its time, Salmon Days was a celebration that brought the community together.[39]

The athletic and social recreational activities that had been such a pivotal part of Malcolm Island's history were being continued through the efforts of the Rec Board. However, as important as these recreational activities were, they were just a small part of the responsibilities the Rec. took on. As Laughlin explains;

> We're not like most Recs. Most Recreations you're providing recreation for the community. We're the fund-raisers, we're the [pause] we have to do everything…Any of these government things that happen - the trail-build-ing [for community hiking]…a project for the museum, nothing can happen without going through the Rec. because there is no other group…There's no group that's been in existence long enough that government agencies are even going to enter into a contract with, so that you can hold insurance.[40]

As an example, Laughlin notes that volunteer groups using the school gym are able to do so for free rather than pay fifty dollars an hour, because the Rec. pays the insur-ance. Like the Co-op in the past, the Recreation Board is viewed as a stable, permanent body in the community.

It is this image that has also led to the Rec's position as the renter and maintainer of community buildings. Laughlin notes that when the FO Hall was up for sale in 1978, the local Lions Club had expressed some interest in purchasing it. However, the Finnish Organization, viewing the Lions as a strictly private group, had insisted the hall go to an organization such as the Rec., which would be able to guarantee that the hall be kept in the community. Seen as a permanent presence in Sointula, the Rec. has also been

79. Upper Right:
Salmon Days ladies in costume, 1979.

80. Lower Right:
Smoking salmon on Salmon Days, 1975.

81: Lower Far Right:
Tractor and float in Salmon Days
Parade, 1970s.

Community House

trusted with control of the fire hall and the Senior's Centre, and managing the buildings that are central to the island's history and present stability.[41]

The Fed-Up Co-op, Treesing, and the Recreation Association, may have been new organizations for Malcolm Island, but they had a long ideological pedigree. The establishment of a food and silviculture co-op on the island must have awoken more than a few memories of the original Co-op Store and the 1926 B.C. Fisherman's Co-operative. Likewise, the Rec. Association was probably understood as a continuation of the recreational activities of the Young Pioneers and the Finnish Organization, with the community leadership of the Co-op Store mixed in. New people and new paths perhaps, but as always, after a period of adjustment, the island absorbed the change, and the equilibrium of the community, if slightly altered, was preserved. It would take a shock of some magnitude to threaten the communitarian values of the island – a shock which the coming years were about to provide.

82: Above Left:
Cubs marching in Salmon
Days parade, 1987.

A clear example of the Rec. Board's role in the community can be seen in the Community House. In the early 1990s the Rec. Board became aware that an older Sointula man was living on his own in a "cold and miserable" trailer. With community help, the Rec. converted a building they owned into a "community home" with a complete kitchen and living room area and had him moved in within a week. In Wanda Laughlin's words,

> It was like he had died and gone to heaven, he just thought this was sooo great!...That was the kind of thing this community is so great at doing. The electrician went down and volunteered his own [time]...the plumber went down....everyone else went down and painted....There was a need, lets go for it!

The house has gone on to be a home for a man suffering from cancer, and a handicapped individual; in both cases rent was waived, the hydro bill being the residents only obligation. Currently, the building has no tenant and it is being used as a Teen Centre, complete with Pool Table and adult supervision; however, there is an understanding with the teens that they will have to vacate if any one individual in the community is in real need.

6.   Calm Before the Storm

In 1980, the Planning Department of the Regional District of Mount Waddington, of which Malcolm Island is a part, met with the Malcolm Island Advisory Planning Commission to come up with a development plan for the island. Emphasizing a common desire to keep Malcolm Island rural through slow and sustainable growth, "The Plan" detailed objectives for the island's physical, environmental, social, and economic development. Distinct from most plans of that era, Malcolm Islanders had come together to agree that preserving their community rights and lifestyle were more important than pure economic growth. No one, however, imagined the economic devastation that was about to befall them through factors completely beyond their control.

While "The Plan" cannot be taken to represent the wishes of all members of the Malcolm Island community, it does reflect the island's prevalant realities and ideals. A look at the members of the Planning Commission reveals a fair cross section of the community, with 1970s newcomers such as Ralph Harris and Mike Fields, post war loggers such as Delmare Laughlin, and the descendants of original settlers, such as Don Anderson.[1] The fact that residents of different backgrounds were able to agree on a direction for their community speaks well for the communitarian values on the island at this time.

As does the direction agreed upon. Concern for one's neighbour was a traditional part of the island's communitarianism, to the extent that one's profit or freedom was not to be obtained at the expense of the community's comfort and well being. "The Plan" was no exception. Distinguishing between the community's best interest and its economic growth, the committee agreed to "provide for a variety of small community and rural lifestyles," and to "discourage large-scale commercial, industrial and tourist developments." In some ways, "The Plan" is another example of Malcolm Islanders' long-standing adherence to socialist values in the face of encroaching capitalist ideals.

The triumph of communitarianism over capitalism, however, should not be over stressed. The community's commitment to "The Plan" was, to some measure, tied to the economic strength of the times. One Sointula fisherman, working in the early 1980s, tells of buying a new car with three days of fishing wages.[2] In 1980, the future ills of the fishing and logging industries were largely unthinkable. With economic success in the fishing and logging industries all but ensured, there was little need for any large scale development on the island – and maintaining the traditional rural character of Sointula, together with its communitarianism, appears to have been a relatively uncomplicated matter.

The Island's loggers and fishermen had long prided themselves on their independence. And, up until this point, adherence to industry unions had generally been their only concession of freedom within their chosen occupations.. However, as changes in the logging and fishing industries occurred later in the decade, Malcolm Islanders' ability to continue their traditional path was severely compromised.

This independence first began to deteriorate in Malcolm Island's logging industry. By the late 1970s the island itself was becoming logged out and locally owned and operating logging businesses began to decline. People such as Elgin Shiels had sold out to larger B.C. companies. At first, it was still possible for Malcolm Island loggers to make a decent living working elsewhere in British Columbia, especially for bigger companies (Elgin Shiels notes that his time working for the larger companies in the 1970s and early 1980s was his most profitable).[3]

In the 1980s, however, international changes would occur that were far beyond Malcolm Islanders' control, constraining them in ways previously unimagined. In the logging industry, the high commodity prices of the 1970s began to plunge with the world recession of 1982, never to return to their original levels. Additionally, the market saw increased competition from countries such as Indonesia, Chile, and the southern US, all of which were able to grow wood fibre at a faster rate than climactically cooler B.C., and all of which had lower labour costs.[4] Facing these challenges, while trying to adapt to new environmental sensibilities, logging profits became constrained. In response, indus-

83: Previous Page:
Fishing ship at Bere Point,
Malcolm Island, 2004.

84: Right:
FO Hall under snow, 1979.

try adopted new technologies and replaced a number of small on-site mills with more efficient centralized mills. The result has been a decline in employment in the logging industry, from employing seven per cent of B.C.'s workers at the beginning of the 1980s to five per cent in 1999.[5] Unemployment rates in the industry hit double digits in the later 1980s, and averaged around seventeen per cent from 1990 to 1998.[6]

This decline in the logging industry no doubt affected Malcolm Islanders to a certain degree – it was an important part of the local economy. But not the most important. As Alfred Williams said of the community so many years previously: "Everything we have here comes from fishing."[7] There is little exaggeration in Williams' statement; as an integral part of Sointula from day one, fishing has helped define the community. For generations of young men on the island, quitting school at sixteen to begin to "make a man's wage" fishing was a rite of passage to adulthood.[8] The fishing lifestyle was also a huge part of life for Malcolm Island women, whether or not they were actively catching fish. Aileen Wooldridge laughingly traces her fishing career to 1934, when she was brought onto her father's boat as an eight month old baby;[9] Muriel Lowry also explored her father's boat as a child; Oiva Halminen, describes it as the one place where she felt most at home;[10] Kelly Edwards (born 1962) recalls that, like a lot of daughters, she and her sisters worked as cooks and deck hands on their fathers' boats. She also notes that even before women fished on their own, many women, like her mom, went out fishing with their husbands, bringing their kids along – adding that the sight of diapers hanging from the mast-lines was not uncommon.[11] Fishing was more than a job on the island; it was a way of life for entire families.

In the 1980s this way of life began to be threatened. As with logging, much of the problem was due to international factors beyond the control of Sointula fishermen. The Malcolm Island fishing economy had always been based around salmon, which was traditionally sold to canning companies (sometimes co-ops). However, through the 1970s and 1980s, the demand for salmon on the world market gradually shifted to fresh fish, the supply of which was dominated by the Japanese. Further, there was a dramatic increase in farmed salmon, which equalled the yearly catch of wild salmon by the late 1980s. The result was a decline in the price of salmon.[12] In an attempt to prevent a dramatic decline in wages and benefits, the UFAWU went on strike in July of 1989.

85: Right:
Unknown newspaper clipping, reporting end of strike.

86: Far Right:
UFAWU strike poster.

Demanding better conditions and prices was as much a part of being a Malcolm Island fisherman and fisherwoman as anything else. Since even before there was a UFAWU, Malcolm Island fishermen had been fighting for what they considered fair wages, doing so even at the height of the depression. Dean Wooldridge, a Sointula resident who fished from the 1940s into the 1990s, recalls with pride the united stand he and other Malcolm Island fishermen displayed: "We had big powerful outfits we were bucking too - B.C. Packers, Nelson Brothers...they were big outfits, so we had lots of fun! The fishermen were solid."[13] Whatever the outcome, Malcolm Island fishermen had a tradition of standing united.

In 1989, however, that tradition ended. After less than a month on strike an agreement was reached in which no real improvements for the workers were gained.[14] Dean Wooldridge sees the failure of the strike as the point when fish prices and fishing in general went downhill. Blaming the lack of solidarity in the union ranks for the collapse of the strike, Wooldridge notes sadly that many young Malcolm Island fishermen were among those who crossed the picket line.[15] Echoing this sentiment, Albert and Norma Williams note that the ideology of the younger Sointula fishermen seems to be radi-

Fish Union Admits Defeat, Calls Off Northern Strike

The United Fishermen and Allied Workers Union Wednesday called off its four-month trawl and halibut strike in Prince Rupert and admitted defeat.

Union secretary Homer Stevens said the "unfair" label was being lifted immediately from Prince Rupert Fishing Vessel Owners Association boats and that shoreworkers would resume handling them.

"The strike is over. It means we don't expect to win," said a dejected Stevens.

'SIGH OF RELIEF'

Prince Rupert mayor Pete Lester said the whole community will "breathe a sigh of relief" at the end of the strike, which split the northern port and had a serious economic effect.

He said the strike failed because the UFAWU was fighting most of the city.

Efforts are to begin today to clear up a side effect of the strike, the future of shoreworkers at two fish plants who refused to handle owner association boats and whose jobs were largely taken over by other workers who crossed union picket lines.

Norm Bellis, manager of the Prince Rupert Fishermen's Co-op, one of the plants involved, said his organization has to know the dispute is completely solved before taking the men back without loss of seniority.

He said the co-op does not want to be caught again in the middle of a jurisdictional dispute.

Stevens announced acceptance of defeat and the end of the strike after a meeting of the union's strike committee.

The decision came only hours after members of the Deep Sea Fishermen's Union rejected a 14-point plan aimed at resolving the jurisdictional dispute between it and the UFAWU.

The plan, arrived at with the aid of Ed Sims, president of Vancouver and District Labor Council, had earlier been accepted by the DSFU executive and the membership of the UFAWU.

It divided owners' association boats between the two unions on the basis of whether they were fishing for private companies or for the Prince Rupert Fishermen's Co-op.

The UFAWU decision to end

Please Turn to Page Two See: "Strike"

cally different that that shown by their grandfathers – the ones who built the union in the first place.[16] This seeming lack of union conviction by many younger fishermen, as demonstrated in the 1989 strike, may have been the beginning of the UFAWU's decline on Malcolm Island.

An even more damaging blow, however, arrived in 1996, in the form of the Pacific Salmon Revitalization Strategy, more commonly known as the Mifflin Plan. Designed and instituted by the federal Department of Fisheries and Oceans (DFO) under Minister Fred Mifflin, the plan was characterized as a "Fleet Rationalization Strategy with three stated objectives: conservation, economic viability, and partnership. Ostensibly, the Mifflin Plan was intended to prevent the desruction of declining salmon stocks and habitat. Towards this end, the plan implemented four key measures: a voluntary license retirement program, commonly referred to as the "buyback" program (funded by DFO);

single gear licensing, allowing a license holder to fish using only one type of gear; area licensing, designating two areas two areas for seine fishing, three areas for gillnet fishing, and three areas for troll fishing; and lastly, a provision that allowed for the purchase of additional licenses in order to fish other areas or using other gear (referred to as "stacking").

The almost immediate results of these measures were the loss of flexibility for fishers in choosing their fishing 'grounds', which in turn severely compromised their ability to be economically viable. Prior to Mifflin fishers had some degree of freedom in deciding where and what to fish (although this had been declining for years through other DFO strategies). Fishers were now being forced to pick one area and they had to buy specific licenses depending on their method of fishing (gillnet, troll, seine) and which fish they were after. Predictably, the price of licenses rose dramatically.

87: Left:
Sointula fishing ship catching 7500 sockeye salmon, before the Mifflin Plan, 1994.

88: Right:
as above.

Speaking out againt this plan at a meeting of the Standing Committee on Aboriginal Affairs and Northern Development, representatives of several communities and groups involved with the fishery noted that the plan was made without consultation with environmental, community, aboriginal, or labour groups – and that it would devastate coastal communities.[17] Not surprisingly, fishers (and others) all along the coast referred to the strategy as "the Muffin Plan" and many had little hope that it would acheive its goals.

The effect of the Mifflin Plan on Malcolm Island has, unquestionably, been extreme. Thirty-one year old former fisherwoman Tosha Nelson notes that after the plan's implementation, she and her husband would have had to pay an additional $600,000 to maintain their shrimp and salmon licenses – an unaffordable option for the young couple.[18] Lennie Pohto estimates that the Mifflin Plan caused the UFAWU to lose half its membership as fishermen and women were driven out of the industry by the increased cost and fishing restrictions.[19]

There is much anger on the island towards the outside forces that many see as having taken their livelihood away from them. With the wide availability of farmed salmon, competition from fisheries in other countries, and restrictions placed upon British Columbia salmon fishers (including fishing quotas and huge license fees), the ability of Sointula to survive as a fishing community has been severely curtailed. Dean and Aileen Wooldridge note that dumped fish from fish farms have "raised hell" with wild salmon fry, decreasing the natural stock;[20] Lennie Pohto singles out both mid-ocean Japanese and Alaskan fishermen for encroaching on B.C. salmon stocks;[21] and Calvin Siider argues that quotas should be eased, stating that the decline in salmon stocks is a cyclical event in the fishing cycle.[22]

While these outside groups have received much of the blame for the near disapearance of the island's fishing industry, some of the disappointment on the island has been directed inward. Albert Williams' has commented that today's fishermen would accept two or three cents a pound for their catch. This might not be much of an exaggeration. Aileen Wooldridge remarks that her son recently sold a load of pink salmon for five cents per pound, less than ten percent of what she received before 1981.[23] Whether or not anything could be accomplished by a strike under today's conditions is question-

able; however, the younger fishermens' seeming lack of commitment to the strength of collective action, as demonstrated during the 1989 strike, clearly baffles and distresses many of the older generation. Aileen Wooldridge recalls a time when a young Malcolm Island fisherman enquired when they were going out on strike; he wasn't about to join them, but was hoping they would drive up the prices while he fished. According to Dean Woolridge, who at the time was in the company of a few old timers, recalls that his response to the younng fisher's presumptuous attitude did not go over very well. "I said, 'We're not going to tie up any more, it's your turn. You guys go and tie together…we're gonna keep fishing for a change.' To which the young fisher announced: 'Oh, well, you can't do that!' They figured we'd keep doing it forever."[24] The belief, shared by more than a few of the older generation, that many of the young fishermen and women have abandoned the ideals of their parents and grandparents, has clearly added to the bitterness created by the economic decline of the fishing industry.

90: Left:
Sointulans demonstrating against
increasing fishing restrictions,
1992

Such a conclusion, however, may not adequately take into account the new post-1980s fishing environment. The older generation's comparison of their generation's ability to support the union during economic strife, versus the younger generation's inability, may be overlooking some fundamental economic and social changes. While earlier generations may have had simpler needs, and been able to meet those needs during strike-time, this is not the case today. It is unlikely that the older fishermen, in an earlier age of home made boats and houses without mortgages, had the same debt load as the young fishermen in the 1989 strike. In the view of Clayton Jordan, who was a young fishermen at the time of the 1989 strike, and who continued fishing up until 2004, the difference in union attitude between the old and new guard is completely understandable, especially when the divisive effects of the Mifflin Plan are taken into account:

> 40 years ago [Sointula fishermen] had one license to fish all fisheries, you
> know. If I had a group of ten friends and we all just needed the one license,
> we had the same license, and we bought it for a dollar and then we helped
> each other build boats, well, I'm sure that would all bring us closer together...
> You take those 10 group of people and you divide them into 10 different
> groups - it's hard to have a strong union, isn't it?[25]

Though pro-union and non-union fishermen on the island cannot be divided by age uniformly (there are many young union activists and several older non-union people), it is not inaccurate to view union attitudes, in general, as products of differing times and environments. Union support on Malcolm Island, particularly in the fishing industry, had come about through the fear that, alone, the common worker would be exploited – by big business, by the government, and by the larger society. Ironically, the economic success achieved by the early unionists helped create a new generation of Malcolm Island fishermen who did not have that same fear. Having succeeded economically without having been face to face with the same exploitation as their forebearers, it seems that this new generation has generally put more faith in the individual economic security that they became familiar with in the present, rather than the communitarian security of the past.

Regardless, in the face of the new challenges posed by farmed salmon, stringent and divisive government regulations, and international pressures unknown to previous generations of fishermen, the fishing environment on Malcolm Island has become economically poorer, and poorer in union support.

An Ideological Adjustment

The communitarian and economic shifts of the island can be seen in many different examples, but it is perhaps most startling to note its presence in the former show-piece of the community: the Co-op. The coming of the 1980s saw the Sointula Co-op trying to maintain its original communitarianism, while at the same time expanding its services to successfully compete with profit-oriented institutions on Vancouver Island. The store benefitted greatly in these efforts from the strong management of Phillip Au, who guided the fortunes of the store until his retirement in 1999. Just as the Co-op had enjoyed stability under the 29-year leadership of Hannes Myntti, the 25 years of Au's management likewise provided the Co-op Store with a steady hand through difficult times. Loretta Rhitamo ranks Mr. Au alongside her father as a true leader who always put the Co-op first.[26] Under Au, the Co-op continued to provide scholarships to Malcolm Island students; gave donations to such events as Salmon Days, bike rodeos, and the island's Christmas party; supported such groups as the Lions, and the Sointula Library; and, at one time, offered a discount of ten per cent on all goods to any non-profit organization in the community.[27] These ventures were an important continuation of the communitarian legacy of the Co-op Store, as practiced since before Hannes Myntti's time.

Arguably, however, the most important contribution that Au made at this time was to ensure the Co-op's economic stability. Competition from larger stores in Port McNeill and from down island, coupled with an increasingly improved transportation system, had combined to put more and more pressure on the Co-op Store as it moved into the 1980s. With the support of the Co-op's board of directors, Au sought to keep the business competitive. One of his first measures to do so was through the acquisition of a liquor outlet for the store in 1984.[28] Though it made sense for the Co-op to have such an outlet as a way of enticing shoppers to shop on island, its approval was not immediately forthcoming. Au recalls a special meeting being held over the issue, the biggest general meeting in his time with the Co-op, during which an undercurrent of opposition to the proposal arose.[29] This pressure against was likely a lingering expression of the community's past temperance beliefs; but tradition lost to the economic realities of the present, and the outlet was approved through a majority vote.

The economic importance of the liquor outlet pales, however, next to the Co-op's purchase of the ESSO gas station on the island in 1986. In the mid-1980s, ESSO indicated to the Co-op that it was planning to leave the island. As Au notes, such a move would have been greatly disruptive to the community, especially in its effects on the shopping habits of residents (who would presumably buy goods elsewhere when they went for gas). Seeing both the need to prevent an out-migration of shoppers, and the potential for profit, the Co-op moved quickly and cleverly. As Au notes, not only was the negotiated purchase price cheap, $5,000 as he remembers, but the purchase agreement between the Co-op and ESSO stipulated that the Co-op was to be supplied with gas at a rate two cents less per litre than the ESSO agent in Port Hardy for a five year period. Importantly, the agreement specified that ESSO had to undertake a soil survey of the ground underneath the gas station, and cover the cost of whatever cleanup was necessary – a stipulation that cost the ESSO and saved the Co-op some $80,000.[30] In Au's estimation, the Co-op has thrived from this arrangement, both from gas revenues and from the patronage refund the Co-op receives from buying its gas through Federated Co-operative – the supplier whom the Co-op Store went to as soon as its five year agreement with ESSO was up. Both the gas bar and liquor agency venture were practical maneuvers through which the Co-op maintained its centrality to a changing community, and in doing so maintained its own economic viability; it was the same manouvering which helped the Co-op become the centre piece of the community in the early days of its existence. In each of the twenty-five years of Au's management, the Co-op always realized a profit.

Yet, this community involvement and economic stability were not enough to prevent the gradual decline of the Co-op's importance in the community. As mentioned earlier, competition from the outside had begun to wear away at the Co-op.

Norma Williams notes that the last ten years or so have made a real difference, with young families increasingly turning to superstores in places such as Nanaimo to do their shopping;[31] With the decline in the fishing industry in the last ten to fifteen years, both the hardware and grocery sales of the Co-op have taken a downturn. Wanda Laughlin, president of the Co-op board of directors for 1989 and 1990, notes that it became too expensive for the store to keep extensive hardware stock for a dwindling number of fishermen, so it had to cut back to save on costs; the "Catch 22" of the situation was that with a decreased selection, it was often quicker for people to just go to a big store in Nanaimo to pick up what they needed.[32] These same fishers, living with reduced incomes due to the lowering of their allowed catch, have had to increasingly look at ways to save money. As Wanda Laughlin notes, "It's our Co-op, you want to support it. But can you afford to pay $10 more [than at a superstore]?" Looking ten years hence, she fears for both the future of the Co-op, and the community as a whole.[33]

However, it may not be the economic decline that has hurt the Co-op so much as a shift in community ideals. As Loretta Rhitamo points out, the economic success of the community between the late 1960s and early 1980s played a key role in changing the community/Co-op relationship: "forty years ago, people bought practically everything through the Co-op. Gave you a good deal. There was a real need at first. Then, when fishing was fantastic, there was not such a need."[34] As with the choice to support co-operative action in the current fishing industry, the choice to support the Co-op Store is difficult; to support co-operative action now means making financial sacrifices which have no guarantee of future pay-off. But, as Loretta notes, this choice might become easier as the economic downturn continues, "Now it seems they should have the Co-op. Maybe people need it more."[35]

Hope and Community

That Malcolm Islanders needed something in the wake of the Mifflin plan and its economic fallout was quite evident, especially to those witnessing the decline in the island's spirit. Marjorie Greensides had first come to Sointula from Vancouver

91: Upper Far Left:
Sointula Esso gas bar, 1970s.

92: Upper Left:
Co-op Store gas bar, 2004.

93: Lower Left:
Co-op gas truck in Sointula, 2004.

in 1990, driven simply by a sense of adventure and a desire to travel to new places. Though Marjorie subsequently left the island to pursue an environmental studies and sociology degree in Victoria, she missed the sense of community she had experienced in Sointula. Returning to the island post-Mifflin, however, Marjorie could not help but notice the change that Malcolm Island had undergone: "You could feel it," she notes, "a big black cloud over the community."[36] People wondered aloud to Greensides why she, with a university degree, would be coming back to live here. Marjorie's friend Susan Harvey, a Malcolm Islander since 1981, notes that the decline was especially evident in the men of the town, who had "attached a lot of their mental health to that job [fishing]."[37] With no sign of an economic turnaround in the near future, it appeared as if that big black cloud might become a permanent part of the landscape.

Not everyone, however, was prepared to accept that outcome. Harvey recalls how Wanda Laughlin, the "unofficial mayor of Sointula," reacted to this decline in community spirit; "Wanda walked into the café one day. Not one single conversation had anything uplifting, good in it. [She thought], 'how the hell can we change everybody's focus?'"[38] What Laughlin came up with was unique, to say the least: the Malcolm Island Treasure Hunt. This contest would begin with a clue designed to lead the participants onto the next clue at some location on the island. Over a period of 8 to 12 weeks (varying from year to year) participants would need to delve back into the island's history, asking old-timers questions about where a certain event happened, or scouring the island themselves to look for clues. With a grand prize of $500 it wasn't going to solve anyone's economic woes (as Marjorie Greensides jokes, you spend $600 in gas just participating[39]), but the project was a complete success. As Harvey recalls, "everyone just *glommed* onto it." Harvey remembers the words of one treasure hunter who followed a clue to a certain out of the way bay on a corner of the island: "'I haven't been down here since I was 15...I'd forgotten how beautiful it is, I'm going to bring the kids camping here this summer'. [The treasure hunt] made them remember things about the town."[40] Both Marjorie and Susan note with sadness the losses that the community has experienced in recent times: a decline in health, out-migration, and even a rise in the suicide rate. While obviously not a cure all, the Treasure Hunt is seen by many as a positive step out of the depression that had settled on the island; "It was the kind of thing that had to happen," Harvey notes. "People started laughing...their focus is more outward."[41] Though not an event to change the material outlook for the island, it may have provided something just as important: hope.

7. Co-operative Comeback

A positive outlook for the future is an important part of any community's spirit; however, maintaining that outlook without something solid and material to back it is extremely difficult. While there was and is still hope on the island for a return of a viable fishing industry, some enterprising members of the community have begun to examine alternative solutions to the island's economic woes. To do so, they have returned to a model that has served the island very well in the past: the co-operative. With both the Malcolm Island Shellfish Co-op (MISC) and the Wild Island Foods Co-op, the community has made a stab at regaining control of its economic future – and has, perhaps, begun to renew a somewhat dormant co-operative ideology.

Malcolm Island Shellfish Co-operative

Will Soltau, onetime president of MISC, is clear when he states that the shellfish co-op began as anything but an ideological venture. In 1990, in the wake of the disastrous 1989 UFAWU strike and a general deterioration of the fishing industry, Soltau and a group of about nine other Malcolm Islanders started to discuss alternate fishing related businesses that might be possible on the island. Will had been involved in salmon aquaculture in the mid 1980s, but discussion regarding a possible farm on the island did not lead anywhere (as more information regarding the environmental dangers of farmed salmon has become available, opinion on the island has turned dramatically against this type of venture). The group began to discuss a less controversial type of aquaculture, one involving shellfish, as an alternative. Eventually, conversation began to be steered towards one particularly valuable species: pinto abalone.

Know as the "gold of the ocean,"[1] this mollusk began to be heavily harvested in British Columbia through the 1970s and 1980s. Almost identical to aso abalone, a Japanese favourite, the pinto was well received in both the important Japanese and Chinese markets, where it can command very high prices.[2] The high demand, however, led to over-harvesting, poaching, and the eventual closing of the B.C. abalone industry in 1990. With the demand for pinto abalone still existing, and with the necessary environmental conditions present on Malcolm Island (pinto abalone has traditionally thrived there) the possible economic benefits of abalone became clear. All that was needed was a small push for the project to get off the back burner.

That push came in the form of a threat and a promise. In 1995, Will Soltau and others on the island began to note federal initiatives aimed at getting fishermen out of the industry and into other ventures. Promised government funds were available, and with the threat of fishing restrictions yet to come, the group's plan began to materialize. Though a private business structure was discussed, the group decided on a co-operative venture for several reasons. First, and most obvious, was the desire to maintain community control. Second, they would have greater access to government funding, which was more readily available for co-operatives than private businesses. Third, on the advice of the then district economic development officer Annemarie Koch, it was decided that the provincial government of the day would be more likely to grant the necessary permits to the venture as a co-operative than a corporation.

The resulting decision centred on what focus the co-op would have. Some members wished to consider making the co-op a wide umbrella shellfish co-op where such products as clams and gooey ducks would be produced alongside the abalone; the chosen name of the co-op (Malcolm Island *Shellfish* Co-op) reflects that desire. This co-op, however, was to take a decidedly more narrow direction. Dave Johnstone, a driving force of this group from the beginning, had been an abalone diver before 1990. With previous knowledge of the industry, Johnstone and his wife Meg Wheeler pushed hard for making abalone the sole focus of the co-op.[3] It was a throw of the dice that would put all of the co-op's hopes on the success or failure of one commercial crop. The disagreement was also a sign of conflicts to come.

94: Previous Page:
Sointula Co-op Hardware Store, 2004.

95: Right:
Abalone, raised by MISC, 2002.

By 1997, Soltau found himself "president of a company that didn't have any assets."[4] The Co-op began to purchase equipment through several sources of income: with federal grant money; with some money that had come in through membership shares, reaching $75,000 by 1999; and with a lesser amount through investment shares. For the project to really get going, however, a great deal more money was needed, money that, at first, would only be available from the deep coffers of the government. In 1999 MISC, along with a number of other coastal community groups, set out to secure funding from the newly formed Community Economic Adjustment Initiative (CEAI), a program set up by the Department of Fisheries and Oceans in partnership with municipal and provincial groups to "assist the fourteen hardest-hit communities affected by the downturn in the salmon fishing industry."[5] At number four on that list, Malcolm Island seemed due for some help. With a theoretically workable alternative to the salmon industry, with some aid from the government, it seemed that MISC might become the white knight of the community.

Which is when the soap opera-like troubles of MISC began. Disagreement arose over the handling of the co-operative's all important business proposal to the CEAI, upon which all financial hopes of the moment rested. The proposal had been placed under the control of Meg Wheeler; however, as the process developed, questions arose as to whether Meg's proposal, as detailed as it was in abalone biology and its worldwide market, was the cost specific business plan that some members felt it should be. At one point, concerned that their proposal might fail, Soltau took it upon himself to go to Vancouver Island without the knowledge of the board and it directors, to meet with officials involved with CEAI funding. Soltau wished to see if MISC could still receive some benefits, such as training or technological information, if their proposal failed.

What might have been a simple fact finding trip turned sour after it was discovered that Soltau had undertaken this initative. Though everyone involved seemed truly to be striving for the same thing – a successful proposal – what arose was a real split in the co-operative; it revolved around the structure of the enterprise, between a more collaborative approach in which the board would help guide the co-operative, and a more executive approach, in which a few strong personalities would decide. Under fire from some of these strong personalities, Will Soltau felt that the only way to preserve the Co-op was to resign.

Raising Abalone

In January of 2000, MISC received a $250,000 loan from CEAI, giving the co-op the necessary funding to move forward and sparking a sense of optimism and success. Even though the loan was only geared towards a limited eighteen month test project, the wider potential that a successful abalone industry had for the island, and in fact the whole region, was already being touted. Meg Wheeler, speaking through the community newspaper *Island Echo*, remarked that "this is a first step towards a lucrative abalone culturing facility that could create 40-60 jobs on Malcolm Island."[6] Meg went on to state her belief that abalone could single handedly replace what the northern island had lost in the salmon industry.[7]

The project appeared to be well viewed in official circles as well. John Rosser, a MISC member who would eventually take over the day to day care of the abalone, noted that there were "20 acronyms of different government things that helped us in one way or another to get started...we've gotten $800,000 in government help."[8] For an area that was still living through the aftermath of the Mifflin Plan, it was somewhat of a

Though pinto abalone are a unique and difficult species to farm, Australian technology has proven effective. Adopted at MISC, the Australian system is modular: juvenile abalone are grown in rows of linked outdoor cultivation tanks, allowing individual tanks to be easily moved and ensuring that any disease outbreak remains isolated. Ocean water is pumped into the cultivation tanks through two eight-inch wide pipes, utilizing sand filters to remove particles longer than 40 micros. While these filters keep out most pollutants, they allow algae to pass through – the primary source of abalone food. Perfecting this system, MISC has found unique ways to specially modify the abalone food and heat the water, creating optimal conditions whereby abalone may reach marketable maturity in four years.

The relatively few mature brood stock, from which the marketed abalone are derived, remain inside the hatchery during the process, with the males and females kept in separate tanks. In August, the brood stock are induced to spawn through externally exposing them to ultra-violet light. The fertilized eggs, which are transferred to hatchery larval development tanks, develop into larva in about one week, after which they are transferred to the outdoor cultivation tanks. There they will stay and grow with the others until hopefully one day becoming part of a main course in a Vancouver, Tokyo, or Hong Kong restaurant.[1]

reach to embrace the government as a potential ally. There was, however, cautious optimism. Noting MISC's success in acquiring government funds, the *North Island Gazette* (a newspaper dedicated to covering events around the north part of Vancouver Island) remarked with some surprise that "sometimes when someone says he's from the government and there to help, he really is."[9] In an article for *Western Aquaculture*, Wheeler noted official support for the project, stating, "even the bureaucrats are enthused."[10]

That bureaucratic enthusiasm and the optimism it inspired would be sorely challenged along the way, however. In the summer of 2000, MISC had the necessary funds in place, and, with the arrival of an abalone expert from Australia, (consultant Darryl Evans of Port Lincoln, Australia), had the necessary know-how to get started. They lacked only one ingredient: abalone. As a former abalone diver, Dave Johnstone knew where to get the necessary brood stock to begin the process; the Co-op also was in possession of a letter from an assistant deputy minister at DFO allowing them to take a specified number of abalone for brood stock.[11] Officials at another level in the DFO, however, were insisting that MISC sign a collaborative agreement before they could receive permission to harvest the brood stock, an agreement Johnstone and other MISC members feared did not guarantee continued access to the brood stock after the 18 month trial period was over. Such a guarantee was essential if MISC was to continue as a viable commercial operation.[12] Equally essential was getting the abalone seeded as soon as possible; Australian expert Evans stressed that August was the best time for abalone to spawn. But talks with the DFO continued stalling. As time ran out, Dave Johnstone made what seemed a necessary choice – he went diving.

The dive took place on July 29, 2000. Two days later, on July 31, 2000, Darryl Evans and Murray Tanner, then MISC president, proudly displayed their facility – complete with recently arrived abalone – to visiting DFO Minister Herb Dhaliwal, who was apparently unaware of any controversy surrounding the whole matter. However, as Johnstone had been very open about his action, it did not take long for other DFO officials to catch on, and a few weeks later Dave Johnstone and MISC were charged with poaching abalone. However, as Murray Tanner relates, the official who most mattered was on their side: "The judge actually got quite annoyed with Fisheries and Oceans over the whole thing…The whole reasoning, I mean, it was like we had to dot a few more i's and cross a few more t's."[13] The case against MISC was thrown out and, though there would be future disagreements with the DFO over access to brood stock, MISC was able to get their initial harvest underway.

Despite their success in receiving government funding, and their victory in court, the directors of MISC were becoming more and more aware that they lacked the knowledge necessary to move their organization forward. John Rosser laughingly describes himself and the other board members of the time as "a bunch of local yokels that didn't know doodley-squat about [co-operatives]."[14] When Marty Frost, a consultant and long time co-op proponent, came to Sointula to help educate MISC's directors, he gave some blunt business advice: "If you guys are gonna march forward from here, you've got to have a [business manager]. You really need one."[15] Realizing that Frost was correct on this point, those most involved with the running of MISC, including Dave and Meg, agreed to put out advertisements for a full time manger. In June of 2001, Pelle Agerup arrived in Sointula.

In many ways, Agerup seemed like an ideal fit for both MISC and Malcolm Island. Though still a young man in his thirties, his credentials – a BA in Environmental Economics followed by an MBA and five years working in the IT industry in his home country of Sweden – gave him instant credibility in business matters. What is more, Pelle had lived on a similar island in Sweden, a fishing community with a small population; to a certain degree he knew what to expect regarding Malcolm Island's pace and lifestyle. Joining the Lions, the choir, the volunteer fire department and just talking to as many people as he could, Agerup attempted to "dive into" the community and make it his own.[16]

Though initially well received in Sointula, it was not long before Agerup realized that he would soon have to make some potentially unpopular decisions. Though he had been aware that the organization needed restructuring, he was taken aback at some of the practices that had been allowed to take place:

> There were 11 people here when I got here and there was one person actually working with abalone. So it was badly managed to say the least. As soon as some grant money came around on the island there were a whole bunch of people assigned jobs, makeshift jobs…Short-term thinking. When I came here there was no business plan - I don't know how they managed to get all

the money [$800,000 in government grants] without a business plan, and there was no scientific experimentation done. There were guesstimates.... The first that they told me when I got here was that it takes three years to grow them from start to finish, the abalone, and just what they had in the shed there would be worth millions of dollars. So, the reality check showed it would take at least seven years to grow them under present conditions, and the whole shed full of abalone would still only be a few hundred thousand at market.[17]

Pelle noted of MISC personel that "there was one strong person and that was Meg. And she was calling the shots and deciding what the board should decide on too."[18] Unable to pay MISC's rent, hydro bills, and its payroll expenses Pelle decided to cross his own Rubicon; in late 2001, he laid off the entire staff of MISC, Meg included. From being a welcomed presence on the island moving easily between different groups and people, Pelle became, for a time, a marked man:

It was a whole ugly mess with letters sent and really trying to get me off the island, and phoning my wife and threatening us. Yeah - it was ugly, really, as bad as can be. We had - police were involved - we had a loaded shotgun under the bed, we had video surveillance, phone taps, the lot.[19]

It was uncertain who was behind these intimidation tactics (and remains so to this day). It was also uncertain how many Malcolm Islanders shared these feelings against Agerup's management. The latter became clear at the MISC general meeting in December of 2001. The meeting basically pitted Meg Wheeler and Dave Johnstone, and their vision for MISC, against Pelle and his. Wheeler and Johnstone spoke against Pelle's leadership, denounced the co-operative model as unworkable, and offered to buy MISC for a dollar, at which point Pelle would be dismissed; Pelle countered with a proposal of patiently building the co-op under competent management.[20,21] It was not a close vote. With over ninety per cent of the seventy-five members voting in his favor, Pelle's vision for the co-op was resoundley accepted by the membership. Though Agerup was greatly comforted by this public display of support, for those most closely involved with MISC it was a bitter-sweet affair. John Rosser notes that there was no intention to lay Meg off permanently, and that she should be commended for having secured so much funding for MISC.[22] Murray Tanner, president of MISC for almost two years in 2000 and 2001, credits Meg and Dave for having had the original dream for the organization and for putting a lot of their time and money into it; he adds, however, that their dominant vision of how to operate the co-op often made it challenging to work alongside them. Tanner's feelings echo the message behind the vote in the December 2001 meeting: MISC members felt more comfortable with the softer and quieter Pelle leading the co-op.

Agerup was to find that having the backing of Malcolm Islanders for his leadership would mean more than just good wishes and moral support. Faced with eviction from Meg and Dave's property, on which the co-op had been situated, Pelle immediately received offers from local fishermen to help find a new location and to tow the hatchery tanks there (the eviction notice was rescinded soon after).[23] As time went on, and MISC's needs grew, Pelle took full advantage of the community's good will. Sending out a letter to each household on the island, Agerup was able to acquire almost all of the equipment needed to keep the MISC hatchery going. He estimates that the "solar wheel," MISC's first experiment in heating water for the abalone in order to quicken their growth, cost a mere four dollars, a few nails being the only item not provided for by community donation.[24] "Its very hard to say where the community and Co-op [end and start]" Pelle notes. It seemed that MISC, like the Co-op Store in bygone days, was becoming *the* institution to be supported.[25]

The Co-op Store, however, had products to sell from its very beginning. Though the abalone industry was well established in Australia and New Zealand (by 2000, Australia's annual abalone export was worth $154,000,000[26]) British Columbian pinto abalone were a unique and almost unexplored variety; no one knew how long it would take to bring them from egg to market size. With no product and little remaining capital, Pelle set out to simply keep MISC going until something more concrete could be established. For a six to twelve month period, John Rosser, his daughter Michelle, Glen Watson (MISC president after Murray Tanner) and Pelle volunteered their hours in exchange for shares to keep MISC going. Though recognizing the group effort, Michelle Rosser credit's Pelle's level-headed thinking and strong but gentle approach for MISC's survival during this period. Her father John adds that Pelle kept them motivated:

[He] had the optimism to just everyday say 'its gonna be all right. It's gonna be alright. It's gonna be alright'...and a lot of times people like me are goin' 'oh my god, how are we gonna - we can't pay the bill next month and blah, blah, blah, blah, blah,' ' It's okay, we're gonna make it'. [he laughs] And sure enough we did. By the skin of our teeth![27]

MISC's survival is a testimony not only to Pelle's leadership and the selfless dedication of people like John and Michelle Rosser and Glen Watson, but to a bit of luck, and, perhaps, shared idealism. As John Rosser tells it, "it's unbelievable how close we were to just - gone!"[28] In September of 2002, MISC was on its last legs – out of money, with no hope of securing the necessary funds to pay hydro and rent. Experiments with heating the water were increasing the abalone growth rate, but the survival rate of the first spawning was low (as it is in nature) and any potential product was still years away. It appeared as if Malcolm Island's latest attempt at co-operative revival might be at an end.

At this point Sharon Charles came into the picture. Introduced to MISC by Peter Van Gills of Ecotrust (a private non-profit group dedicated to promoting environmentally sound economic opportunities for rural B.C. communities) Charles was president of the Semiahmoo Development Corporation, an organization working out of the Semiahmoo First Nations reserve near Surrey. In many ways, the MISC project seemed like an ideal fit for Charles and her organization: economically, abalone production looked like a viable business for the Malcolm Island region; spiritually and culturally, abalone have a special significance to many coastal first nations people; and lastly, the co-operative arrangement itself seemed to conform to Charles' and her group's own business ideology.[29]

It was this last point that was so important to MISC and its members. The democratic nature of the co-op structure had been a stumbling block in attracting other investors, as the co-operative principle of "one person, one vote" meant that large investors would receive no more say in business matters than small investors. But, the fear of losing control of MISC and having it moved off the island made this the only acceptable structure for the time being. Charles and her development corporation, however, seemed not at all put off by that. Saying that she thought the island had a great future and that she could accept MISC retaining fifty-one per cent control of the organization,

Charles immediately began to pay off MISC's outstanding bills. The creditors were satisfied and the immediate crisis was over.

And for the future, well, it seemed as if the optimism of MISC's past was back again. The Co-op and the Semiahmoo discussed the details of partnership – with $5,000,000 being floated as a possible investment figure.[30] Such an investment would allow MISC to move from its rather limited area to an expanded facility, increasing the scale of the operation and its potential for profit. Pelle and John Rosser's experiments with heating the water were beginning to pay off in accelerated growth, and though only tens of thousands of abalone remained from the original spawning, the isolated tank structure of their arrangement helped insure that no water born diseases would wipe out MISC's entire harvest (as had occurred in the California abalone industry). In the early months of 2003, MISC appeared to be on the ascent. The co-op had gotten itself to the point where it knew how to grow and maintain a healthy abalone crop; what is more, it had the financial backing for expanding its crop. And, finally, co-op members were secure in the knowledge that they had a dedicated, competent manager in Pelle Agerup to help guide them through the process.

The problem, however, was that MISC was still a dream that was years away from reality. Success depended upon continued good fortune and the cementing of the financial framework for the organization. The coming year would see failure in both fronts. The first misfortune would be the most unexpected – the departure of Agerup. Having survived the unrest of the first layoffs, and a lean year of working for free, Pelle was suddenly forced to leave the island due to an illness in the family. It is difficult to overestimate the importance that having someone like Pelle at the head of MISC held. Though co-operatives are by definition under the control of the membership, past experience had taught Malcolm Islanders to value the strong leadership of their co-op managers. Hannes Myntti, Harold MacMillan, and Phillip Au had the experience and knowledge to help steer the Co-op Store through bad times, and capitalize during the good. Likewise, Pelle had been a large factor in stabilizing MISC's uncertain future. Given the unsettled nature of MISC's finances at this point, the absence of management did not bode well.

Unfortunately, it was not long before the financial structure underneath MISC would begin to give out too. The future investment of the Semiahmoo Development

Corporation had been much touted on the island, but nothing official had ever been signed. Malcolm Islanders had a long tradition of simply doing things on trust (one recent Sointula resident describes buying his house on a simple "handshake agreement"[31]); however, a large business partnership such as this was not simply a matter of an informal general agreement. As MISC board member Art Swanson noted early in 2003, "you and me can sit around a table and hash things out and say, 'this is good'. But now, give it to the lawyers…?"[32] Swanson's words would turn out to be prophetic. When the time came for MISC and the Semiahmoo to formalize their agreement the conditions had changed; the Semiahmoo were now talking about greater control and the possibility of moving MISC off of the island.[33]

Ironically, as John Rosser relates, it may have been his and MISC's own research that changed the Semiahmoo Development Corporation's perspective. Focusing on the all important water heating question, Rosser and MISC discovered a method being used with other shellfish (though not yet, to their knowledge, with abalone) to cheaply and efficiently heat water: re-circulation. Instead of constantly taking in seawater through filtered pipes and heating it (only to have it run back out to the ocean), re-circulation would see water brought in and simply kept going around in a circle, staying at a consistent temperature, with only a very small amount of top up water needed to compensate for evaporation and minor leekage; this would keep the water "pristinely clean in its own system," while also massively cutting down on the heating bill. In fact, evidence suggested that because of friction, the process may even result in a need to slightly *cool* the water in the tank.[34] According to Rosser, the old method of constantly taking in fresh water would not have worked nearer to the Semiahmoo reservation because the water down there is too polluted; but with the re-circulation method, Rosser believes the Semiahmoo Development Corporation may have made a realization: "Oh, we can do it down there cheaper than we can do it [on Malcolm Island]. Bingo!"[35] It is important to note that the Semiahmoo Development Corporation has not stated this as a factor in their business decisions surrounding MISC – it is simply conjecture on John Rosser's part. Regardless of the reasoning, the major investment that MISC was looking for from Sharon Charles and her organization has not been forthcoming.

What might have been the final blow to the co-op occurred in April of 2004, when Meg and Dave finally sold the property MISC was on. In true Malcolm Island fashion,

96: Right:
MISC abalone tanks, with
recirculating sea water, 2004.

however, the community came to the rescue. Lennie Pohto, a member of MISC and a longtime co-operative supporter, just happened to have an ideal piece of property near the water. As long as the abalone didn't mind sharing their habitat with a couple of highland cows, the new location would not only ensure the continued existence of MISC, it would also provide the space for the co-op to attempt a five tonne farm – said by Australian experts to be the financial break even point. The five tonne experiment could prove to potential investors that MISC is a viable operation, one worth investing

in; from there, a fifty tonne farm, a six million dollar investment, would be possible and profitable.[36]

And so MISC remains, not the forty job salvation that the island once envisioned, but not an abandoned hope either. The obstacles are well chronicled, but the possibilities and plusses seem just as strong, if not stronger: currently, the Mount Waddington Regional District is busy helping MISC prepare a grant that, if successful, would fund their five tonne model;[37] still years away from saleable product, MISC has already had a large shellfish marketer knocking at their door, ready to take their product the moment it is ready;[38] a consultant for the regional district has labelled MISC as the most investment ready project on the North Island;[39] and, as board member Art Swanson sees it, MISC has two irreplaceable assets: the best water in the world, and John Rosser.[40] Starting with no real knowledge of abalone, Rosser has, by research and experiment, made himself one of the foremost experts in the raising of pinto abalone. His year long experiment in water heating has helped establish the ideal temperature for pinto abalone growth, and his constant fine tuning of abalone feed has created the potential for a future side industry for MISC (pinto abalone feed production).[41] Even experts from Australia have remarked at his innovative experiments in storing and raising the abalone.[42] Rosser believes that with access to more brood stock (still a tricky proposition with DFO) and with the proper financial backing, he can have a lucrative abalone crop (from spawn to finish) in four years or less; the ability is there, all that is needed is the chance.[43]

For now, MISC plays the waiting game, hoping for what has been euphemistically referred to by board members as "a big brother," "a friend," and even "a sugardaddy" – a big investor who can help launch the co-op and ensure it makes it to its first big harvest. Though there has been disagreement along the way over how much say to give the big investor, or even whether to remain a co-operative in the long run, every MISC member contacted seems to agree on one basic goal: keep MISC a thriving Malcolm Island based institution. While this desire stems from an economic sensibility to keep the jobs local and thus help pump the local economy, it also comes from something more. As John Rosser puts it;

> I'd like to see this business get off the ground and be what all the other [MISC] members hope...a way for local people in a community to change

97: Right:
MISC at current location, 2004.

their own destiny, to shape their own destiny...so that they aren't totally reliant on the outside world to be what they want to be.[44]

It is a statement that could have been made a hundred years earlier by a member of the Kalevan Kansa. The basic desire of Malcolm Islanders to lead lives free from outside control remains one of the defining points of the community, and may be the strongest underlying force behind this new co-operative.

Wild Island Foods Co-op

Though economic concerns have certainly been central to the development of the Wild Island Foods Co-op, it too is a co-operative that has been shaped by an underlying community ideal. In its July 2002 newsletter, *The Wild Island Advantage*, two year old Wild Island made a pitch to Malcolm Island that was based as much on community values as on economics: "So often you may feel powerless, controlled by people, forces and events that are far from home. An investment in Wild Island Foods is a way to make something positive happen in a community that has - and will continue - to rise to every occasion."[45] Arising at roughly the same time as the shellfish co-op, Wild Island Foods was formed for many of the same reasons as MISC, went through a similar development pattern, and faced some familiar problems.

Like MISC, Wild Island is a project that may owe its existence to the impact of the Mifflin Plan. Reacting to the potential devastation that this plan held for the community, Human Resources Development Canada (HRDC) representative Rick Roberts initiated the community's incorporation of the Interacting Resource Society (IRS), a group whose primary goal was to explore other non-fishing economic possibilities for Malcolm Island. Sending out a survey to every household on the island, the IRS solicited suggestions for local economic alternatives; of the 229 responses received, ninety-six per cent identified value-added food processing as a possible solution.[46] That so many people should have arrived at the same conclusion speaks to the importance that food had and still has in the community. The preponderance of Finnish baked goods at the old FO Hall dances and community events, as well as the traditional mulligans for the Co-op Store Meetings, has been well documented.

One of the initial leaders of the Wild Island Foods Co-op was Liette Lavoie, a transplanted Quebec native who moved to the island in 1966, imbued with the co-operative ideals so common in her home province.[47] An active member of the IRS, Liette was brought on as Wild Island's project manager, largely responsible for the initial business and marketing plans that would help get Wild Island started. She notes that Malcolm Islanders' enthusiasm for food and food preparation continues today:

> [Sointula] per capita has the best cooks I have ever encountered anywhere. The potlucks in this town are out of this world. To please people with food

is difficult here because if you're going to sell food - it better be really good!
It is the heart of the community, it really is. The food has always been what
brings people together.[48]

With tradition, and a fairly clear mandate behind them, the IRS was able to get
HRDC and the Provincial Ministry of Advanced Education (MAETT) to fund $50,000 for
development costs, including a feasibility study to help a planning committee develop a
business plan, search for funding, and develop marketing strategies for a food processing
facility.[49] Here, before Wild Islands even truly began, the first snag appeared. The firm
chosen to do the $30,000 feasibility study did not seem to understand their client's
wishes, and concentrated on the idea of a traditional fish processing plant, ignoring the
idea of value added food.[50] Perhaps this focus was based on and spoke to a larger problem – that Malcolm Island was a fishing community, and that many on and off the island
could not imagine it as anything else. Regardless, with the only remaining fish plant soon
to close, and with government officials making it clear that they did not even wish to
hear about value added fish,[51] the firm's efforts were clearly headed in the wrong direction. Both in terms of misapplied money, and in initial momentum, the feasibility study
was an inauspicious start to the co-op.

That an outside group may not have shared the same business vision of Malcolm
Islanders was perhaps not so hard to conceive, particularly if seen as a nod to a past
when Malcolm Islanders were not in step with most other B.C. communities. There was
also, however, some apparent division in the community over the new business, with
some Malcolm Islanders wondering aloud if Sointula really needed another co-op.[52] As
Lavoie recalls, however, a co-op structure was seen by many of those involved as the
one which would do the most for the community, and ensure the fairest distribution of
profits; also, as at MISC, Lavoie and others realized that having a co-op structure would
be a boon when applying for government grants.[53] Aided by co-op developer Marty
Frost, the Wild Island Foods Co-op was incorporated in February 2000.

Right from the beginning, Wild Island differed from MISC, and most of Malcolm
Island's past co-ops, in the preponderance of women in its ranks. Whether this was due
to the fact that food preparation had been a traditionally female occupation on the
island, or simply to the existence of a network of like-minded women attempting to

carve an economic niche for themselves (as with Treesing so many years ago) is unclear; however, the story of Wild Island's leadership was to be, with few exceptions, the story of a select group of Malcolm Island women.

Attempting to pinpoint their best course of business development, Lavoie and other Wild Island members conducted two surveys in 2000, one geared towards producers, the other towards consumers. The first survey questioned ten potential producers interested in using a Wild Island production facility to put through such items as antipasto, coffee, jam, seafoods, and even dog biscuits.[54] Based on the survey's results, Wild Island decided not only to develop a central processing kitchen with the necessary equipment (there was great overlap in producers equipment needs), but extend their services to include assistance in individual business and marketing plans, product development and processing, federal certification, as well as packaging and labeling. It was hoped that Wild Island would provide a community brand under which each product would be more effectively marketed.[55] Eventually, Wild Island arranged, with the British Columbia Institute of Technology (BCIT), to offer an intensive course to locals through which several Sointua residents would become certified Micro Food Processors – giving them the knowledge they would need to best use the facility.[56] When the food processing facility was actually built, Wild Island would be ready to help the community take full advantage of it.

The second survey, taken later in 2000, concerned the possible development of a bakery and specialty foods section of Wild Island. Contacting the 300 households in Sointula at the time, the survey found that ninety per cent of the respondents would purchase locally baked goods if they did not use preservatives and additives, and that more than ninety-six percent would purchase traditional Finnish items such as Pulla, a Finnish sweet bread.[57] The bakery opened in April of 2002, doing fair business in not only breads, pastries and in-store roasted coffee (organic and fair trade), but also as a restaurant (with a fairly limited menu). As Lavoie recalls, the restaurant/bakery was meant to be the "cherry on the cake,"[58] a way to get cash flow moving and provide some jobs while the production facility got underway. The reality of the situation was to be quite different.

Like MISC, Wild Island was basically rich in ideas and community enthusiasm, but cash poor. In order to get a workable facility built and running, they needed a large infusion of capital, perhaps a few hundred thousand dollars. Given the high proportion of women at Wild Island, Liette Lavoie decided that the Women's Development Bank might be the ideal place to secure the needed funds; this group, however, informed Lavoie that they did not do business with co-operatives.[59] Like MISC, Wild Island would find it difficult to secure private sector money for a co-operative venture.

This left government agencies as the main source for securing the necessary capital. Over the next few years the HRDC, three provincial ministries, the CEAI, and the Community Futures Development Corporation of Mount Waddington would all help the co-op get going through its initial stages, providing grants and loans, some of which were only available to co-operatives.[60] There was a price though. As part of their initial grant, Wild Islands was able to secure $192,000 from CEAI; the catch, however, was that CEAI would not give the money unless Community Futures agreed to provide a $50,000 loan to the co-op;[61] and before Community Futures would agree to the $50,000 loan, the Wild Island board had to sign a personal guarantee for $50,000 *each*.[62] It was a sign of their devotion to the co-op that each board member was willing to do so, and so the funds were acquired.

This entire process, however, was also a sign that securing capital from the government and from other funding agencies was not going to be a straightforward process. As Lavoie notes, there is an entire lingo associated with grant getting that is completely foreign to the plain-talking islanders.[63] Long-term directors Kathy Parton and Lorraine Williams believe that grant getting is also a preferential process, remarking that MISC seemed to be favoured by certain funding organizations, while Wild Island was all but shut out from these same opportunities.[64] Outspoken co-op director Susan Harvey adds that it is a deeply flawed process, one in which the organization receiving the funding is encouraged to quickly spend it, effectively promoting wasteful and hasty purchasing and artificially high wages.[65] Of course, there are other opinions on the matter as well. Some involved in the grant process suggest that Wild Island's funding proposals did not have the financial and statistical figures that grant organizations needed for proper analysis.[66] Regardless, whether it was unnecessary government red tape, the failure of Wild Island to submit diligent applications, or some combination of the two, the underlying result was the same: the initial process of receiving grants was frustrating for Wild Island and its directors.

Compounding the co-op's funding problems was an internal division. As Susan Harvey recalls, in late 2000, or early 2001, Wild Island was negotiating to get a large amount of capital from Van City Savings, a Vancouver based credit union with a well developed program for providing capital to groups with limited collateral.[67] Harvey states that negotiations between Van City and Wild Island had reached the point of discussing where exactly the cheque should go – when things fell apart. Two Wild Island board members, harbouring some doubt over the co-op's ability to manage the planned loan, privately approached Van City with their reservations. Predicatably, the deal collapsed, with, as Harvey notes, devestating effect: "It took a huge toll...if [we] had that money initially, the rest of the stuff would've been finished and this probably would not have started with a restaurant. It would have started with a processing plant."[68]

It is unclear what exactly the disagreement at Wild Island was about, but the co-op's inability to internally resolve it was directly responsible for delaying, and perhaps preventing the completion of Wild Island's processing plant, the core around which the entire co-op was supposed to exist. As with MISC, the food co-op ironically found itself facing difficulties with co-operation within its own group.

Management has been another key trouble spot for the co-operative. As Pelle Agerup's example had shown in MISC, a good manager can revive the spirit of a faltering co-op, helping to smooth over difficulties and, most importantly, keeping control over the bottom line. In its initial years, Wild Island seems to have not been blessed with a manager of Pelle's skills, as unfortunate purchasing decisions left the co-op with a collection of antiquated kitchen equipment that has mostly sat unused in the basement – further postponing their plans for a production facility. Moreover, the bakery and restaurant's early managers did not stay for the long haul, taking with them whatever experience they had developed.

Like MISC, Wild Island had the unenviable task of attempting to learn about the co-operative method while also learning about a completely new business – four new businesses, as Lorraine Williams points out, when one considers the restaurant, the

98: Right:
Wild Island Foods, 2004.

bakery, the coffee roasting, and the production plant as separate entities. Given all the obstacles, needs, and time considerations involved with their new co-op, Kathy Parton concludes that Wild Island was, "like a needy baby, conceived with a huge debt load."[69] It was an infant that would need considerable support from its board, staff, and members to get to walking speed.

As difficult as the first few years of the co-op's development were, however, they were not without successes, not the least of which was the creation of the Wild Island bakery and restaurant itself. Built on the sight of a defunct fish processing plant the $200,000 facility is the first major building a visitor encounters upon disembarking from

the Sointula-Port McNeill Ferry. Instead of seeing a symbol of a stalled fishing industry, visitors are struck by a beautiful, high roofed wooden chateau designed to be welcoming from both sides and a view of the harbour. Located literally a stones throw from the Co-op Store (from whom it leases the property), and several other centrally located facitities, Wild Island has become more than a business; it has become the town meeting place. Brenda Swanson, Sointula representative to the Regional District of Mount Waddington, notes that without Wild Island she would have no real place on the island to meet with other district reps, or with any other key group.[70] Barely two years old, Wild Island has already established a role for itself in the community.

Further, the bakery and restaurant has created approximately twenty-seven jobs through its construction and operations, accomplishing a large part of the co-op's original purpose to help provide jobs and stimulate the island's economy.[71] And this while the processing plant has yet to take form. While many of these jobs are admittedly short term, in a community faced with a huge economic downturn, any business actually providing jobs on island has clearly achieved something positive.

Wild Island has also enjoyed success in the somewhat intangible areas of internal co-operative structure and community spirit. Despite the setbacks that occurred with board members, staff, and management in the first few years of the co-op's development, it successfully established solid guidelines to help Wild Island members understand and appreciate their co-op, and their individual place in it. The co-op structure consists of four classes of membership, representing the four types of people benefiting from the co-op: consumers, investors, producers, and workers. Each type of member receives some type of direct compensation for their involvement: Worker training, an RRSP program, and an above minimum wage job for worker members; the aforementioned list of co-op provided services for producer members; a fixed five per cent return rate for investor members; and, as mentioned, the existence of a central convenient restaurant/bakery for consumer members.

Each of these groups was also to have a representative or two on the board of directors.[72] By 2003, the board had held three full time training sessions and, in Liette Lavoie's view, each participant had grown to understand what it meant to be a director and what to expect from a perspective manager.[73] The directors also seem to have learned what to expect from each other. In contrast to some of the board problems of the past, Lavoie notes that by 2003 the Wild Island board was running by group consensus, and that no board member was ever left discontented after a vote.[74] Lorraine Williams and Kathy Partons add that by late 2002, the position of board meeting chairperson was a rotating one, functioning to both help give everyone experience in leading the process and to more equitably distribute authority in the co-op.[75] Though it may have been atypical of most top down business structures, it was a set up very much in line with co-operative ideals, and one in which some of the divisions that had plagued Wild Island in the past could be avoided.

98: Left:
Wild Island Foods in foreground, with Co-op Store in background, approaching Sointula dock, 2004.

Regarding that other intangible asset, community spirit, this was something that Wild Island leaned heavily on in its first years. As with MISC, community support manifested itself not only in terms of actual investment money (early in 2003, $37,000 was raised in one drive alone),[76] but in donated material and free labor. Wild Island's wheelchair ramp and fire escape were put together by volunteer workers using donated timber (the cost of the fire escape appears to have been two pieces of fresh cheesecake, one for each labourer).[77] In terms of monetary value, an estimate given by one director to a business magazine, put the worth of volunteer hours to the co-op between 1997 and 2000 at $36,750.[78] This figure was just in terms of agreed on volunteer time. In reality, almost every paid employee of Wild Island has been so busy volunteering to work beyond their paid time, as Lorraine Williams and Kathy Parton note, that they have not had time to keep exact track of their volunteer hours.[79]

Susan Harvey's personal approach came in the lines of an old song: "The economy was so bad I had to lay myself off - but I just kept turning up anyway."[80] Having experience in the restaurant business, Harvey realized that the day-to-day running of the restaurant could benefit from a strong guiding hand (she notes the bakery's failure to run cost estimates on such items as cinnamon buns as an example of practices that needed to be changed). Susan arranged to have herself laid off, and just kept turning up as a volunteer, without pay or shares. Together with Mirm Trimmer, another resident with restaurant experience, Susan became a co-manager. Through improved inventory methods, product costing, and general restaurant know-how, the two managers helped improve the co-op's financial situation. By the end of the year the restaurant/bakery was running more smoothly and Wild Island's aged payables debt had gone from $29,000 to $13,000.[81] It was, however, a bittersweet achievement, with both Mirm and Harvey resigning later in the year due to overwhelming stress and exhaustion.

Though the restaurant was on a better footing now, Wild Island decided to close it down for the slower winter months in order to save on costs. Like MISC, Wild Island appeared to be going through a hibernation mode in late 2003, attempting to simply survive the hard times, while hoping for a more hospitable climate in the spring.

Before the co-op could reach that favourable spring, however, the fall of 2003 had one more unpleasant obstacle to throw at them: Wild Island's Annual General Meeting

(AGM). The co-op had been in financial difficulty for sometime, and it was common knowledge that some members were disgruntled with some of the co-op's past management, board decisions, and its general direction. The AGM, however, took Wild Island's directors by surprise. Three days before the meeting took place, each board member received what Lorraine Williams describes as a hostile letter from a group of Wild Island members, basically stating that the board members did not know what they were doing, and were making many errors in judgment.[82] The meeting itself was somewhat chaotic, with ex-managers making pointed remarks, and other members not only questioning the board's general competency, but deriding the rather informal running of the AGM, going so far as to start to give instructions to the Chair from the floor. It was not, as Lorraine Williams and Kathy Parton recall, Wild Island's finest hour.

Yet, through the turmoil, the co-operative spirit survived. Instead of being defensive and striking back at its critics, the co-op board was able to use the moment as an opportunity to explain Wild Island's needs, and to ask for help. The disgruntled group of members agreed to organize a Mexican themed fundraising dinner for Wild Island, raising $1300 for the co-op. Other community members stepped in as well. Tom Roper, curator of the Sointula Museum, agreed to head a fundraising committee for the co-op, involving himself not only with subsequent fundraising dinners, but also helping to organize future Wild Island funding proposals; and Barb Bugoy, manager of the Evergreen Credit Union (formally, the Sointula Credit Union) agreed to do the financial books for the bakery/restaurant, accepting one or two investment shares in lieu of the usual $3500 charge.[83] While the co-op's debt and lease payments would make the winter's finances difficult, and though some community resentment remained over the co-op's decision to close for the winter, Wild Island had reason to be optimistic as it headed into 2004 – it had emerged from a potentially disastrous general meeting with substantial evidence of community support.

As Marjorie Greensides notes, both Wild Island and MISC have seen ebbs and flows in the level of this community support.[84] While the majority of Malcolm islanders have been hopeful that both co-ops could make a successful go of their enterprises, the continual delaying of success can not have helped but foster doubt. In the case of Wild Island, the early intervention by discontented board members in the Van City Savings

loan situation had provided the first indications that there were individuals who would transfer their doubts into action. The 2003 Wild Island Foods AGM had given the next. The third would come in the new year, and from a quite unexpected source.

As previously mentioned, the Wild Island property is actually owned by the Co-op Store, which leases it out to the food co-op at a monthly rate. With its financial troubles, Wild Island had gotten quite behind in its payments and by early 2004 was left owing

99: Left:
Sointula Evergreen Savings
Credit Union, 2004.

the Co-op Store some $20,000 in back rent. Attending a February 18, 2004 Co-op Store meeting that was largely centred on this issue, several Wild Island members were taken aback at the attitude of some of the Co-op Store's members.

As Wild Island has shares in the Co-op, Parton and Williams were surprised when the Co-op chair appeared to separate them off as guests at the meeting, giving them little chance to explain the situation to Co-op Store members who suggested that the debt must be settled immediately (the implication being that foreclosure might ensue).[85] While Parton admits that she understands the cold logic of those who simply saw the co-op's debt as any ordinary delinquent account, she feels that this view totally misses the bigger picture. To begin with, she notes that the thousand dollar per month rent was an unreasonable expectation given the island's economy and the limited size of the bakery's clientele. Further, Parton notes that Wild Island financially contributes to the Co-op Store, both directly and indirectly. Having Wild Island as an attraction may well mean visiting summer boaters staying for supper and then shopping at the Co-op Store, rather than bypassing the island for Port McNeill. And, not only was Wild Island providing jobs for locals who then had money to spend on Co-op groceries, but Wild Island itself was estimated to have spent $50,000 at the Co-op Store for various supplies.[86] Moreover, though Wild Island might owe $20,000 in rent, it has invested $200,000 into the property, greatly raising its overall value to the Co-op Store. It should be noted, though, that this value has not been realized by the Co-op Store, and has in fact had the adverse effect of raising the Co-op Store's taxes.

In past years, the Co-op Store had acted as a benefactor in the community. Adhering to that key co-operative princple, "co-operation among co-operatives," it had charged nominal rents to businesses it felt were good for Sointula and helped its fellow co-operatives in various ways. In contrast, though the Co-op Store clearly had the right to receive its rent from Wild Island, its seemingly hard-line approach appeared out of character with its past role as a community builder. Kathy Parton feels that the answer may lay in the hard times that have befallen the island: "When you're living in a place with a depressed economy then you get people vying for what little bits of money there are, and it is more divisive."[87] Part of the answer also may have been the obvious: that there were members of the community who did not believe that Wild Island could succeed.

The Co-op Store meeting adopted the resolution that the two co-op boards were to negotiate a settlement. But negotiations were problematic. Conflict ensued over the delay of a Co-op Store offer, as it arrived by mail *after* its stated deadline, complicated by the fact that the Co-op had put it on the table as a final offer without, apparently, indicating that this was the case. Additionally, Wild Island board members had vague suspicions that some Co-op Store board members were negotiating with the intent to foreclose.[88] In the end, however, common ground was discovered and a suitable negotiation, complete with reduced rent, was worked out. The most obvious common ground shared by the two co-ops, as Brenda Swanson points out, was that many Co-op Store members are also Wild Island members, so where was the sense in them voting to foreclose?[89] Further, there was no real benefit to be had for the community in a failed Wild Island.

And so, Wild Island finds itself still alive, but in a difficult situation. "This summer [of 2004] is the last kick of the ball for this co-op," says Lorraine Williams, "A good busy season for the restaurant could see it begin to make enough to get by, a poor season..."[90] In that area, the co-op received an unexpected blessing, a Chinese engineer who makes wonderful Finnish pulla – Ken Choi. Having been hired as the co-op's baker in 2003 through an unusual chain of events, the untrained Choi emerged as the bright spot of the co-op.[91] With Choi basically managing the bakery, Wild Island began exporting bread to Port McNeill, as well as enjoying brisk sales through the Co-op Store. Not only a good baker, Choi also worked on the board of directors and helped to make decisions based on his practical knowledge of what the bakery section needs. Like John Rosser at MISC, he was an example of the right person stepping forward at the right time, helping the co-op get through a rough time. Unfortunately, Choi's stay was not as permanent as the co-op would have liked. Choi relocated to Port McNeill in the summer of 2004.

A second example of such a person is HRDC representative Rick Roberts. Having helped Wild Island work on funding proposals in the past (and present), Roberts is currently attempting to get what Susan Harvey describes as a "not-manager" to help both Wild Island and MISC with their finances and organization (there is apparently some resistance with some for having a government appointed manager, hence the person will be a not-manager, or financial advisor).[92] Describing him as a saint for all that he has

attempted to do for Wild Island, Susan Harvey notes that on an island where government officials and 'guys in suits' are viewed with some suspicion, Roberts is accepted and trusted. "He's as good as his word," Harvey notes.[93] With the aid of government official Rick Roberts, baker Ken Choi, fund-raiser Tom Roper, and what appears to be a driven and co-operative board of directors, there is still hope that Wild Island can eventually secure a processing plant, and thus bring their co-op to the next level.

Whether these strengths can overcome Wild Island's large debt load, and lack of a current manager and production facility, is a matter of time. In some ways, the question is as old as Sointula itself: can people make a living growing food on the island? Lorraine Williams notes that there is a spirit of *sisu* which remains on the island, a determination that keeps her and others going with the belief that growing and producing food on the island is a real and current possibility.[94] It is the original dream of the Finnish settlers emerging once again on Malcolm Island.

101. Below: Sointula Centenial Flag, originally designed by Dr. Beckman in 1902.

Stubbornly Co-operative

The two most recent attempts to revive Sointula's co-operative past can be seen as the most natural of occurrences on an island with nearly one hundred years of experience with co-operative ventures. As Marjorie Greensides notes, Malcolm Islanders take a certain amount of pride from their co-operative history and identity;[95] she also notes that this is a community that loves to collectively organize.[96] The two tendencies have long played out together on Malcolm Island, with volunteerism and community spirit underlying many business ventures. By organizing themselves and looking after their own affairs, Malcolm Islanders have been able to control the direction of their community. Locally owned, supported and managed co-operative ventures will not sell out and move to a more financially profitable location. Thus, the community outlook can be seen as a mix of the ideal and the practical, a simple continuation of past Malcolm Island practices at work in a more modern, and more financially troubled time.

There is, however, another way of looking at the new co-ops and at the current co-operative tendancy on the island, one that is not so uniformly positive or cohesive. Brenda Swanson believes that while there is a co-operative spirit on the island surrounding personal day to day interaction, there has been a distinct lack of co-operation surrounding the new ventures and new ideas in general. With the post-Mifflin downturn in the economy, Swanson sees third or fourth generation fishermen as forced to change and adapt to a new economy and new ideas. Yet, she notes that there is not only a resistance to that change, but a suspicion of those advocating it.[97] Laura Mitchell, a Sointula resident who can trace her family's roots in the community back to 1915, proudly points out that stubbornness is a community trait and that people who don't appreciate what the community is and want to make a lot of changes generally don't last long.[98]

8.   Sointula: Present and Future

While wishing to maintain a unique lifestyle may well be an admirable quality, this resistance to change (well chronicled in Sointula's past) may also be seen as a hinderance to development. MISC and Wild Island may have generally escaped censure on this point due to the fact that they are closely related to two lonstanding island activites – fishing and food production. Other areas of new economic and social development may not, however, be welcomed in the same way. Much of their success will depend on how well they fit into the existing community. Thus, as much as change might seem necessary in an economically struggling area with a variety of social problems, Malcolm Island's future development will still very much be influenced by the community's past practices. Community support on Malcolm Island can be considerable; who or what get to be considered a part of the community, however, is not that straight forward.

The Sointula Resource Centre

In 1998/1999, a group of Malcolm Island residents saw a need in the community for a centrally located information center, a place where both residents and visitors alike could go to be updated on the community. With the help of then regional district representative Theresa Ransom, a volunteer group was set up in a typical, old-style Sointula manner: a need was recognized on the island, people rallied to fill the need, and another volunteer organization is formed – one that not only serves the community but is built up and supported by the it. This time, however, the pattern would change slightly. HRDC representative Rick Roberts approached the community and asked if they were interested in doing a feasibility study on this issue, one that would involve a government grant and a permanent organization. Marjorie Greensides, who was doing some private consulting work on the island, was brought on board as executive director, and by January 2002, the Sointula Resource Centre Society was formed.[1]

The Centre was not intended to be an informal island-financed group, but a more structured non-profit organization, with its own board of directors. It had owed its start to government grants ($80,000 from HRDC in its first year, $60,000 the next), and an abrupt and unexpected end to HRDC funding in 2003/2004 caused financial strain, resulting in the near dissolution of the organization.[2] However, the Centre has persevered by carving out a niche for itself as *the* place to go for information; providing internet access, small business facilitation and support, a local labour registry, maps, bylaws, zoning information, a selection of government forms, and many other services.[3] The Centre has also concerned itself with the cultural needs of the community through Artopia, a yearly art show that brings the community's artists together in a summer island festival. Filling many roles, the Resource Centre has become a focal point of Sointula; a place, as Greensides notes, where people not only stop by for specific purposes, but drop in to simply keep in touch with their community.[4]

Given the variety and extensive use of the Centre's services, it would appear at first glance that the organization had been integrated fairly seamlessly into the community. As Greensides explains, however, there are issues surrounding past practices, established community groups, and unwanted change that make this assessment a little premature. To begin with, she notes, her organization is new, and all things new on Malcolm Island must prove themselves (she notes that Malcolm Islanders have seen a lot of new people come and go, unable to adapt); second, the Resource Centre is helping people make career and social changes to cope with a harsh economy – and has, to some degree, been associated with this unwelcome change and resented because of it; third, the center does things that volunteers used to do, and gets paid for it (a practice Greensides defends as necessary due to declining volunteer numbers). What is more, the Centre has received much of its money from government grants, a practice negatively seen by some as akin to accepting welfare.[5]

And so the Centre remains very much a part of Malcolm Island in transition. Its ability to become completely successful and integrated may be a matter of addressing the above concerns. If it can survive financially without government assistance, show that it has the best interests of the majority of the population at heart, and simply stick around until it is no longer "new," then it may yet become like the Co-op Store or Rec. Association: part of the island.

102. Previous Page:
Cruise boat passes by Malcolm Island, local fishing boat in foreground, 2004.

103. Right:
Local youth hanging out at the Sointula Resource Centre, 2004.

Old Craft, New Craft

104. Left:
Heron Carving on Kaleva Road, 2004.

105. Right:
Carvings of Tim Motchman.

In the mid-1970s, as Sointula's growing artistic community decided they needed a venue for their work, Winterfest was born. This volunteer-run November arts and crafts show has included artists and artisans from a number of neighbouring communities and has showcased a wide variety of works, from Port McNeill pottery, to locally made gillnet rugs. The event ends with a coffee house that brings artisans, patrons, visitors and residents together to socialize. Current organizer Carmen Burrows estimates that last year over 250 people came to see works by 40-50 artisans.[1]

This same need to provide an outlet for the arts community led resident Iris field to concoct the idea for Artopia, a new summer festival that focuses more on art than the craft driven Winterfest. Due to decreasing volunteer ranks, the Resource Centre was enlisted to organize Artopia, which has helped to bring in summer tourists.[2] Two prominent local artists whose work has become celebrated at Artopia are resident artists Tim Motchman, and his wooden animal carvings, and the nature pastels of Bob Field.[3]

Though having a government funded non-profit group promote island culture is a departure from the volunteer ethos of old, Artopia, like Winterfest, has become a showcase for the artistic community — an example of Malcolm Islanders continuing to support their own.

The Environment

Ever since Kurikka designated a certain Malcolm Island bay as a place where no animals would be killed, there has been an environmental tradition on the island. The wild and rural nature of the island in which generations of Sointulans have been raised has been etched into the community's way of life. This ethos, however, has necessarily been affected by certain economic realities. As an environmentally aware individual, Carmen Burrows notes that logging on the island through the 1950s, 1960s, and 1970s has helped to destroy most of the island's old growth forest.[6] Defending the practice, old time logger Elgin Shiels unapolegetically states that logging is what the island is really made for and that many of the enviromentalists speaking out against logging practices are simply "off track."[7] This traditional logger's viewpoint is one that Marjorie Greensides, who has a BA in environmental studies, is familiar with. She recalls being teased for being a tree-hugger by many of the loggers and fishermen of the island, people who perceived a threat to their livelihoods in the environmental campaigns of some activists; Greensides goes on to note, however, that many of these people turned out to be the best envi-

Community Forest

106. Left:
Sunset at Bere Point, Malcolm Island, 2004.

As the BC Ministry of Forests describes, community forests are locally managed operations reflecting local goals. Typically, they promote the local economy while still maintaining recreational opportunities and protection for the environment.[1] As resident Gordon McDougall relates, a previous attempt by Malcolm Islanders to secure a community forest license in 1998 failed due to their overemphasis on environmental and protectionist aspects in their logging plan. As McDougall dryly notes, "If your going to make some money, your gonna have to cut down a tree once in a while."[2]

Starting anew in 2003, a core group dedicated to an economically viable community forest created the Malcolm Island community Forest Initiative. Though they picked a corporation model as the one that stood the best chance of securing a government license, as member Dennis Swanson notes, with the Lions, the Rec Association, and even the environmental OGMA group (Old Growth Management Area) as equal partners, the project really is a co-operative and communal affair; hiking, tourism, and the environment will not be overlooked.[3] With much second growth timber on the island, McDougall and Swanson are convinced that in time, the Malcolm Island Community Forest Initiative can be successful, a reason for future generations to stay on the island and benefit from its forests.

ronmentalists she had ever met.[8] Among those who work and live in nature there is a knowledge and appreciation of the same; that appreciation is tempered, however, by a history of logging as a livelihood, and by the fear that change will mean the destruction of one's economic base and lifestyle.

Thus, in order to function as part of the island, environmental groups have had to prove that they are adding something to the community, not taking away. The support by the Old Growth Management Area (OGMA - see above) for the Malcolm Island Community Forest Initiative is an example of this, as is OGMA's general collaborative relationship with the logging industry. While they have a mandate to preserve eleven to twelve per cent of the old growth forest land, Carmen Burrows, a representative of the group, notes that her members are not against logging. In fact, the group is allowing a local logger to maintain control over a wood lot within a designated OGMA area, certain that he will be a good environmental steward for the area.[9] Further, the group is pushing for increased secondary manufacturing on the island so that potential economic benefits can be developed rather than lost through raw resource sales. As Marjorie Greensides has suggested, environmentalism and the actions of resource industries are not mutually exclusive.

Another example of an environmental group working well within the larger community has been the Malcolm Island Environmental Protection Society (MIEPS), active in the late 1990s and early 2000s. It has provided educational material on preserving fish stocks without engaging in blockades or disruptive gestures. The group was also instrumental in preventing the Ministry of Forests from spraying pesticides on the island[10] – an action consistent with the island's tradition of both celebrating the purity of its environment and distrusting the government. MIEPS would also express its general support for MISC and Wild Island, pleased with the low pollution alternative to fish farms offered by the first and by the stress on organic and wild agricultural production by the second. Though MIEPS disbanded in 2002, its ability to work alongside the Malcolm Island community, not against, helped to ensure that it would find acceptance on the island.

Similarly, the efforts of "whale warden" Troy Bright allowed him, despite being both a newcomer and environmentalist, to work effectively in Sointula. Originally from Nova Scotia, Bright has been on Malcolm Island since 1998, spending three years as director for MIEPS. His original reason for coming to the island, however, and his current focus, are the whales of Bere Point. Bere Point is a regional park with a camping ground and a very special beach – one that killer whales come to rub themselves on. Having taught himself about the habits and needs of these creatures, Bright has undertaken to ensure that these animals remain as undisturbed and protected as possible.

Here, he has found a lot of local support. Recently, a number of trees were overturned by a big blowout in the park; the regional district wished to come in and log the blowout, something that would disturb the local environment in general, and the whale rubbing beach in particular. Spearheading the movement against this, Troy found he had the backing of both Department of Fisheries and Oceans officials, and in particular, the community.[11] He has also led a movement to inform tourists about proper whale procedure, attempting to teach people to quietly watch and appreciate the whales rather than running up to the beach and frightening them away. Bright compares the Malcolm Island experience, where generations of people have quietly appreciated this area and

107. Right:
Bere Point Regional Park entrance, 2004.

the orcas who come here, to a place like Victoria, where, on a recent day, 130 boats competed with each other to get close to a pod of eighty-three killer whales.[12] Though he is frustrated at the lack of concrete effort on the part of the regional district to contribute towards the proper informational signs or a viewing platform, he is hopeful that the tourists who come to Bere Point will leave with a greater understanding and respect for the mammals. For Bright, the fact that "nothing too drastic" in the way of change occurs on the island is a good thing. He sees Sointula as having developed a wonderful view of nature and humanity, a view that the rest of the world could learn from.[13]

The Tourists

Camping at Bere Point practically twenty-four hours a day, seven days a week during the orcas prime rubbing season (June to September), Troy Bright has ample opportunity to meet with and talk to tourists coming to the island. He believes that the tourism at Bere Point is generally good for the community, not only bringing in money, but allowing for greater education for the general public about killer whales; Bright also notes that "old timers" on the island will go and park at the beach and sit and talk with the campers there.[14] It is a comforting scenario: nature-loving visitors enjoying Sointula's natural beauty, while learning about the community from its senior members, all the while putting money into the local economy. An easy and subtle change to accept, one might think. The reality, however, is that the idea of tourism as a desired part of the island economy and social makeup, is a controversial and sometimes divisive subject.

It is not difficult to uncover incidents in the past twenty years or so that speak to a general suspicion of outsiders. Susan Harvey, who became a resident in 1981, recalls one of her first trips to the island. Getting off the ferry Susan was approached by a local and basically asked, "Who are you and why are you here?"[15] As soon as it was established that Susan knew people on the island her reception was much warmer. Ironically, as she describes, Harvey recently found herself on the flip side of this scenario when she encountered a visitor describing the view he was enjoying to someone off island, via his cell phone. She remembers having the greatest urge just to grab the phone out of his hand and throw it into the ocean. Susan explains her reaction in two ways: one, as a bewildered reaction to someone who would rather describe something beautiful then personally enjoy it; and two as "the drawbridge syndrome," a desire to keep the island and the life enjoyed on it a secret from the outside world.[16]

It is not that Malcolm Islanders have not welcomed temporary visitors to the island in the past, but it has predominately been a certain type of visitor. Susan Harvey notes that when the fishing was good the island used to get a huge influx of fishermen from up and down the coast in the fishing season, a type of visitor who fitted well with the locals.[17] Such guests unobtrusively fed the local economy, particularly the local Co-op Store which, as previously mentioned, had a large supply of fishing gear in its hardware section. Now, however, that type of visitor is largely gone and a new type has come

108. Left:
Sunset at Bere Point, Malcolm Island, 2004.

in. Kathy Parton recalls her disgust at a cruise ship that came to Sointula, flooding the restaurant with customers so that the locals could not get in, and later contacted Wild Island with an offer to bring in more tourists for a ten per cent cut of the restaurant's profit.[18] Locals excluded from their social gathering place, noisy crowds of visitors, and a blatant capitalist grasping for unearned commission; this is exactly the scenario that repels Malcolm Islanders from the whole tourist experience.

As Wanda Laughlin notes, this reaction against outside visitors has hurt Malcolm Island economically. Laughlin recalls what happened when a cruise ship stopped off one summer and a group of tourists came to explore the island: "It was embarrassing. People were so rude to them. It was like, 'what are you doing in our town?!'…So why stop here? They go to Alert Bay where they are treated like royalty."[19] Laughlin notes that this attitude has changed quite a bit in the last five years, as people have realized the economic need for a tourist industry. Bed and Breakfasts and guest cottages have sprung up, and local shops have capitalized on tourist dollars. Kelly Edwards has an ice cream/grilled food stand on the beach by the ferry; the Co-op Store sells "Sointula" tee-shirts, and, as noted on the Vancouver Island North Visitors Association website (VINVA), Sointula offers visitors everything from bicycle and kayak rentals, to a tour of Finnish history and culture in the local museum.[20] It is the type of low key tourism that Laughlin and others hope to develop further, a planned approach that will keep the island from becoming a "tourist Mecca" like Salt Spring Island, a model many Malcolm Islanders have cited as one to avoid.[21] This plan will have to overcome the island's lingering distaste of obtrusive forms of tourism, and the anger aroused in some Sointulans in perception that they have no choice in the matter. As Harvey admits, Malcolm Islanders feel that the economics of the situation is forcing them to accept tourism.[22] Lennie Pohto conveys many islanders' fear in his response to this perception: "if that's what we've got to depend on, well then, God help us!"[23] Lennie's response is only partially tongue in cheek.

Increased tourism has been a debated topic on the island for some time now, but in a sense it has not become truly divisive. For one thing, tourism offers a real economy to be developed, albeit a fluctuating seasonal one. A rainy winter climate with little snow and few indoor activities does not lend itself well to tourism. For another, no real boom

109. Right: First Street, Sointula, with ferry approaching dock, 2004.

has as yet taken place. While residents may argue about the desirability of a tourist trade, and while a small one may have already developed (with a Sointula Tourist Association to promote it), there are not currently hoards of visitors outnumbering the locals every summer, nor any project in the works now that would attract such visitors. Further, of the tourists who come to enjoy the simple beauty of the island, some return year after year, forming friendships and close ties.[24]

Newcomers and New Times

It is not the temporarily visiting newcomers who are giving the long time Malcolm Islanders the most reason to pause, however; it is the permanently residing newcomers that are doing so. With the downturn in the fishing industry, many young families have been forced to leave the island in order to find work. This has led to an increase in both the number of houses for sale, and consequently, a previously uncommon new resident – the American retiree. Attracted by low house prices and the serenity of the island, American couples at or near retirement age are buying up a large number of Malcolm Island homes. While the fact that new people (some relatively well off) are coming into a declining community might well be viewed as a positive development, the issue is more complicated than that.

One aspect has to do with the newcomers' ages. Retired couples are less likely to have school aged children, and are thus not going to be filling holes in the school enrollment left by departed young families. Also, there may be some question as to how well they will fill the holes in the community's volunteer ranks. Campbell Wilson has noted that the Lions Club members of Malcolm Island are generally the younger "doers" of the community, volunteering for physically demanding community work. While there were over seventy members of the Lions in the 1970s, there are now only thirteen.[25] Similarly, Wanda Laughlin describes that while volunteers have been indispensible to keeping the community going, a core group of them (including herself) are getting older and there is no one to take their place.[26] Whether a group of semi-retired and retired newcomers will have the same energy, or the same desire to be the next wave of Lions' or Rec. Centre volunteers, remains to be seen.

110. Left:
Sointula Heritage Public Buildings, from left: Superior School (now housing the museum), F.O. Hall, and Athletic Hall, 2004.

Whether such people will be accepted when they do volunteer is another matter. Marjorie Greensides recalls the controversy that surrounded the community's recent research into incorporation, and how the input of newcomers came into question. This research involved a provincially funded restructuring process where-by a private consultant, in consultation with the community, would investigate the social and economic changes that would occur should the community incorporate. While Marjorie saw this process as a golden opportunity to get valuable information about the community for free (regardless of whether the community decided to incorporate or not) others did not see it that way. As Greensides recalls, the discussion over the issue turned into a nasty shouting match. In one telling incident, she remembers an irate resident yelling at the volunteer chair of the restructuring process: "You're not even local! You're just an American who's moved here...Who do you think you are coming in trying to change our community!?"[27]

Part of this verbal attack may well have stemmed from an anti-American, or at least anti-American-on-Malcolm-Island mentality. The existence of such a mentality had been seen before during the hippie era, when American newcomers in the 1970s were accused of attempting to buy up the island. Brenda Swanson has confirmed that such an attitude exists currently in some circles, and needs to be overcome.[28] This dormant anti-Americanism may also be subtly tied to an undercurrent of fear of outside domination. The long standing Malcolm Island desire to live free of authority, particularly without the authority of layers of government, has been well documented in the past and is said by some to be very much alive today.[29] Reaction against a process that could lead to another layer of government would likely have been voracious no matter who was chair; the fact that an American newcomer was in the position may have added to the feeling that "outsiders are trying to change the island," a convenient fact to seize on for those already completely opposed to the process.

Part of the reaction against an American newcomer attempting to lead the community onto a new path may also be tied up with a subtle hierarchy on the island. Sointula is a place with a long history. Logger Mickey Edwards notes that there are factions and rivalries that have passed down through families on the island for a hundred years – to the point, Edwards notes, where, if he sees a particular resident with a new pickup truck

111. Left:
Sointula Harbour in
Rough Bay, 2004.

one week, he can be sure to see two or three certain other residents with slightly bigger pickups in the weeks to come.[30] Susan Harvey remarks that, in a community with such a deep memory, you might be trying to get to the bottom of a dispute and find out it has to do with an event that happened twenty-five years ago.[31] It takes some time to sort out the intricacies of such a community; a newcomer might well be seen as being presumptious for speaking out on an issue or for a particular direction when they do not know the full history behind it. As Marjorie Greensides explains, "it takes you thirty years to become a local, and even then you're not guaranteed."[32]

So how do newcomers start to become part of the community? "Cautiously," Greensides remarks. Though now an outspoken and self described "thorn" at most community meetings, she notes that, when she first started to participate as a newcomer, she took care to simply listen and say very little.[33] Echoing this sentiment, Brenda Swanson remarks that you can't demand leadership here; it comes to you.[34] It is a tricky process. Nearly every interview subject has touched on the idea of volunteerism and community, how those who are successful in integrating themselves into island life are those who actively participate. Yet, if one attempts to take the lead too quickly as a newcomer, one can find oneself on the outside looking in.

It is a contradiction that has been worked out before on the island, specifically in the case of the conservative church-going Finns of the 1950s and the hippies of the 1970s. Both of these groups experienced an initial fear and opposition to the changes they represented (religious and social in nature). It was only when these people began to prove themselves individually as willing and able to become involved within the community that they began to be accepted, eventually assuming leadership roles in the community. Changes did, of course, ensue, but they were gradual changes that either fitted an established framework, or, as with the coming of religion, changes that would not force others to change their way of doing things.

This desire not to change what exists on Malcolm Island is perhaps the easiest way to explain the reaction to the American retirees, and the general island philosophy as well. Clayton Jordan contrasts the "frightening" city life he knew as a child to the carefree, caring, and very tight knit community on Malcolm Island. He notes that it is not always easy for others to fit into that mold:

> Its tough for outsiders to come in and feel and think and judge, I guess, the way [we live]…People in a smaller community, they're more judgmental 'cause [we] chose to live here and live our lives the way we do and the outside influences are not always acceptable.[35]

John Rosser figures that life unfolded the way it was supposed to when he came from Nanaimo to Sointula. He states that the character of the place is not going to change and that it attracts only people who respect that; he has noticed that peo-

Belly Dancing

ple who don't respect or accept that lifestyle do not stay.[36] Brenda Swanson remarks that there is a long-standing tradition on Malcolm Island that newcomers must prove themselves. While she believes that Malcolm Islanders have to get past their distrust of the newcomers who are coming and, in her view, helping to build up the community, she does note that the traditional stress on a close-knit, somewhat insular community, makes Sointula unique. Traveling to places like Port McNeill and Alert Bay, Swanson says she doesn't get the same sense of distrust and protectionism as she does in Sointula; but neither does she get the same sense of community.[37]

Rosser, Swanson, and Jordan were all at one time new arrivals to the island (mid 1970s, 1985, and 1996 respectively); given the "30 year" rule of thumb for acceptance, they might still be considered newcomers by some. All three, however, have come to see the island as home, appreciating the communitarianism to be found here. While it might be easy to assume that the new retirees will follow the same path as past immigrants and either adapt to the island or leave (and that Malcolm Islanders will forgo their

It was at Winterfest 2001 that belly dancer Kathryn Burgess-Griffith first performed in Sointula. An island newcomer, Kathryn was uncertain how her classical Egyptian Raks Al-Sharqui style of dance would go over in the small community. After ten minutes of dead silence a terrified Burgess-Griffith paused before her finale — and 400 people rose in a spontaneous standing ovation! She had found her audience.

Since that time, Kathryn has taught that audience noisy appreciation (clapping and whistling is encouraged), and has taught over 50 Sointula women to express themselves through dance (even the Sointula Girl Guides have taken workshops, achieving their dance badges in the process). As a newcomer, belly dancing was Burgess Griffith's way into the community.

Many goals still remain for her in the belly dancing field, including building her own dance studio and creating an instructional video. As she sees it, however, her most important goal may already have been realized: "I've been hearing comments actually from the men in the community about how...the women that are belly dancing are walking taller and prouder and more confidentially...And if that's all I ever accomplish in teaching belly dance in this community - that's fabulous!"

distrust and accept them as they have past newcomers), this time it may be a different scenario. A fair number of the houses bought by retired or nearly retired outsiders are being used simply as summer homes. Such part-time residents are unlikely to help maintain the same tight knit community, unlikely to be absorbed into a communitarian lifestyle, the way that past newcomers were.

Marjorie Greensides imagines a possible nightmare scenario for the future, whereby fifty to sixty per cent of properties are owned by absentee landlords and the community is divided between wealthy semi-residents, and a poorer service class of permanent residents.[38] Already, subtle economic changes on the island have pointed to that type of trend. Campbell Wilson notes that, while teenagers once worked on seine boats for the summer, making as much as their teachers did in the year, now they're cutting grass for someone who lives on the island only three months of the year.[39] Wilson himself is managing well with a construction business, noting that even part-time residents need things built, but it is the next generation that he worries about.

112. Above Left:
Fisherman's Memorial, at
Sointula Harbour - donated
by the Lions Club, 2004.

113. Right:
Sointula Beach, 2004.

As Campbell Wilson, secretary of the Malcolm Island Lions Club notes, his group is not your typical Lions Club. In 1980, the group took over the administration and maintenance of the breakwater docks owned by the Department of Fisheries and Oceans, enabling them to collect substantial moorage fees. As a result, they have been able to employ four part time workers, clear $1000 a month, and still have ample ability to support many community projects. Campbell notes that Lions groups elsewhere are typically composed of older men who fundraise through weekly bingos. In Sointula, however, the organization's involvement in initiatives that fall outside the organization's usual mandate have allowed them to skip the bingo, attracting a younger crowd — more given to work parties and a beer.

When local businesses were threatened by the closure of another important dock in 2001, this time by Transport Canada, the club went beyond its mandate again, taking over administration. In their 31 year history, the Lions Club has also helped fund and organize a seniors housing project, organized an international exchange program, helped build the Sointula Ball Field, created the Lions Park, and built a ski cabin at Mt. Cain for the use of the community and youth groups. In a community with no municipal government, the Malcolm Island Lions have taken it upon themselves to ensure that the community's needs are filled, whatever the mandate.[1][2]

Conclusion

When Sointula remained a hard to reach island, with an ethnically uniform population, a defined socialist leaning, and a bias towards co-operative dealings over centralized authority, social change was unlikely. Over the years, better access through transportation, a change in ethnic and political makeup, and the intrusion of both capitalist leanings and government interaction (through both grants and increased regulations) have made social transition inevitable. Economically, as long as fishing was able to provide a stable livelihood for the majority of the population, the financial security of the island was ensured and economic change was unnecessary. But Mifflin and the 1989 strike assured that economic change would occur as well.

The question then remains – change towards what? If the community no longer has a set ethnic, political, or co-operative identity, what keeps it together socially? If men and women whose families have been fishing for generations can no longer be Malcolm Island fishermen than what are they – and can they afford to remain on the island.[40] Malcolm Island is still a relatively isolated place, not particularly rich in valuable timber, local fishing, or any scarce resources. It is a harsh reality to contemplate, but Sointula would not be the first small B.C. community to slowly fade away as its economy faultered, and its citizens found opportunities elsewhere.

There is a character to the community of Sointula, however, that speaks against that result. It is seen in the words of John Rosser, Brenda Swanson, and Clayton Jordan as they explain a feeling for Sointula that they have not felt for other communities. The original identifying marks of the community, Finnishness, socialism, union support etc., have faded. But the sense of community that began around these factors has not only remained, but grown through the dozens of volunteer and service organizations that have arisen on the island, and through a general communitarian ethos. It was part of what attracted the hippies of the 1970s, and it is a large part of what attracts and holds people to Malcolm Island now. As Marjorie Greensides and Susan Harvey explain, it is a simple philosophy:

> **Marjorie Greensides**: [There are] two kinds of people in the world - those who'll follow opportunities wherever they take them and those who will do whatever it takes to stay where they are.

114. Left:
Sointula, from across Rough Bay, 2004.

Susan Harvey: ...and we're of the latter variety.[41]

A cynic might view this as a slightly "Pollyanna" type viewpoint: the desire to live someplace does not automatically translate into the financial ability to do so. And if the economy becomes dependent on a wealthy class of summer residents, what kind of community will remain anyway? This is where, once again, the practical nature of the islanders coincides with their idealism. MISC and Wild Island are two of the obvious responses to the need to develop a local economy, but more are being proposed. Aside from his efforts in the Community Forest Initiative, Dennis Swanson owns an industrial sight on the island that he has turned into a basically co-operative effort: a sawmiller, a construction worker, and an individual who makes wood flooring and panneling share the cost of the site in return for space. Swanson has other schemes afoot, including the possibility of an eighteen hole golf course for the island, currently in the conceptional stage.[42]

Brenda Swanson (a relative to Dennis by marriage) believes that it will be a number of local initiatives such as MISC, Community Forest, and these other ventures that will keep Malcolm Island from ever becoming a ghost town.[43] Exhibiting the attitude spoken of by Marjorie Greensides, she has embraced the matter of "new residents" as an opportunity. Swanson and a friend are considering opening a property management business to take care of the homes of the temporary residents during the winter months (a local newspaper report regarding increased youth vandalism may make such a venture possible). As for the new permanent residents, Swanson notes that they are definitely contributing their skills to the community. She point to one of these semi-retired couples who sell medical supplies and run a real estate office off of the island; she notes another new couple that sells tools and runs the local burger stand, Lula's – currently the only nighttime eatery on the island.[44] They have fit their skills and know-how into the community.

Where to Next?

When you know where you want to live, you do what it takes to do so – from the original Kalevan Kansa pioneers who saw Malcolm Island as their opportunity for a free life, to the 1970s hippies looking for an alternative to capitalism and Vietnam, up to the new semi-retired and retired residents today who see something in Malcolm Island life that is worth having. Though they have been here thirteen years now, Dan and Laura Klingbiel were new American retirees in 1992. Dan notes that he was tired of so much "civilization," so many rules and people telling you what you could and couldn't do. They explored many different communities looking for a different type of place to retire, before they came to look at Sointla:

> We wanted some place that was peaceful and beautiful and had a sense of
> freedom in it, and a sense of pride in its heritage. As soon as we got off of
> the ferry we knew this was the place…[it was] a sense of coming home.[45]

117. Above Left:
Boathouse in Mitchell Bay, 2004.

118. Following Page:
Mural along First Street, 2004.

18 year-old Fraser Swanson would appear to be following the migration pattern of today's young Malcolm Islander: coming from a fishing family Swanson plans to leave Sointula to explore different options for his life. Is he simply another example of a mass movement of young Malcolm Islanders, who, unable to make a living in the fishing industry, are forced to make their way elsewhere? Not exactly.

First of all, Fraser has already been fishing since he was eight, in recent years making between $4,000 to $12,000 a summer (a fair student wage). While he recognizes the possibility of making money in the industry, he is simply "not sure [he] enjoys fishing as much as [he] would enjoy something else."

Second, it is not clear that he is part of a pattern. Swanson notes that the young people all say they are going to leave Sointula, but many remain, becoming 'lifers.' In fact, he believes that the number of young families has begun to creep up in recent years.

Lastly, though education and career possibilities will take him from the island for now, Swanson plans to return some day. Expressing his love of "island life" - a relaxed environment where you know everybody and everybody knows you - Swanson notes that whatever career he ends up undertaking, he can just as easily practice it in Sointula. It has been noted that some people will do "whatever it takes to stay where they are." Fraser Swanson appears to be one of many Malcolm Islanders who have decided to take a longer path to do just that.[1]

Dan and Laura bought their property on a handshake agreement and moved to a remote location in Mitchell Bay. Leaving behind the urban landscape and the sound of squealing tires they had known in California, they wake to the sound of wild birds, and the sight of the couple's two oxen, Doc and Otter, in the back yard. The couple stresses the free, yet communal life on the island, of someone tracking their truck down in town to drop off an overdue library book because the librarian told them Laura was looking for it, of neighbours calling in concern because the couple broke with routine and went into town on Tuesday rather than Thurday. To supplement their retirement fund the couple has set up a Bed and Breakfast and guest cottage on their property and Dan, an ex-Industrial Arts teacher, has taken to blacksmithing. Revising a Malcolm Island tradition that goes back to Kalevan Kansa days, Dan includes some of his works in the Artopia festival.

Describing life on the island as close to utopia, the Klingbiels have made sure to give back to Sointula. Aside from supporting the local economy by shopping on island, the couple has been active in community organizations, including membership in MISC. Their communitarianism, however, also extends to informal gestures. Dan relates the story of a young boy named Luke, a neighbour's child who was home taught and seemed to lack direction. Noting the boy's affinity for building, Dan took him under his wing and taught him architectural drafting. Describing him as the most precocious student he had ever had, Klingbiel notes that Luke went on to draw at least three residential houses and two businesses, as well as the extension for the Sointula museum (his design was accepted by the architect hired without correction). For the museum project, Dan informed Luke that he should do the project pro bono, as a way to give back to his community.[46] It is not only a preservation of the communitarian values of the island, but a passing on of these values to the next generation. It is a community-over-capital mentality that has existed on the island since its inception – one being fostered by a couple of American retirees.

The example of the Klingbiels does not, of course, remove all doubt regarding the commitment of new residents to communitarian values, any more than the plans and efforts of MISC, Wild Island, or the Swansons removes all doubt about the island's economic future. What it does do, however, is provide a modicum of hope. Much has changed on the island in a hundred plus years, but Sointula still attracts people for its rural beauty, its lifestyle of living as free as possible from rules and regulations, and a communitarianism that creates for many a feeling of being home. The economic hopes of the island are, in some respects, outside of the islander's hands, dependent on outside investment, industry prices, government regulations, and international treaties. There are a fair number of Malcolm Islanders, however, who are doing everything they can, including volunteer effort, to make sure the economic possibilities that the island does possess have every chance of success. Kurikka dreamed of utopia, and did not remain when he saw it fail. Makela worked for a viable community that looked after its own, and stayed to see it succeed. The residents of Malcolm Island, whether newcomers or old-time Finns, are the descendents of Makela – the practical dreamers of Sointula.

Photo Credits

"SMC" indicates Sointula Museum Collection

Cover Ron Dueck, photo is of a boat owned and located at Sea 4 Miles Cottages, Kaleva Rd.
1. Ron Dueck, taken at the Sointula Museum.
2. Ron Dueck, taken at the Sointula Museum.
3. Albert & Fran Tarkanen, from the SMC.
4. Norma and Albert Williams, from the SMC.
5. Unknown, from the SMC.
6. Unknown, from the SMC.
7. Unknown, from the SMC.
8. Unknown, from the SMC.
9. Ray and June Peterson, from the SMC.
10. Norma and Albert Williams, from the SMC.
11. Unknown, from the SMC.
12. Unknown, from the SMC.
13. Unknown, from the SMC.
14. Robert & Ingrid Belveal, from the SMC.
15. Norma and Albert Williams, from the SMC.
16. Unknown, from the SMC.
17. Unknown, from the SMC.
18. Unknown, from the SMC.
19. Ron Dueck, taken at the Sointula Museum.
20. Ron Dueck, taken at the Sointula Museum.
21. Norma and Albert Williams, from the SMC.
22. Unknown, from the SMC.
23. Loretta Rihtamo, from the SMC.
24. Unknown, from the SMC.
25. Unknown, from the SMC.
26. Linda Sjoberg, from the SMC.
27. Doris Potts, from the SMC.
28. Lenny Pohto, from the SMC.
29. Lenny Pohto, from the SMC.
30. Unknown, from the SMC.
31. Carl Nelson, from the SMC.
32. Carl Nelson, from the SMC.
33. Eddie and Sylvia Johnson, from the SMC. 34.
Norma and Albert Williams, from SMC.
35. Unknown, from the SMC.
36. Lee Anderson, from the SMC.
37. Andy Anderson, from the SMC.
38. Unknown, from the SMC.
39. Albert & Fran Tarkanen, from the SMC.
40. Unknown, from the SMC..
41. Unknown, from the SMC..
42. Doris Wirta, from the SMC..
43. Andy Anderson, from the SMC.
44. Unknown, from the SMC.
45. Wilma Laughlin, from the SMC.
46. Wilma Laughlin, from the SMC.
47. Doris Potts, from the SMC.
48. Lee Anderson, from the SMC.
49. Unknown, from the SMC.
50. Unknown, from the SMC.
51. Doris Potts, from the SMC.
52. Carol Poff, from the SMC.
53. Wilma Laughlin, from the SMC.
54. Wilma Laughlin, from the SMC.
55. From the SMC.
56. Wilma Laughlin, from the SMC.
57. Robert Turner, from the SMC.
58. Robert Turner, from the SMC.
59. Ron Dueck.
60. Aileen Woolridge, from the SMC.
61. Ron Dueck, taken at the Sointula Museum.
62. Ray and June Peterson, from the SMC.
63. Eddie and Sylvia Johnson, from the SMC.
64. Dave Siider, from the SMC.
65. Wilma Laughlin, from the SMC.
66. Courtesy, *The Fisherman*.
67. Liisa and Matti Syrjala, from the SMC.
68. Robert & Ingrid Belveal, from the SMC.
69. Unknown, from the SMC.
70. From the SMC.
71. Lenny Pohto, from the SMC.
72. Ron Dueck.
73. R.J. Kayfetz, from the SMC.
74. R.J. Kayfetz, from the SMC.
75. Carol Poff (Sommer), from the SMC.
76. Robert Turner, from the SMC.
77. Courtesy Ralph Harris.
78. Courtesy Ralph Harris.
79. Carol Poff (Sommer), from the SMC.
80. Carol Poff (Sommer), from the SMC.
81. Liisa and Matti Syrjala, from the SMC.
82. Linda Sjoberg, from the SMC.
83. Ron Dueck.
84. Ray and June Peterson, from the SMC.
85. From the SMC.
86. From the SMC.
87. Linda Sjoberg, from the SMC.
88. Linda Sjoberg, from the SMC.
89. Unknown, from the SMC.
90. Eddie and Sylvia Johnson, from the SMC.
91. Rob Boyes, from the SMC.
92. Ron Dueck.
93. Ron Dueck.
94. Ron Dueck.
95. Courtesy T. DeJager.
96. Ron Dueck.
97. Ron Dueck.
98. Ron Dueck.
99. Ron Dueck.
100. Ron Dueck.
101. Ron Dueck, taken at the Sointula Museum.
102. Ron Dueck.
103. Ron Dueck.
104. Ron Dueck.
105. Courtesy Tim Motchman.
106. Ron Dueck.
107. Ron Dueck.
108. Ron Dueck.
109. Ron Dueck.
110. Ron Dueck.

111. Ron Dueck.
112. Ron Dueck.
113. Ron Dueck.
114. Ron Dueck.
115. Ron Dueck.
116. Ron Dueck.
117. Ron Dueck.
118. Ron Dueck.

Endnotes

Chapter 1

1. Pekka Halmalainen, *In Time of Storm: Revolution, Civil War, and the Ethnolinguistic Issue in Finland* (Albany: State University of New York Press, 1978), 6.
2. L. A. Puntila, *The Political History of Finland* (London: William Heinemann LTD. 1975), 46.
3. Sylvie Nickels, Hillar Kallas, and Phillipa Friedman, *Finland: an Introduction* (London: George Allen & Unwin Ltd., 1973), 185.
4. W. R. Mead, *Finland* (London: Ernest Benn Limited, 1968), 137.
5. *North Island Gazette*, (October 16, 1980).
6. Puntila, 71.
7. *Ibid.*, 61.

The Kalevala

1. Elias Lonnrot, *The Kalevala: An Epic Poem After Oral Tradition*, translated by Keith Bosley Ed. (Oxford: Oxford University Press, 1989).

Minna Canth

1. Katharina M. Wilson, Ed., *An Encyclopedia of Continental Women Writers, Vol 1*, (London: Garland Publishing Inc., 1991).
2. Claire Buck, Ed., *Bloomsbury Guide To Women's Literature*, (Great Britain : Bloomsbury Publishing Ltd., 1992).

Chapter 2

1. Matti Halminen, *The History of Sointula and the Kalevan Kansa*, translated by Allan Henry Salo, (Helsinki: Kustantaja Mikko Ampuja, 1936) 246, 247.
2. *Ibid.*, 245.
3. *Ibid.*, 241.
4. Alan H Salo, "The Kalevan Kansa Colonization Company Limited: A Finnish Canadian Millenarian Movement in British Columbia" (MA. Thesis, University of British Columbia, 1978).
5. Halminen, Matti, 243.
6. *Ibid.*, 244.
7. Mead, 125.

8. Halminen, Matti, 250.
9. *Ibid.*, 260.
10. *Ibid.*, 260.
11. Interview with Arvo Tynjala, (BC Archives, Aural History Programme, 1967), 1016:2-2.
12. Halminen, Matti, 255.
13. Paula Wild, *Sointula: Island Utopia* (Madeira Park: Harbour Publishing, 1995) 40, noting *Nanaimo Daily Herald* (1901).
14. Wild, 41, noting *Victoria Daily Colonist* (1901).
15. *Aika* (August 23,1901).
16. Wild, 43.
17. Halminen, Matti, 285.
18. *Aika* (February 28, 1901), 1.
19. Donald Wilson, "Matti Kurikka and A. B. Makela: Socialist Thought Among Finns In Canada." *Canadian Ethnic Studies Vol. X, no. 2* (1978), 15.
20. *Aika* (May 9, 1902), 1.
21. *Aika* (November 1, 1903), 13-17.
22. Wild, 19.
23. *Ibid*, 51.
24. Wild, 51.
25. Gordon Fish, *Dreams of Freedom, Bella Coola, Cape Scott, Sointula* (Provincial Archives of British Columbia, Victoria: 1982), 77.
26. "I Lived in a BC Utopia", *Ladysmith Chronicle*, (January 11, 1962), 1, 6.
27. *Aika* (March 28, 1902), 51, 54.
28. *World Book Encyclopedia, Volume 19* (Chicago: World Book Inc., 1983), 191.
29. *Aika* (December 1, 1903), 51, 54.
30. Wild, 59, 60.
31. *Ibid.*, 56.
32. *Aika* (July 11, 1901), 1.
33. Wild, 95.
34. *Aika* (July 8, 1902), 28-62.
35. Halminen, Matti, 327-331.
36. *Ibid.*, 332.
37. *Ibid.*, 331.
38. *Aika* (December 15, 1903), 91-93.
39. Wild, 81, 82.
40. Halminen, Matti, 358.

41. *Aika* (August 22, 1902), 2.

42. Wild, 93.

43. *The People of Sointula*, Karvonen Films LTD., 2001.

44. Wild, 94.

45. *Aika* (April 1, 1904), 289-295.

46. *Aika* (March 15, 1904), 257-262.

47. Wild, 89.

48. Halminen, Matti, 365, 366.

49. *Aika* (June 15, 1904), 8-10; (July 1, 1904), 40-44; (July 15, 1904), 84-87.

50. *Ibid.*

51. Fish, 67.

Makela

1. *The People of Sointula*, Karvonen Films LTD., 2001.

2. A.B. Makela, "Something about Canada", tyokansan Kalenteri, 1913 (Port Aurthur: Tyokansa Press, 1913) 95, 96.

3. Wild.

Chapter 3

1. Interview with Dave Siider, (BCICS, February 20, 2003).

2. Interview with Sally Peterson, (Gordon Fish, BC Archives, February 11, 1982).

3. Fish, 75.

4. *The Fisherman*, (December 18, 1959).

5. *Ibid.*

6. Fish, 76.

7. "Little Section of Finland", *Vancouver Sun*, (May 25, 1927).

8. Interview with Arvo Tynjala, (Murray Kennedy, BC Archives, May 16, 1972).

9. Fish, 76.

10. Interview with Tauno Salo (Paula Wild, BC Archives, July 7, 1988).

11. "Rules and By-laws of the Sointula Co-operative Store Limited", 1909.

12. *Co-operative Consumer*, 1978.

13. Interview with Dave Siider, (BCICS, February 20, 2003).

14. Interview with Lennie Pohto, (BCICS, February 18, 2003).

15. Interview with Diane Hufnagel, (Paula Wild, BC Archives, June 22, 1988).

16. Interview with Lennie Pohto, (BCICS, February 18, 2003).

17. *Ibid.*

18. Interview with Tauno Salo (Paula Wild, BC Archives, July 7, 1988)

19. "Sointula Co-operative Store Annual Report", 1918, 1927.

20. "Sointula Co-operative Store Annual Report", 1928, 1939.

21. "Sointula Co-operative Store Annual Report", 1910.

22. Interview with Dave Siider, (BCICS, February 20, 2003).

23. *The Fisherman*, (December 18, 1959).

24. "Amendments to the Rules and Bylaws of the Sointula Co-operative Store Limited", 1912, 1916, 1917, 1925, 1932.

25. *The Fisherman*, (December 18, 1959).

26. Petition of Bruno Kaario, (December 27, 1933).

27. Copy of petition and oath, dated December 1, 1933, submitted to Supreme Court of British Columbia, Docket 106747.

28. Fish, 72

29. "Sointula Co-op Store Annual Report", 1917.

30. Fish, 67

31. *Ibid.*

32. Interview with Arvo Tynjala, (Murray Kennedy, BC Archives, May 16, 1972).

33. Salo, Alan H. "The Kalevan Kansa Colonization Company Limited: A Finnish Canadian Millenarian Movement." MA. Thesis, University of British Columbia, 1978, 14.

34. Interview with Alfred Williams, (Gordon Fish, BC Archives, 1979).

35. Fish, 68.

36. *Ibid.*

37. Wild, 135.

38. Fish, 70.

39. Wild, 119.

40. *Ibid.*, 120, 123.

41. A.V. Hill: *Tides Of Change: A Story of Fishermen's Co-operatives in British Columbia* (Prince Rupert: Prince Rupert Fishermen's Co-operative Association, 1967), 11-32.

42. Hill, 11-32.

43. Interview with Dave Siider, (BCICS, February 20, 2003).

44. Hill, 11-32.

45. Hill, 11-32.

46. Hill, 11-32.

47. Fish, 71.

48. Interview with Victor Wirkki, (BCICS, February 17, 2003).

49. Fish, 71.

50. *The Fisherman*, (December 20, 1993), 24.

51. "Anderson letter to Premier Richard McBride", (Sointula Museum, Sointula British Columbia, 1909).

52. *Aika*, (December 1, 1903).

53. Interview with Arvo Tynjala, (Imbert Orchard, BC Archives, June 22, 1967).

54. Ronald Grantham, "Some Aspects of the Socialist Movement in British Columbia, 1898-1933" (MA. Thesis, University of British Columbia, 1942), 50.

55. A. B. Makela, "Something about Canada", Tyokansan Kalenteri, 1913 (Port Arthur: Tyokansa Press, 1913) 95, 96.

56. *Western Clarion*, (December 4, 1909).

57. Alan Neil Kuitunen, "The Finnish Canadian Socialist Movement, 1900-1914" (M.A. thesis, University of Calgary, 1982), 92.

58. Wild, endnote 56, noting *Western Clarion*, (May 30, 1908), 1-3.

59. Kuitunen, 92.

60. Wild, 127.

61. *Ibid.*, 80, 81.

62. Kuitunen, 113, 114.

63. William Eklund, *Builders Of Canada: History of the Finnish Organization of Canada, 1911-1971* (Toronto: Vapaus Publishing Company Limited, 1987), 1.

64. *Ibid.*, 106.

65. Wild, 107, 171.

66. Eklund, 143

67. Aili Anderson, *History of Sointula* (Sointula: Sointula Centennial Committee, 1958), 75.

68. Wild, 130, 131.

69. Interview with Sally Peterson, (Gordon Fish, BC Archives, February 11, 1982).

70. "Little Section of Finland", *Vancouver Sun*, May 25, 1927.

71. Fish, 73.

72. Fish, 73.

73. Eklund, 192.

74. Wild, 129.

75. Interview with Wayne Homer, (Gordon Fish, BC Archives, March 6, 1982).

76. Interview with Tauno Salo, (Paula Wild, BC Archives, July 7, 1988).

77. Interview with Albert and Norma Williams, (BCICS, February 19, 2003).

78. Interview with Victor Wirkki, (BCICS, February 17, 2003).

79. Interview with Dave Siider, (BCICS, February 20, 2003).

80. Fish, 75.

81. Interview with Albert and Norma Williams, (BCICS, February 19, 2003).

82. Interview with Arvo Tynjala, (Imbert Orchard, BC Archives, June 22, 1967).

83. Wild, 148.

84. Interview with Arvo Tynjala, (Imbert Orchard, BC Archives, June 22, 1967).

85. Wild, 150.

86. Interview with Dave Siider, (BCICS, February 20, 2003).

87. Wild, 111, 151.

88. Fish, 70.

89. "Harmony Island", *Canada Journal* 89.

90. Interview with Ole Anderson, (Gordon Fish, BC Archives, 1979).

91. Interview with Irene Michelson, (Gordon Fish, BC Archives, 1979).

91. "I Lived in a BC Utopia", *Ladysmith Chronicle*, January 11, 1962, 1, 6.

Soviet Karelia

1. Reino Kero, "The Canadian Finns in Soviet Karelia in the 1930s" *Finnish Diaspora I, Canada, South America, Africa, Australia, and Sweden.* Ed. Michael G Karni, (Toronto: The Multicultural History Society of Ontario, 1981).

2. Wild.

Chapter 4

1. Wild, 165, 166.

2. "Sointula Co-operative Store Annual Report", 1945.

3. National Archives of Canada (NAC), *Finnish Canadian Communities during World War II*, RG 13 A-2: File 127 117-90-109, 1939-1944.

4. Wild, 165.

5. Interview with Albert and Norma Williams, (BCICS, February 19, 2003).

6. Interview with Diane Hufnagel, (Paula Wild, BC Archives, June 22, 1988).

7. *Co-operative Consumer*, (February 28, 1978).

8. Wild, 166

9. Interview with Albert and Norma Williams, (BCICS, February 19, 2003).

10. Interview with Victor Wirkki, (BCICS, February 17, 2003).

11. *Co-operative Consumer*, (February 28, 1978).

12. *Ibid.*

13. Varpu Lindstrom, *From Heroes to Enemies: Finns in Canada, 1937-1947*

(Beaverton: Aspasia Books, 2000), 121.

14. *Alert Bay Bulletin*, October 15, 1940.

15. Lindstrom, 195.

16. National Archives of Canada (NAC), *Canadian Security Intelligence Service*, RG 146, Vol. 3501- part I, File 130.

17. National Archives of Canada (NAC), *Canadian Security Intelligence Service*, RG 146, Vol. 3501 - part I, Files 125, 66; RG 146, Vol. 3501 part II, File 155.

18. Lindstrom, 184.

19. Interview with Muriel Lowry, (BCICS, May 26, 2003).

20. Interview with Tula Lewis, (BCICS, July 5, 2003).

21. Interview with Albert and Norma Williams, (BCICS, February 19, 2003).

22. Interview with Lennie Pohto, (BCICS, February 18, 2003).

23. Wild, 171, 172.

24. *Ibid.*, 172.

25. *Ibid.*, 173.

26. Interview with Albert and Norma Williams, (BCICS, February 19, 2003).

27. Edward W. Laine, "Community in Crisis: The Finnish-Canadian Quest for Cultural Identity, 1900-1979", *Finnish Diasporai: Canada, South America, Africa, Australia and Sweden*. Ed. Michael G. Karni. (Toronto: The Multicultural History Society of Ontario, 1981).

28. Interview with Wanda Laughlin, (BCICS, July 3, 2003).

29. *Ibid.*

30. Interview with Elgin Shiels, (BCICS, May 12, 2004).

31. Interview with Delmare Laughlin, (BCICS, July 4, 2003).

32. Interview with Victor Wirkki, (BCICS, February 18, 2003).

33. "Dreams of a Socialist Utopia on a Rainforest Island" *North Island Gazette*, (16 October, 1980).

34. Interview with Albert and Norma Williams, (BCICS, February 19, 2003).

35. "Dreams of a Socialist Utopia on a Rainforest Island" *North Island Gazette*, (16 October, 1980).

36. *Alert Bay Bulletin*, (May 1, 1940).

37. British Columbia Archives (BCA), *Inspector of Credit Union Correspondence*, B00262, File 7, (March 29, 1941).

38. Ian MacPherson, *Building And Protecting The Co-operative Movement: A Brief History of the Co-operative Union of Canada 1909-1984* (Ottawa: The Co-operative Union of Canada, 1984), 116.

39. Interview with Diane Hufnagel, (Paula Wild, BC Archives, June 22, 1988).

40. Interview with Muriel Lowry, (BCICS, May 26, 2003).

41. *Ibid.*

42. Interview with Tauno Salo, (Paula Wild, BC Archives, July 7, 1988).

43. Interview with Wayne Homer, (Gordon Fish, BC Archives, March 6, 1982).

44. Interview with Muriel Lowry, (BCICS, May 26, 2003).

45. Interview with Victor Wirkki, (BCICS, February 17, 2003).

46. Interview with Dave Siider, (BCICS, February 20, 2003).

47. *Aika*, (January 1, 1904).

48. *Aika*, 1902.

49. Interview with Victor Wirkki, (BCICS, February 17, 2003).

50. Interview with Lennie Pohto, (BCICS, February 18, 2003).

51. Interview with Loretta Rhitamo, (BCICS, February 20, 2003).

52. Interview with Lennie Pohto, (BCICS, February 18, 2003).

53. Wild, 164

54. Interview with Alfred Williams, (Gordon Fish, BC Archives, February 11, 1982).

55. Rhitamo, BCICS Interview, 20 February, 2003.

56. Interview with Muriel Lowry, (BCICS, May 26, 2003).

57. Interview with Albert and Norma Williams, (BCICS, February 19, 2003).

58. University of British Columbia, Department of University Extension, *Educational Programme for British Columbia Fishermen, Report on Period from September 1, 1939 to March 31, 1940.*

59. *Alert Bay Bulletin*, (May 1, 1941).

60. Interview with Olga Landsdowne, (BCICS, July 4, 2003).

61. "Credit Union Annual Report", 1949, 1960.

62. British Columbia Archives (BCA), *Inspector of Credit Union Correspondence*, B00262, File 7, 29, (Oct. 28, 1960).

63. Interview with Lennie Pohto, (BCICS, February 18, 2003).

64. Interview with Phillip Au, (BCICS, August 26, 2003).

65. British Columbia Archives (BCA), *Inspector of Credit Union Correspondence*, B00262, File 7, 29, (April 5, 1957).

66. "Malcolm Island Superior School Parent-Teacher Association (PTA) Minutes", (May 9, 1952).

67. *The Fisherman*, (July 1987), 24.

68. *Ibid.*, 25.

69. Alicja Muszynski "Class Formation" *Political Economy, 20, Summer 1986*, 101, 102.

70. Interview with Victor Wirkki, (BCICS, February 17, 2003).

71. *The Fisherman*, (July 1987), 31.

72. Interview with Dave Siider, (BCICS, February 20, 2003).

73. *The Fisherman*, (July 1987), 29.

74. *Ibid.,*17.

75. Interview with Lennie Pohto, (BCICS, February 18, 2003).

76. *The Fisherman*, (April 23, 1948).

77. *The Fisherman*, (March 5, 1948; November 19, 1948; December 10, 1948).

78. "Malcolm Island Superior School PTA Minutes", 1938-1966.

79. Anderson, 15.

80. "Malcolm Island Superior School PTA Minutes", (October 7, 1949).

81. *Ibid.,* (June 9, 1950; October 13, 1950).

82. British Columbia Archives (BCA), GR 2569, Box 10, File # 3.

83. "Malcolm Island Superior School PTA Minutes", (December 11, 1953).

84. *Ibid.,* May 11, 1951.

85. *Ibid.,* 1938-1966.

86. *Ibid.,* November 12, 1953.

87. *Ibid.,* October 7, 1949.

88. *Ibid.,* April 10, 1954.

89. *Ibid.,* February 8, 1957.

90. *Ibid.,* November 11, 1938.

91. *Ibid.,* May 19, 1939.

92.. *Ibid.,* January 12, 1951.

93. *Ibid.,* November 9, 1966.

94. *Ibid.,* May 9, 1952.

95. *Ibid.,* December 1, 1949.

96. *Ibid.,* February 14, 1958.

97. Interview with Kevin Neish, (BCICS, May 20, 2003).

98. *Sointula Scuttlebutt*, (January 23, 1953).

99. Interview with Kevin Neish, (BCICS, May 20, 2003).

100. *Ibid.*

101. British Columbia Archives (BCA), *Canadian Security Intelligence Service*, RG 146, Vol. 3501 part I, File 58.

102. Interview with Kevin Neish, (BCICS, May 20, 2003).

103. *Ibid.*

104. *Ibid.*

105. *Ibid.*

106. Wild, 154, 155.

107. "Sointula Co-operative Store Minutes", 1939; 1945.

108. Interview with Aileen and Dean Wooldridge, (BCICS, July 4, 2003).

109. Interview with Albert and Norma Williams, (BCICS, February 19, 2003).

110. Interview with Loretta Rhitamo, (BCICS, February 20, 2003).

111. *Ibid.*

112. "Sointula Co-operative Store Minutes", 1963.

113. *Vancouver Sun*, (March 23, 1953).

114. British Columbia Archives (BCA), *Canadian Security Intelligence Service*, RG 146, Vol. 4090, File 229.

115. *Ibid.,* RG 146, Vol. 4090, File 171.

116. *Ibid.,* RG 146, Vol. 4090, File 218.

117. *Ibid.,* RG 146, Vol. 4090, File 158.

118. *Ibid.,* RG 146, Vol. 4090, File 170.

119. *Ibid.,* RG 146, Vol. 4090, File 157.

120. "Sointula Co-operative Store Minutes", 1950-1969.

121. Interview with Landsdowne, (BCICS, July 4, 2003).

122. "Sointula Co-operative Store Minutes", (April, 1956).

123. British Columbia Archives (BCA), *Canadian Security Intelligence Service*, RG 146, Vol. 3501, Part II, File 168.

124. "Sointula Co-operative Store Minutes", (December 11, 1968; 30, October, 1970).

125. *Ibid.,* (May 12, 1969).

126. *Ibid.,* (September 30, 1970).

127. Interview with Dave Siider, (BCICS, February 20, 2003).

128. "Sointula Co-operative Store Minutes", (January 30, 1965).

129. *Ibid.,* (September 28, 1951; February 8, 1964; January 30, 1965).

130. *Ibid.,* (September 27, 1967).

131. *Ibid.,* (November 19, 1967).

132. *Ibid.,* (March 11, 1968).

133. *Ibid.,* (July 20, 1968).

134. *Ibid.,* (April 17, 1965).

135. "Minister of Highways Annual Report", 1966/67, 1971/72.

136. Interview with Landsdowne, (BCICS, July 4, 2003).

137. "Sointula Co-operative Store Minutes", (March 26, 1973).

138. *Ibid.,* (February 11, 1974).

139. Interview with Dave Siider, (BCICS, February 20, 2003).

140. Interview with Landsdowne, (BCICS, July 4, 2003).

141. "Sointula Co-operative Store Minutes", (November 30, 1970).

142. *Ibid.,* (April 27, 1973).

143. *Ibid.,* (February 11, 1974).

Community Justice

1. Interview with Dave Siider, (BCICS, February 20, 2003).
2. Interview with Victor Wirkki, (BCICS, February 17, 2003).
3. Wild.

Chapter 5

1. Interview with Landsdowne, (BCICS, July 4, 2003).
2. Wild, 177, 178.
3. Interview with Albert and Norma Williams, (BCICS, February 19, 2003).
4. Wild, 180.
5. Interview with Kelly Edwards, (BCICS, July 2, 2003).
6. Interview with Wanda Laughlin, (BCICS, July 3, 2003).
7. Interview with Victor Wirkki, (BCICS, February 17, 2003).
8. Interview with Albert and Norma Williams, (BCICS, February 19, 2003).
9. Wild, 177.
10. *Ibid.*, 182.
11. *Ibid.*, 181, 182.
12. Interview with Victor Wirkki, (BCICS, February 17, 2003).
13. Wild, 192.
14. *Ibid.*, 193.
15. *Ibid.*, 192.
16. *Ibid.*, 181.
17. Interview with Albert and Norma Williams, (BCICS, February 19, 2003).
18. Interview with Loretta Rhitamo, (BCICS, February 20, 2003).
19. Wild, 186.
20. Interview with Wanda Laughlin, (BCICS, July 3, 2003).
21. Wild, 186.
22. *The People of Sointula*, Karvonen Films LTD., 2001.
23. Interview with Albert and Norma Williams, (BCICS, February 19, 2003).
24. Interview with Wanda Laughlin, (BCICS, July 3, 2003).
25. Wild, 188.
26. Interview with Loretta Rhitamo, (BCICS, February 20, 2003).
27. Interview with Ralph Harris, (Paula Wild, BC Archives, August 12, 1988).
28. BCICS Galleria Profile, "Lardeau Valley Co-operative", Retrieved in October, 2004 http://bcics.uvic.ca/galleria/bc.php?tourtype=1&group=15&story=22.
29. BCICS Galleria Profile, "Treesing Treeplanting Co-operative", Retrieved in October, 2004 http://bcics.uvic.ca/galleria/bc.php?tourtype=1&group=6&story=43#
30. *Ibid.*
31. *Ibid.*
32. *Ibid.*
33. *Ibid.*
34. Wild, 189.
35. Interview with Wanda Laughlin, (BCICS, July 3, 2003).
36. Interview with Kelly Edwards, (BCICS, July 2, 2003).
37. Interview with Wanda Laughlin, (BCICS, July 3, 2003).
38. *Ibid.*
39. *Ibid.*
40. *Ibid.*
41. *Ibid.*
42. *Ibid.*

Community House

1. Interview with Wanda Laughlin, (BCICS, July 3, 2003).

Chapter 6

1. "Official Malcolm Island Settlement Plan", Sointula Museum
2. *The People of Sointula*, Karvonen Films LTD., 2001.
3. Interview with Elgin Shiels, (BCICS, May 12, 2004).
4. "The British Columbia Economy", Retrieved in July 2004 www.bctop100.com/economy.htm.
5. Hallin, Lillian. "A Guide to the BC Economy and Labour Market", Retrieved in July 2004 www.guidetobceconomy.org
6. *Ibid.*
7. Interview with Alfred Williams, (Gordon Fish BC Archives, 1979).
8. Interview with Loretta Rhitamo, (BCICS, February 20, 2003).
9. Interview with Aileen Wooldridge, (BCICS, July 4, 2003).
10. Interview with Murial Lowry, (BCICS, May 26, 2003).
11. Interview with Kelly Edwards, (BCICS, July 2, 2003).
12. Charles R. Menzies, "Us and Them: The Prince Rupert Fishermen's Co-op and Organized Labour, 1931 - 1989", *Labour/Le Travail*, Fall 2001.
13. Interview with Aileen Wooldridge, (BCICS, July 4, 2003).
14. Menzies.
15. Interview with Aileen Wooldridge, (BCICS, July 4, 2003).
16. Interview with Albert and Norma Williams, (BCICS, February 19, 2003).

17. *Parliamentary Internet*, Standing Committee on Aboriginal and Northern Affairs, 30 April, 1996.

18. Interview with Tosha Nelson, (BCICS, February 20, 2003).

19. Interview with Lennie Pohto, (BCICS, February 18, 2003).

20. Interview with Aileen Wooldridge, (BCICS, July 4, 2003).

21. Interview with Lennie Pohto, (BCICS, February 18, 2003).

22. *The People of Sointula*, Karvonen Films LTD., 2001.

23. Interview with Aileen Wooldridge, (BCICS, July 4, 2003).

24. *Ibid.*

25. Interview with Clayton Jordan, (BCICS, April 14, 2004).

26. Interview with Loretta Rhitamo, (BCICS, February 20, 2003).

27. "Sointula Co-operative Store Minutes", (November 7, 1983; May 20, 1986; January 19, 1987; June 23, 1988).

28. *Ibid.*, (November 6, 1984).

29. Interview with Phillip Au, (BCICS, August 26, 2003).

30. *Ibid.*

31. Interview with Albert and Norma Williams, (BCICS, February 19, 2003).

32. Interview with Wanda Laughlin, (BCICS, July 3, 2003).

33. *Ibid.*

34. Interview with Loretta Rhitamo, (BCICS, February 20, 2003).

35. *Ibid.*

36. Interview with Marjorie Greensides, (BCICS, February 19, 2003).

37. Interview with Susan Harvey, (BCICS, February 19, 2003).

38. *Ibid.*

39. Interview with Marjorie Greensides, (BCICS, February 19, 2003).

40. Interview with Susan Harvey, (BCICS, February 19, 2003).

41. *Ibid.*

Chapter 7

1. Interview with Pelle Agerup, (BCICS, February 21, 2003).

2. *Ibid.*

3. Interview with Will Soltau, (BCICS, February 19, 2003).

4. *Ibid.*

5. *Island Echo*, (February, 2000).

6. *Ibid.*

7. "Abalone: A Message of Hope" *Western Aquaculture*, (August, 2000).

8. Interview with John Rosser, (BCICS, February 17, 2003).

9. *North Island Gazette*, (October 17, 2001).

10. "Abalone: A Message of Hope" *Western Aquaculture*, (August, 2000).

11. *North Island Gazette*, (August 16, 2000).

12. *Ibid.*, (August 2, 2000).

13. Interview with Murray Tanner, (BCICS, February 19, 2003).

14. Interview with John Rosser, (BCICS, February 17, 2003).

15. *Ibid.*

16. Interview with Pelle Agerup, (BCICS, February 21, 2003).

17. *Ibid.*

18. *Ibid.*

19. *Ibid.*

20. *Ibid.*

21. *North Island Gazette*, (February 6, 2002).

22. Interview with John Rosser, (BCICS, February 17, 2003).

23. Interview with Pelle Agerup, (BCICS, February 21, 2003).

24. *Ibid.*

25. *Ibid.*

26. *The Barometer*, (October, 2000).

27. Interview with John Rosser, (BCICS, February 17, 2003).

28. *Ibid.*

29. *Ibid.*

30. *Ibid.*

31. Interview with Dan and Laura Klingbiel, (BCICS, July 4, 2004).

32. Interview with Art Swanson, (BCICS, February 20, 2003).

33. Interview with John Rosser, (BCICS, February 17, 2003).

34. *Ibid.*

35. *Ibid.*

36. *Ibid.*

37. *Ibid.*

38. *Ibid.*

39. Interview with Art Swanson, (BCICS, February 20, 2003).

40. *Ibid.*

41. Interview with John Rosser, (BCICS, February 17, 2003).

42. *Ibid.*

43. *Ibid.*

44. *Ibid.*

45. *Wild Island Advantage*, (July, 2002).

46. Interview with Liette Lavoie, (BCICS, February 20, 2003).

47. *Ibid.*

48. *Ibid.*

49. BCICS BC Provincial Galleria, "Wild Island Foods Co-operative", Retrieved on October 2004 http://bcics.uvic.ca/galleria/bc.php?tourtype=1&group=6&story=45.

50. Interview with Liette Lavoie, (BCICS, February 20, 2003).

51. *Ibid.*

52. *Ibid.*

53. *Ibid.*

54. Laura Sjolie, *Wild Island Foods Co-operative*, 27 January, 2004.

55. *Ibid.*

56. *Ibid.*

57. *Ibid.*

58. Interview with Liette Lavoie, (BCICS, February 20, 2003).

59. *Ibid.*

60. Accessed June, 2004 www.wildfoods.com.

61. Interview with Kathy Parton and Lorraine Williams, (BCICS, April 14, 2004).

62. *Ibid.*

63. Interview with Liette Lavoie, (BCICS, February 20, 2003).

64. Interview with Kathy Parton and Lorraine Williams, (BCICS, April 14, 2004).

65. Interview with Susan Harvey, (BCICS, April 15, 2004).

66. Confidential E-mail, 19 April, 2004.

67. "Van City capital Corporation", Accessed in September 2004 http://www.bctia.org/members/VanCity_Capital_Corporation.asp.

68. Interview with Susan Harvey, (BCICS, April 15, 2004).

69. Interview with Kathy Parton and Lorraine Williams, (BCICS, April 14, 2004).

70. Interview with Brenda Swanson, (BCICS, April 15, 2004).

71. Laura Sjolie, Wild Island Foods Co-operative, 27 January, 2004.

72. Interview with Liette Lavoie, (BCICS, February 20, 2003).

73. *Ibid.*

74. *Ibid.*

75. Interview with Kathy Parton and Lorraine Williams, (BCICS, April 14, 2004).

76. *Ibid.*

77. "Minutes of Wild Island Board Meeting", 14 April, 2004.

78. Liette Lavoie, *Business Incubator: A Community Initiative Proposal prepared for Wild Island Foods Co-operative.* (July 11, 2000).

79. Interview with Kathy Parton and Lorraine Williams, (BCICS, April 14,

80. Interview with Susan Harvey, (BCICS, April 15, 2004).

81. Interview with Kathy Parton and Lorraine Williams, (BCICS, April 14, 2004).

82. *Ibid.*

83. *Ibid.*

84. Interview with Marjorie Greensides, (BCICS, April 16, 2004).

85. Interview with Kathy Parton and Lorraine Williams, (BCICS, April 14, 2004).

86. *Ibid.*

87. *Ibid.*

88. "Minutes of Wild Island Board Meeting", (April 14, 2004; May 5, 2004).

89. Interview with Brenda Swanson, (BCICS, April 15, 2004).

90. Interview with Kathy Parton and Lorraine Williams, (BCICS, April 14, 2004).

91. *Ibid.*

92. Interview with Susan Harvey, (BCICS, April 15, 2004).

93. *Ibid.*

94. Interview with Kathy Parton and Lorraine Williams, (BCICS, April 14, 2004).

95. Interview with Marjorie Greensides, (BCICS, April 16, 2004).

96. Interview with Marjorie Greensides and Susan Harvey, (BCICS, February 19, 2003).

97. Interview with Brenda Swanson, (BCICS, April 15, 2004).

98. Interview with Laura Mitchell, (BCICS, February 20, 2003).

Raising Abalone

1. *Hatchery Magazine*, (November/December 2000), 22, 23.

Chapter 8

1. Interview with Marjorie Greensides, (BCICS, April 16, 2004).

2. *Ibid.*

3. Accessed in June, 2004 www.sointula.net.

4. Interview with Marjorie Greensides, (BCICS, April 16, 2004).

5. *Ibid.*

6. Interview with Carmen Burrows, (BCICS, April 16, 2004).

7. Interview with Elgin Shiels, (BCICS, May 12 , 2004).

8. Interview with Marjorie Greensides, (BCICS, April 16, 2004).

9. Interview with Carmen Burrows, (BCICS, April 16, 2004).

10. Interview with Troy Bright, (BCICS, April 15, 2004).

11. *Ibid.*

12. *Ibid.*

13. *Ibid.*

14. *Ibid.*

15. Interview with Susan Harvey, (BCICS, April 15, 2004).

16. *Ibid.*

17. *Ibid.*

18. "Minutes of Wild Island Board Meeting", (April 14, 2004).

19. Interview with Wanda Laughlin, (BCICS, July 3, 2003).

20. "Sointula", Accessed in June, 2004 www.vinva.bc.ca/sointula.htm.

21. Interview with Wanda Laughlin, (BCICS, July 3, 2003).

22. Interview with Susan Harvey, (BCICS, April 15, 2004).

23. Interview with Lennie Pohto, (BCICS, February 18, 2003).

24. Interview with Marjorie Greensides, (BCICS, April 16, 2004).

25. Interview with Campbell Wilson, (BCICS, April 16, 2004).

26. Interview with Wanda Laughlin, (BCICS, July 3, 2003).

27. Interview with Marjorie Greensides, (BCICS, April 16, 2004).

28. Interview with Brenda Swanson, (BCICS, April 15, 2004).

29. Interview with Marjorie Greensides, (BCICS, April 16, 2004).

30. Interview with Mickey Edwards, (BCICS, February 21, 2003).

31. Interview with Susan Harvey, (BCICS, April 15, 2004).

32. Interview with Marjorie Greensides, (BCICS, April 16, 2004).

33. *Ibid.*

34. Interview with Brenda Swanson, (BCICS, April 15, 2004).

35. Interview with Clayton Jordan, (BCICS, April 14, 2004).

36. Interview with John Rosser, (BCICS, February 17, 2003).

37. Interview with Brenda Swanson, (BCICS, April 15, 2004).

38. Interview with Marjorie Greensides, (BCICS, April 16, 2004).

39. Interview with Campbell Wilson, (BCICS, April 16, 2004).

40. Interview with Dennis Swanson, (BCICS, April 15, 2004).

41. Interview with Marjorie Greensides and Susan Harvey, (BCICS, February 19, 2003).

42. Interview with Dennis Swanson, (BCICS, April 15, 2004).

43. Interview with Brenda Swanson, (BCICS, April 15, 2004).

44. *Ibid.*

45. Interview with Dan and Laura Klingbiel, (BCICS, July 4, 2004).

46. *Ibid.*

Old Craft, New Art

1. Interview with Carmen Burrows, (BCICS, April 16, 2004).

2. Interview with Marjorie Greensides, (BCICS, April 16, 2004).

3. Interview with Tim Motchman, (BCICS, April 16, 2004).

Belly Dancing

1. Interview with Kathryn Burgess Griffith, (BCICS, April 15, 2004).

Community Forest

1. "Community Forests Pilot Agreements", British Columbia Ministry of Forests, (June, 2003).

2. Interview with Gordon McDougall, (BCICS, April 14, 2004).

3. Interview with Dennis Swanson, (BCICS, April 15, 2004).

Lions Club

1. Interview with Cambell Wilson, (BCICS, April 16, 2004).

2. "The Malcolm Island Lions Club Report", (October, 2003).

Where To Next?

1. Interiew with Fraser Swanson, (BCICS, May 28, 2004).

Bibliography

Newspapers and Magazines

Aika, 1901 - 1905.

Barometer, The, October, 2000.

Alert Bay Bulletin, 01 May, 1940, 15 October, 1940, 01 May, 1941.

Co-operative Consumer, 28 February, 1978.

Fisherman, The: 50th Anniversary Edition, July, 1987.

Fisherman, The, 05 March, 1948, 23 April, 1948, 19 November, 1948, 10 December, 1948.

Hatchery Magazine, November/December 2000.

In Sointula: Island Utopia. Madeira Park: Harbour Publishing, 1995.

Island Echo, February, 2000.

Ladysmith Chronicle, 11 January, 1962

Nanaimo Daily Herald, 1901. In *Sointula: Island Utopia*. Madeira Park: Harbour Publishing, 1995.

North Island Gazette, 16 October, 1980, 02, 16 August, 2000, 06 February, 2002.

Vancouver Sun, 25 May, 1927, 23 March, 1953.

Victoria Daily Colonist, 1901. In *Sointula: Island Utopia*. Madeira Park: Harbour Publishing, 1995.

"Abalone: A Message of Hope", In *Western Aquaculture*, August, 2000.

Western Clarion, 30 May, 1908, 04 December, 1909.

Books

Buck, Claire, Ed., *Bloomsbury Guide To Women's Literature*, Upper Saddle River, New Jersey: Prentice-Hall, 1992.

Halmalainen, Pekka. In *Time of Storm: Revolution, Civil War, and the Ethnolinguistic Issue in Finland*. Albany: State University of New York Press, 1979.

Muszynski, Alicja. *Cheap Wage Labour: Race and Gender in the Fisheries of British Columbia*, McGill-Queen's University Press, July 1996.

Puntila, L. A.. *The Political History of Finland*. London: William Heinemann Ltd., 1975.

Nickels, Sylvie, Hillar Kallas, and Phillipa Friedman. *Finland: An Introduction*. London: George allen & Unwin LTD., 1973.

Mead, W. R.. *Finland*. London: Ernest Benn Limited, 1968.

Halminen, Matti (translated by Allan Henry Salo). *The History of Sointula and the Kalevan Kansa*. Helsinki: Kustantaja Mikko Ampuja, 1936.

Wild, Paula. *Sointula: Island Utopia*. Madeira Park: Harbour Publishing, 1995.

Fish, Gordon. *Dreams of Freedom, Bella Coola, Cape Scott, Sointula*. Victoria: Provincial Archives of British Columbia, 1982.

Hill, A. V. *Tides Of Change: A Story of Fishermen's Co-operatives in British Columbia*. Prince Rupert: Prince Rupert Fishermen's Co-operative Association, 1967.

Eklund, William. *Builders of Canada: History of the Finnish Organization of Canada, 1911-1971*. Toronto: Vapaus Publishing Company Limited, 1987.

Lindstrom, Varpu. *From Heroes to Enemies: Finns in Canada, 1937-1947*. Beaverton: Aspasia Books, 2000.

MacPherson, Ian. *Building And Protecting The Co-operative Movement: A Brief History of the Co-operative Union of Canada, 1909-1984*. Ottawa: The Co-operative Union of Canada, 1984.

Anderson, Aili. *History of Sointula*. Sointula: Sointula Centennial Committee, 1958.

Lonnrot, Elias, *The Kalevala*. Bosley, Keith (translation), Oxford: Oxford university press, 1989.

Wilson, Katharina M., Ed. *An Encyclopedia of Continental Women Writers, Vol. 1*, London: Garland Publishing Inc., 1991.

Thesis

Grantham, Ronald. "Some Aspects of the Socialist Movement in British Columbia, 1898-1933." MA. Thesis, University of British Columbia, 1942.

Kuitunen, Alan Neil. "The Finnish Canadian socialist movement, 1900-1914." MA. Thesis, University of Calgary, 1982.

Salo, Alan H. "The Kalevan Kansa Colonization Company Limited: A Finnish Canadian Millenarian Movement." MA. Thesis, University of British Columbia, 1978.

Articles

Wilson, Donald. "Matti Kurikka and A. B. Makela: Socialist Thought Among Finns In Canada." In *Canadian Ethnic Studies Vol. X, no. 2* (1978): 9-21

Scott, Andrew. "Canada Journal, Sointula B.C., Harmony Island" In *Equinox*,

Vol 10, No. 2, March/April 1991.

Laine, Edward W. "Community in Crisis: The Finnish-Canadian Quest for
Cultural Identity, 1900-1979." In *Finnish Diasporia: Canada, South
America, Africa, Australia and Sweden*, edited by Michael G. Karni.
Toronto: The Multicultural History Society of Ontario, 1981.

Kero, Reino, "The Canadian Finns in Soviet Karelia in the 1930s" in *Finnish
Diaspora I, Canada, South America, Africa, Australia, and Sweden*.
Ed. Michael g Karni. Toronto: The Multicultural History Society of
Ontario, 1981.

Menzies, Charles R. "Us and Them: The Prince Rupert Fishermen's Co-op and
Organized Labour, 1931-1989." In *Labour/Le Travail* (Fall 2001).

Makela, A. B. "Something About Canada", In *Tyokansan Kalenteri*. Port
Arthur: Tyokansan Press, 1913, 95-96.

Encyclopedia

World Book Encyclopedia, Volume 19, Chicago: World Book Inc., 1983.

Correspondence

Anderson, Andrew "Anderson Letter to Premier Richard McBride." 1909,
Sointula Museum, Sointula British Columbia.

Confidential e-mail, 19 April, 2004.

Rules, Minutes, Reports (Sointula)

"Rules and By-laws of the Sointula Co-operative Store Limited." 1909

"Amendments to the rules and By-laws of the Sointula Co-operative Store
Limited" 1912, 1916, 1917, 1925, 1932.

"The Sointula Co-operative Store Annual Report", 1918, 1927, 1928, 1929,
1932, 1939, 1945.

"Malcolm Island Superior School Parent Teacher Association (PTA) Minutes."
1938-1966, Sointula Public Library

Sointula Credit Union Annual Reports, 1917 - 1960.

Sointula Co-operative Store Minutes. 1950-2000.

The Malcolm Island Lions Club Report, October, 2003.

Official Documentation

Petition of Bruno Kaario to the Supreme Court of British Columbia, 27
December, 1933.

File 106747, Supreme Court of British Columbia

British Columbia Archives, Inspector of Credit Union Correspondence,
B00262, File 7

British Columbia Archives, Letter to the Board of Health & Hospital Services,
GR 2569, Box 10, File # 3.

"Minister of Highways Report for the Year 1966/67", Victoria: A. Sutton,
Printer to the Queen's Most Excellent Majesty in Right of the
Province of British Columbia, 1967; "Minister of Highways Report for
the Year 1971/72", Victoria: K. M. MacDonald, Printer to the Queen's
Most Excellent Majesty in Right of the Province of British Columbia.

"Community Forests Pilot Agreements", British Columbia Ministry of Forests,
June, 2003.

National Archives of Canada. Canadian Security Intelligence Service, Rg 146
Vols. 3501, 4090.

Official Malcolm Island Settlement Plan: Regional District of Mount Waddington, Port McNeill: The District, 1980.

Interviews

Agerup, Pelle, BCICS Interview, 21 February, 2003, 17 February, 2003.

Anderson, Ole, Gordon Fish Interview, 1979, BC Archives.

Au, Phillip, BCICS Interview, 26 August, 2003.

Bright, Troy, BCICS Interview, 15 April, 2004.

Burgess-Griffith, Kathryn, BCICS Interview, 15 April, 2004.

Burrows, Carmen, BCICS Interview, 16 April, 2004.

Edwards, Kelly, BCICS Interview, 2 July, 2003.

Edwards, Mickey, BCICS Interview, 21 February, 2003.

Greensides, Marjorie, and Susan Harvey, BCICS Interview, 19 February, 2003.

Greensides, Marjorie, BCICS Interview, 16 April, 2004.

Harris, Ralph, Paula Wild Interview, 12 August, 1988.

Harvey, Susan, BCICS Interview, 15 April, 2004.

Homer, Wayne, Gordon Fish Interview, 6 March, 1982, BC Archives.

Hufnagel, Diane, Paula Wild Interview, 22 June, 1988, BC Archives.

Jordan, Clayton, BCICS Interview, 14 April, 2004.

Klingbiel, Dan and Laura, BCICS Interview, 04 July, 2004.

Landsdowne, Olga, BCICS Interview, 04 July, 2003.

Laughlin, Delmare, BCICS Interview, 4 July, 2003.

Laughlin, Wanda, BCICS Interview, 3 July, 2003.

Lavoie, Liette, BCICS Interview, 20 February, 2003.

Lewis, Tula, BCICS Interview, 5 July, 2003.

Lowry, Muriel, BCICS Interview, 26 May, 2003.

McDougall, Gordon, BCICS Interview, 14 April, 2004.

Michelson, Irene, Gordon Fish Interview, 1979, BC Archives.

Mitchell, Laura, BCICS Interview, 20 February, 2003.

Motchman, Tim, BCICS Interview, 16 April, 2004.

Neish, Kevin, BCICS Interview, 20 May, 2003.

Nelson, Tosha, BCICS Interview, 20 February, 2003.

Parton, Kathy, and Lorraine Williams, BCICS Interview, 20 February, 2003.

Parton, Kathy, and Lorraine Williams, BCICS Interview, 14 April, 2004.

Peterson, Sally, Gordon Fish Interview, February 11, 1982, BC Archives.

Pohto, Lennie, BCICS Interview, 18 February, 2003.

Rhitamo, Loretta, BCICS Interview, 20 February, 2003.

Rosser, John, BCICS Interview, 17 February, 2003.

Rosser, John, BCICS Interview, 16 April, 2004.

Salo, Tauno, Paula Wild Interview, 7 July, 1988, BC Archives.

Shiels, Elgin, BCICS Interview, 12 May, 2004.

Siider, Dave, BCICS Interview, 20 February, 2003.

Soltau, Will, BCICS Interview, 19 February, 2003.

Swanson, Art, BCICS Interview, 20 February, 2003.

Swanson, Brenda, BCICS Interview, 15 April, 2004.

Swanson, Dennis, BCICS Interview, 15 April, 2004.

Swanson, Fraser, BCICS Interview, 28 May, 2004.

Tanner, Murray, BCICS Interview, 19 February, 2003.

Tynjala, Arvo, Aural history Programme Interview, 1967, BC Archives.

Tynjala, Imbert Orchard Interview, 22 June, 1967, BC Archives.

Tynjala, Arvo, Murray Kennedy Interview, 16 May, 1972, BC Archives.

Williams, Albert and Norma, BCICS Interview, 19 February, 2003.

Williams, Alfred, Gordon Fish Interview, 1979, BC Archives.

Williams, Alfred, Gordon Fish Interview, 1982, BC Archives.

Wilson, Campbell, BCICS Interview, 16 April, 2004.

Wirkki, Victor, BCICS Interview, 17 February, 2003.

Wooldridge, Aileen and Dean, BCICS Interview, 04 July, 2003.

Internet

"Economy". www.bctop100.com/economy.htm

"Logging and Forest Products" in A Guide to the BC Economy and Labour Market, www.guidetobceconomy@workinfonet.bc.ca

Wild Island Foods, www.wildfoods.com

Vancity Savings, http://www.vancity.com

Sointula Resource Centre Society, www.sointula.net

Vancouver Island North Visitors Association, www.vinva.bc.ca/sointula.htm

BCICS Galleria Profile, "Treesing", http://web.uvic.ca/bcics

BCICS Galleria Profile, "Wild Island Foods Co-operative", http://web.uvic.ca/bcics

Miscelaneous

"Standing committee on Aboriginal and Northern Affairs" in Parliamentary Internet, 30 April, 1996.

Lavoie, Liette, "Business Incubator: A Community Initiative Proposal prepared for Wild Island Foods Co-operative". 11 July, 2000.

"Community Forestry in British Columbia, Canada: A Socio-Economic and Ecological Perspective", Cheri Burda, Eco-Research chair of Environmental Law and Policy, University of Victoria, British Columbia.

Wild Island Board Meeting, 14 April, 2004, 05 May, 2004.

Unpublished

Sjolie, Laura, "Wild island Foods Co-operative", 27 January, 2004.

Video

The People of Sointula, Edmonton: Karvonen Films LTD., 2001.

Index

Y